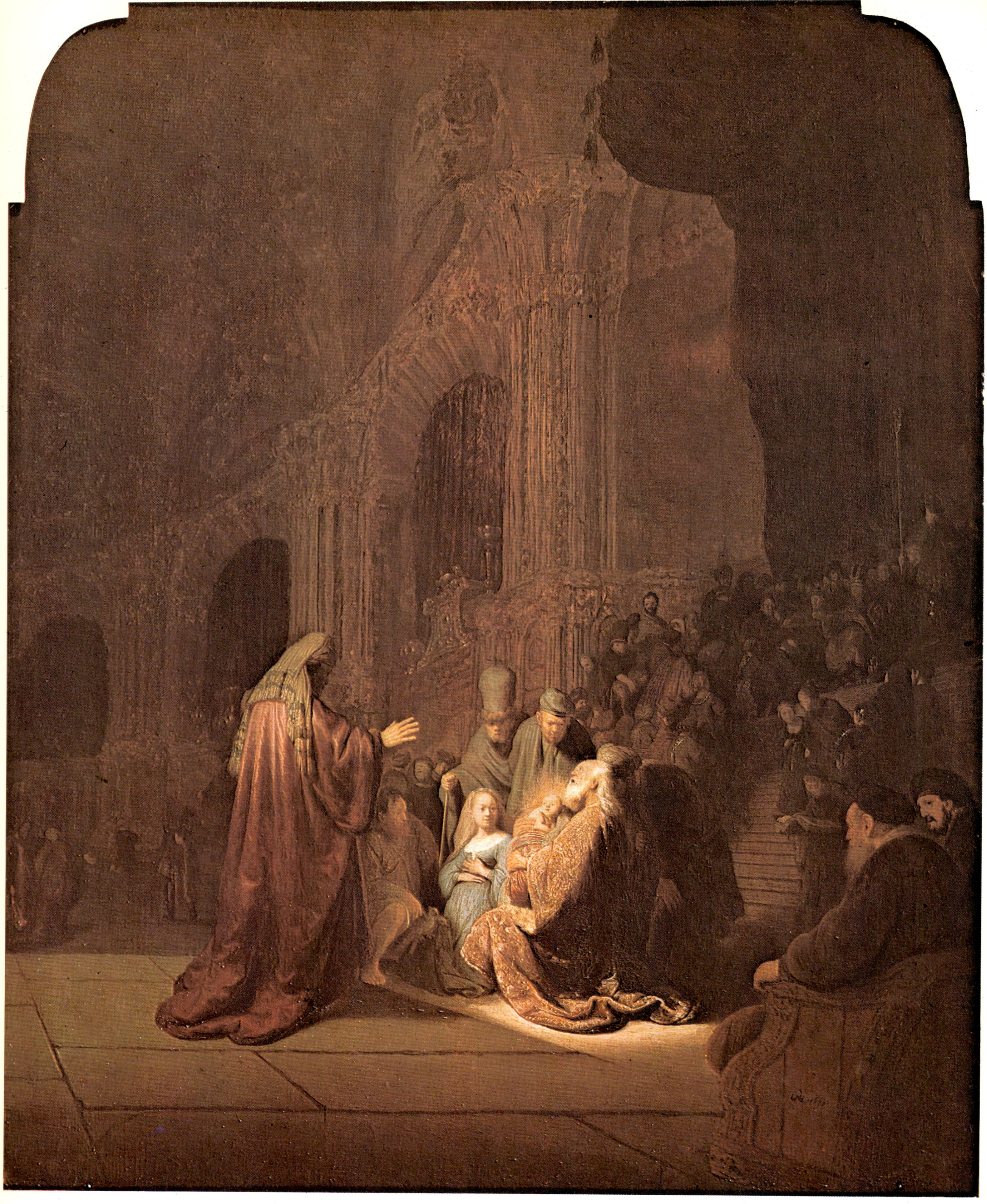

Plate 1 *see page 4*

REMBRANDT and his art

Christopher Wright

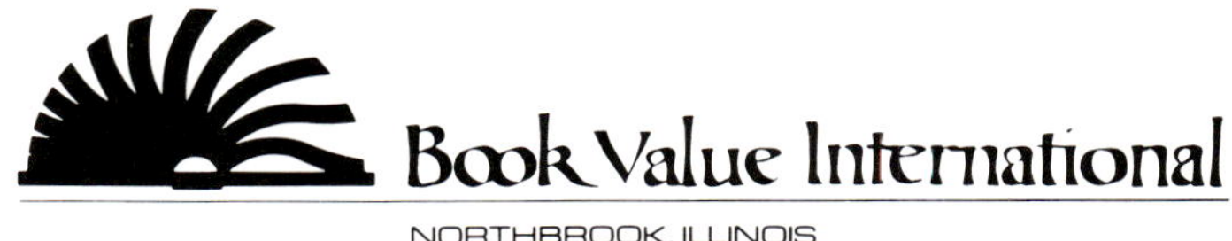

NORTHBROOK, ILLINOIS

Plate 1
The Presentation in the Temple
dated 1631
oil on panel
$24 \times 18\frac{7}{8}$ in (61×48 cm)
Mauritshuis, The Hague

Sold several times at auction in The Hague in the 18th century and finally acquired by the Stadtholder William V in 1763. Removed to France in 1795 by the French occupying forces and returned to The Hague after 1815 where it has remained ever since.

First published in the United Kingdom by The Hamlyn Publishing Group Limited
London · New York · Sydney · Toronto
Astronaut House, Hounslow Road, Feltham, Middlesex, England

This edition published 1981 by
Book Value International, Inc.
A registered imprint of
Quality Books, Inc.
400 Anthony Trail
Northbrook, Illinois 60062 U.S.A.

ISBN 0-89196-089-9

Printed and bound in Spain
by Graficromo, S. A. – Córdoba

Contents

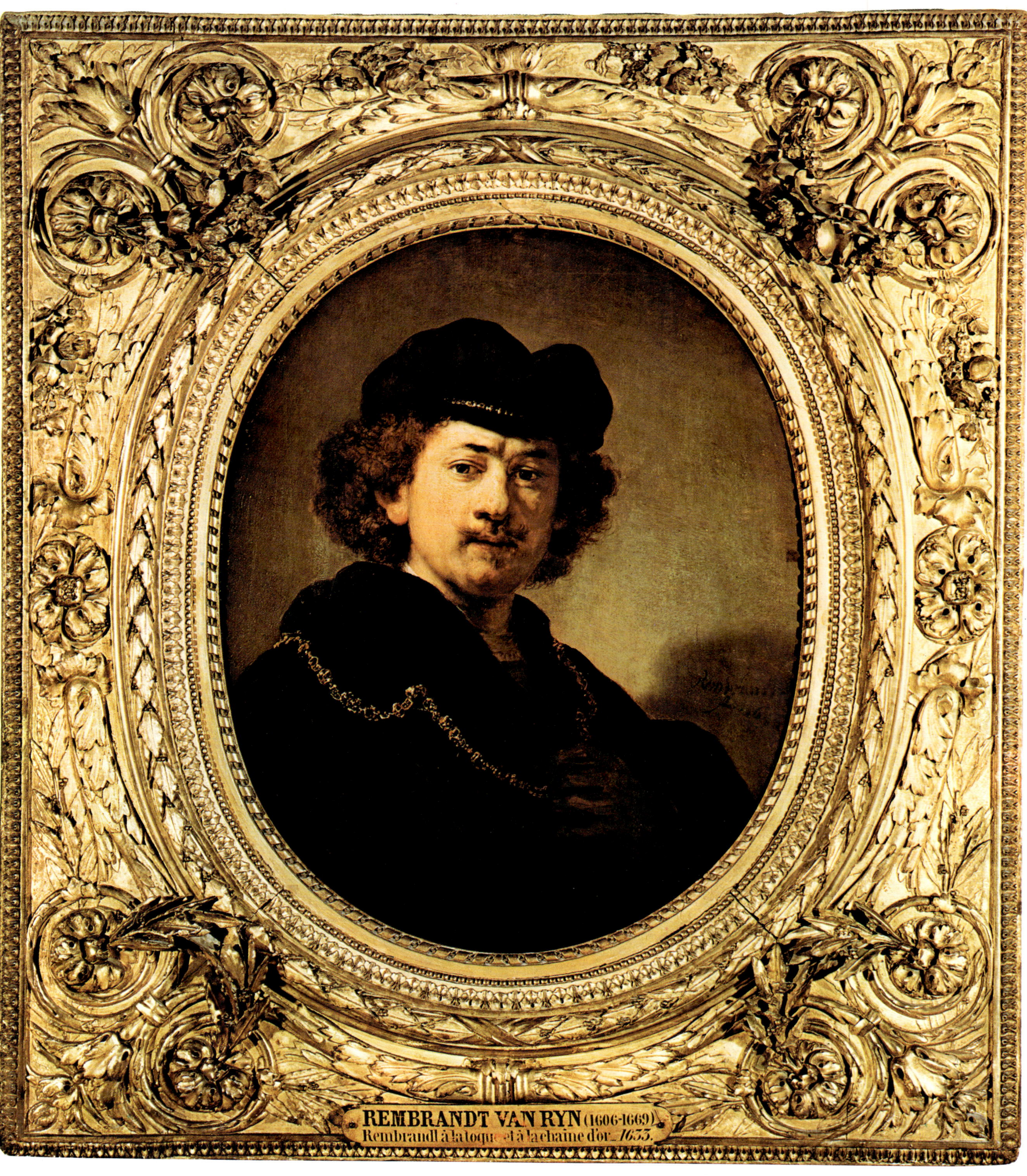
REMBRANDT VAN RYN (1606-1669)
Rembrandt à la toque et à la chaine d'or _1633.

Brief biography of Rembrandt

1606 July 15: Born in Leyden, the son of a miller, full name Rembrandt Harmenszoon van Rijn.

1620 May: Enrolled at the University of Leyden for a short period.

1621 Apprenticed to the obscure painter Jacob Isacsz. van Swanenburgh with whom he remained for three years.

1624 Moved to Amsterdam where he was apprenticed to the then well-known painter Pieter Lastman.

1625 Returned to Leyden where he seems to have collaborated with Jan Lievens for a number of years.

1628 Gerard Dou appeared in Rembrandt's studio.

1631 First important commission, *The Anatomy Lesson of Dr Tulp* (Mauritshuis, The Hague) completed the following year.

1632 Moved to Amsterdam where he was to remain for the rest of his life.

1634 June: Married the wealthy Saskia van Uylenburgh, daughter of a burgomaster from Leeuwarden in Friesland.

1635 First child baptised, died the following year.

1638 Baptism of second child who died less than a month later.

1639 Rembrandt moved into a much larger house.

1640 Baptism of third child who died almost immediately.

1641 Birth of Titus.

1642 Painted *The Night Watch* (Rijksmuseum, Amsterdam). Death of Saskia.

*c.*1645 Hendrickje Stoffels, who was to act as a model for so many pictures, entered his household.

1654 Baptism of his illegitimate daughter Cornelia, the mother being Hendrickje.

1656/57 Sale of his property to avoid bankruptcy.

1658 Sale of his house

1660 Hendrickje and Titus establish an art dealing company with Rembrandt as their employee in order to avoid further creditors.

1661 Painted *The Conspiracy of Claudius Civilis* (Nationalmuseum, Stockholm) for the new Town Hall, Amsterdam.

1662 Removal of the *Claudius Civilis* from the Town Hall. Painted *The Syndics* (Rijksmuseum, Amsterdam).

1663 Death of Hendrickje.

1668 Marriage of Titus, followed almost immediately by his death.

1669 October 4: Death of Rembrandt.

Plate 2
Self-Portrait
dated 1633
oil on panel
$22\frac{3}{4} \times 17\frac{3}{4}$ in (58×45 cm)
Musée du Louvre, Paris

In the collection of the Duc de Choiseul in Paris and in his sale in 1772. Then in the collection of the Duc de Brissac from whom it was confiscated at the time of the Revolution and placed in the Louvre where it has remained ever since.

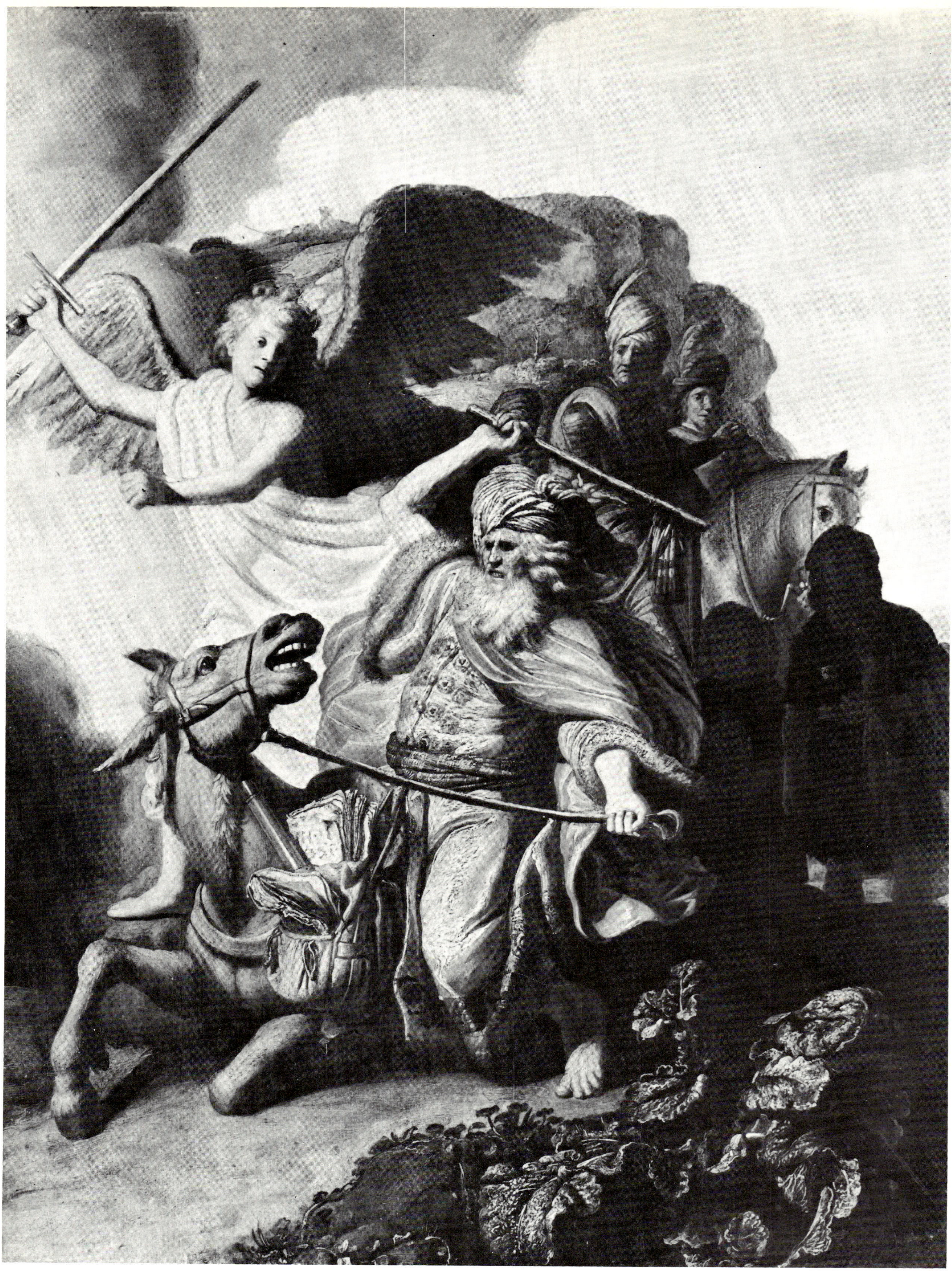

Rembrandt and his art

Plate 3
The Ass of Balaam
dated 1626
oil on panel
$24\frac{3}{4} \times 18\frac{1}{4}$ in (63×46.5 cm)
Musée Cognacq-Jay, Paris

One of the few pictures by Rembrandt to be in France at an early date. It was mentioned in a letter written by the French painter Claude Vignon in 1641. For the next two and a half centuries the picture was unknown until it appeared in an Amsterdam collection in 1905. On the Amsterdam art market in the same year and in 1907 in a private collection in Prague. In Paris two years later and then sold in New York in 1918. Then belonged to Ernest Cognacq who bequeathed it to the museum which bears his name in 1928.

Rembrandt is so much a part of the present-day cultural scene, so much respected, indeed revered, that the man himself, and his paintings, are seen through an agreeable but distorting haze. His contemporaries misunderstood him for they failed to see the way his art was developing. This is not in the least surprising as the artist stood so far apart from the accepted tastes of the Amsterdam of his time.

Dutch 17th-century painting is still regarded by collectors and connoisseurs as the moment when craftsmanship can be taken seriously as an end in itself. This was also the general attitude of Rembrandt's contemporaries and patrons. They had exacting standards and demanded that the artist portrayed, as carefully as possible, and within narrowly defined limits, the objects or people in front of him. This led quite naturally to specialisation–each artist achieving his reputation and making his living in the field of still-life, portraiture, seascape, landscape, or genre. Rembrandt began his career in just this manner, his first fruitful apprenticeship being to Pieter Lastman in Amsterdam. Lastman had a good reputation for religious and mythological pictures, which, even in the strongly Protestant Holland of the time, had a certain respectability above the other types of painting. This is also shown by the fact that Cornelis Cornelisz. van Haarlem, who also specialised in the same type of painting as Lastman, had a much higher reputation than his genre- or landscape-painting contemporaries in Haarlem.

It is easy to see that as a young man Rembrandt imitated his master by producing large religious pictures of an irritatingly pedestrian nature where the art of Lastman is caricatured. The earliest to survive is *The Stoning of Stephen* which is dated 1625 and has recently been discovered in the Musée des Beaux-Arts at Lyon. In fact, of course, Rembrandt soon turned to portraiture, which was lucrative. It seemed to satisfy him personally in the sense that it was in the field of uncommissioned portraiture, that is, of himself, that he was to create some of his most memorable canvases.

The causes of Rembrandt's failure in his own lifetime cannot be entirely explained away by his inability to please his patrons but it constitutes an important factor. The idea of the misanthropic artist creating masterpiece after masterpiece in isolation in an Amsterdam garret disappeared long ago, for it has often been shown that in his last years the artist received several important commissions, although he never had the general success he had enjoyed in the 1630s. Today the very difference between the art of Rembrandt and that of his contemporaries is seen as the chief cause of his great reputation. So many of the 'specialists', however clever, appear to modern eyes utterly predictable. It is perhaps worth adding that this was not so in the 18th and 19th centuries when collectors prized the work of a Dou or a Dujardin simply because it was both well painted and predictable. Interestingly enough, when a specialist in gentle light-soaked landscapes with cows like Aelbert Cuyp grew bored with his particular department and painted, for instance, a seascape, it succeeded in looking like all the other seascapes of his seascape specialist contemporary Jan van Goyen. It was this rigidity which Rembrandt broke down. When he painted a landscape, although there are points of reference to other artists, notably the German Adam Elsheimer, whose art was known to him through the engravings of Hendrick Goudt, the landscapes remain uniquely the vision of Rembrandt and stand quite apart from all the other landscapes painted in Holland at the time.

Rembrandt is often described as a genius which is usually taken to mean a talent so exceptional as to be unique. This is not entirely a fair interpretation, as a considerable number of his contemporaries had an exceptional talent. Those who have stood in that memorable room in the Frans Halsmuseum at Haarlem, where hang the two group portraits of the Governors and the Governesses of the old men's and old women's almshouses (plate 93) by Frans Hals, realise that they are in front of an exceptional talent, which by sheer force of emotion can drain the spectator of his own particular preoccupations and cause him to be, whether he likes it or not, at one with the picture. In this case Hals had what Rembrandt almost always has–the ability to make the spectator stop in his tracks and force him to look. Similar parallels could be drawn with other Dutch artists of the time. Jacob van Ruisdael and Meindert Hobbema, in their respective ways, were occasionally able to make statements about landscape which awaken some extra realisation about nature: thus they bring an extra dimension into the spectator's life by giving an experience which cannot be gained from nature itself.

Rembrandt had just this quality in most of his work. Even taking into account disputed works, some 400 paintings, 1,500 drawings and nearly 300 etchings, many in several states, have come down to us. Not a lot has been lost, but the incredible fact remains that most of the works that survive have what has been described as a 'life changing' quality.

On the problem of authenticity so much has been written, and will continue to be written, that the question seems both endless and fruitless. Yet logic would suggest that his work is relatively easy to recognise in spite of the fact that he had so many clever pupils in his own lifetime. They never really understood his art, and the spirit of Rembrandt was absent from all of them. Some of the pupils created distinguished pictures in their master's manner, like Jan Lievens (who probably collaborated with Rembrandt) and Gerard Dou, who, having got Rembrandt out of his system as a young man went on to specialise very successfully in a certain type of bourgeois interior painting. The controversies continue to rage, usually over pictures which everyone, scholars and public alike, accepts as work of high quality. The reasons for this are not always easy to see. Every generation re-interprets the art of the past, and new favourites emerge, while once-famous pictures are toppled from their pedestals by a change in taste. But this should not really affect the problem of authenticity, as, contrary to what is often believed, it is usually based on historical or scientific data (i.e. it is scientifically possible to determine whether a Rembrandt signature on a picture was added recently or goes back to the 17th century). Sometimes a picture which a recent scholar has decided to reject with much attendant publicity and with embarrassment and vexation on the part of the owner will be found on careful examination to have been doubted in the past. Nevertheless, recent attempts to purge Rembrandt's work of the dross which surrounds it has resulted in many a masterpiece being left in the miserable limbo of the anonymous. Two such paintings are here reproduced in colour – the Aix-en-Provence *Self-Portrait* (plate 80) and the Dresden *Sacrifice of Manoah* (plate 37) in order that the reader may consider the question himself.

The unfolding of Rembrandt's art, as it is to be told here, has concentrated on a selection of his best and most interesting pictures from all periods of his long and varied career, with a brief selection of his drawings and etchings, which have been chosen to show his talents rather than consider his development as an artist in these media.

As the son of a respectable miller of Leyden, which was the most important university town of Holland, Rembrandt attended the local university at a surprisingly early age, and then it appears that he was apprenticed to the obscure topographical painter Jacob Isaacsz. van Swanenburgh. The change from Swanenburgh to the fashionable Pieter Lastman in Amsterdam is the first turningpoint–and there were to be many–in the artist's career. Lastman's reputation evaporated with his death, and today he remains an elusive artist–his works are scattered–but his relatively few surviving pictures have a solid traditional character derived from Italian models and also from his reputed master Cornelis Cornelisz. van Haarlem. Lastman was not alone in practising this kind of art, and this academic style seems to have held sway among artists in most of the other Dutch cities as well, Wtewael and Bloemaert in Utrecht and the previously mentioned Cornelis Cornelisz. in Haarlem. Lastman created rather unsubtle pictures with fairly strong light and shade and quite thickly applied paint–the general impression he gives being rather coarse. Most of Rembrandt's very early pictures are pale and slightly less aggressive imitations of this style, *The Ass of Balaam* (plate 3) in the Musée Cognacq-Jay in Paris being typical. Interestingly enough, there has recently appeared on the London art market a previously unknown Lastman of 1622 of the same subject from which Rembrandt clearly derived his composition.

A far more important influence, but one difficult to assess, of Rembrandt's early artistic life is his association with Jan Lievens. They were virtually the same age, and it can be surmised that they set up a studio together in Leyden whence Rembrandt had returned after his short time with Lastman. They must have used the same models and even collaborated on the same pictures, but the confusing fact which emerges is that, when the picture is clearly by Lievens himself, it appears far more daring and accomplished than when it is by Rembrandt. A case in point is Rembrandt's *The Raising of Lazarus* (plate 4), recently acquired by the Los Angeles County Museum, which has all the marks of his early style although it cannot be specifically dated. The colours are exceptionally delicate and there is a certain smoky blue haze. But when this is compared to Jan Lievens' treatment of the same subject in the Brighton Art Gallery (plate 5), which is dated 1631, the year before Rembrandt's final return to Amsterdam, it is easy to see how much Lievens had profited from Rembrandt from the point of view of the drama of the scene, but what is so tantalising is the introduction of the idea that understatement is more effective than the striving after the obviously dramatic effect. Lazarus's hands only are visible and the winding sheet is pulled up in a great curve. It is just this sort of understatement coupled with drama that

Plate 4
The Raising of Lazarus
about 1630
oil on panel
$36\frac{3}{4} \times 31\frac{7}{8}$ in (93.5×81 cm)
County Museum of Art, Los Angeles
Gift of H. F. Ahmanson and Co. in memory of H. F. Ahmanson

Formerly in the Dübi-Müller collection at Solothurn and later in the Ahmanson collection, Los Angeles. Recently acquired from the latter by the County Museum of Art.

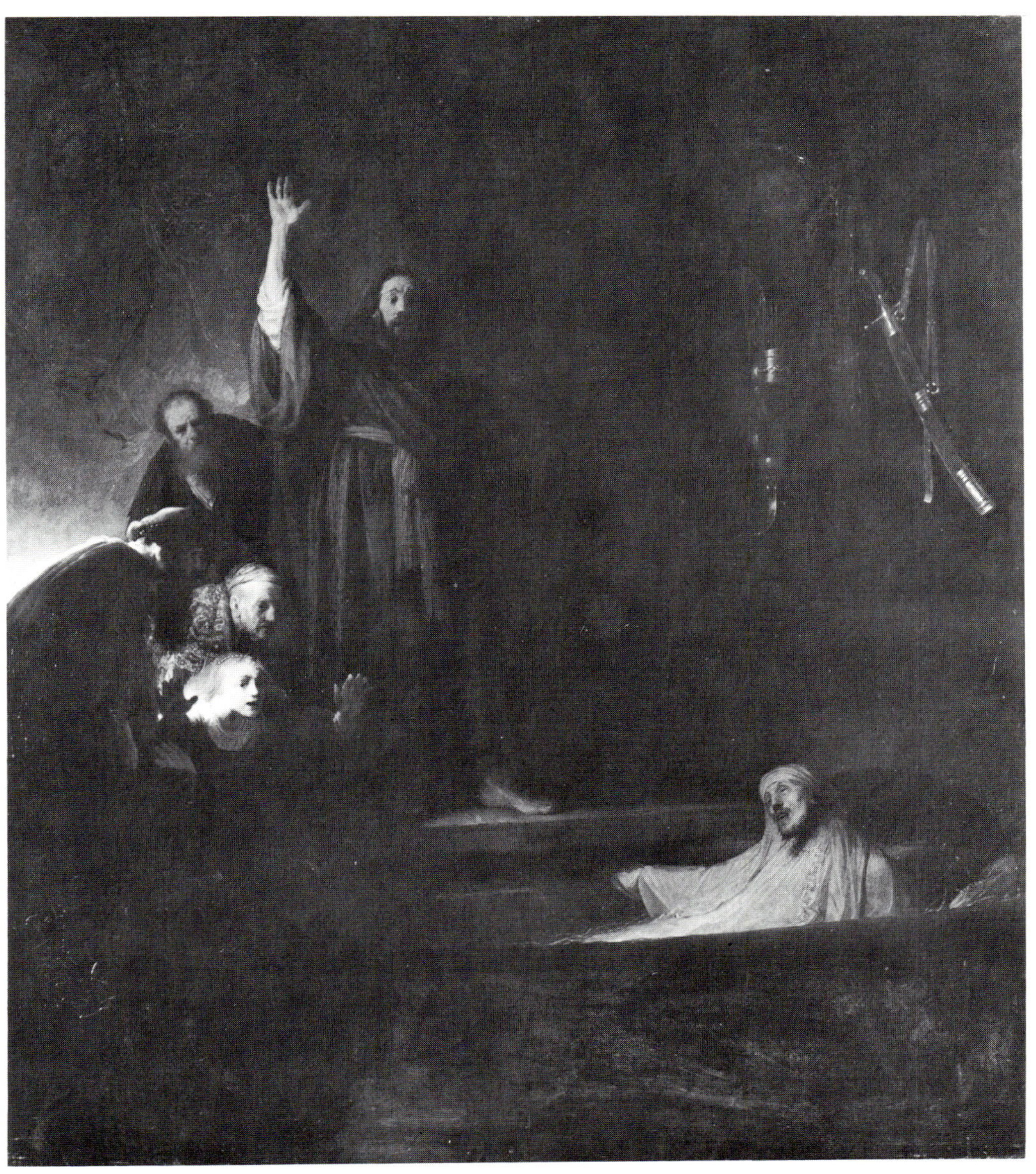

Plate 5
Jan Lievens
The Raising of Lazarus
dated 1631
oil on canvas
$42\frac{1}{8} \times 44\frac{7}{8}$ in (107×114 cm)
Art Gallery and Museums, Brighton

It is very likely that this painting belonged to Rembrandt himself as a picture answering its description appears in the inventory of his goods drawn up at the time of his bankruptcy in 1656. Recorded in the collection of Jan Jacobsz. Hinloopen in Amsterdam in 1662, who also owned Rembrandt's *Christ and His Disciples on the Sea of Galilee* (plate 12). Subsequently appeared in several Dutch sales in the 18th and 19th centuries and for the last time at Christie's in June 1884. It was acquired soon after by Henry Willett of Brighton, a noted collector of Italian pictures. Presented by him to the gallery in 1903.

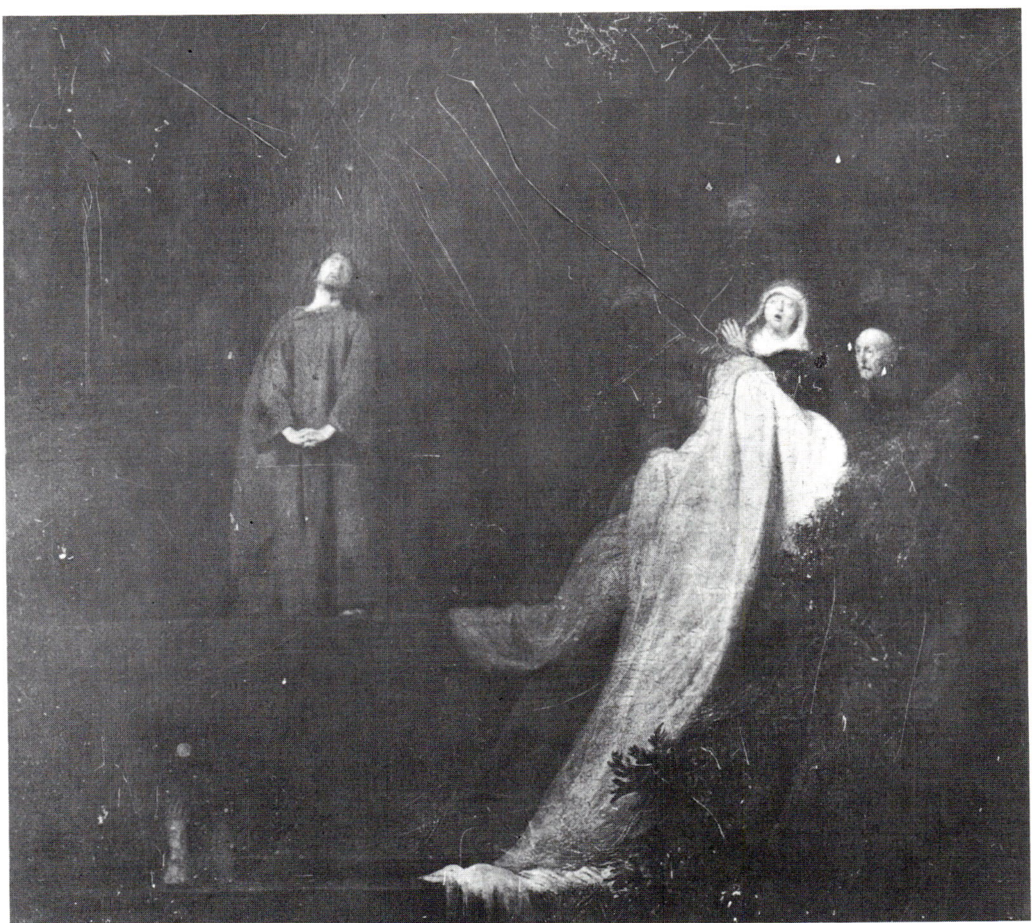

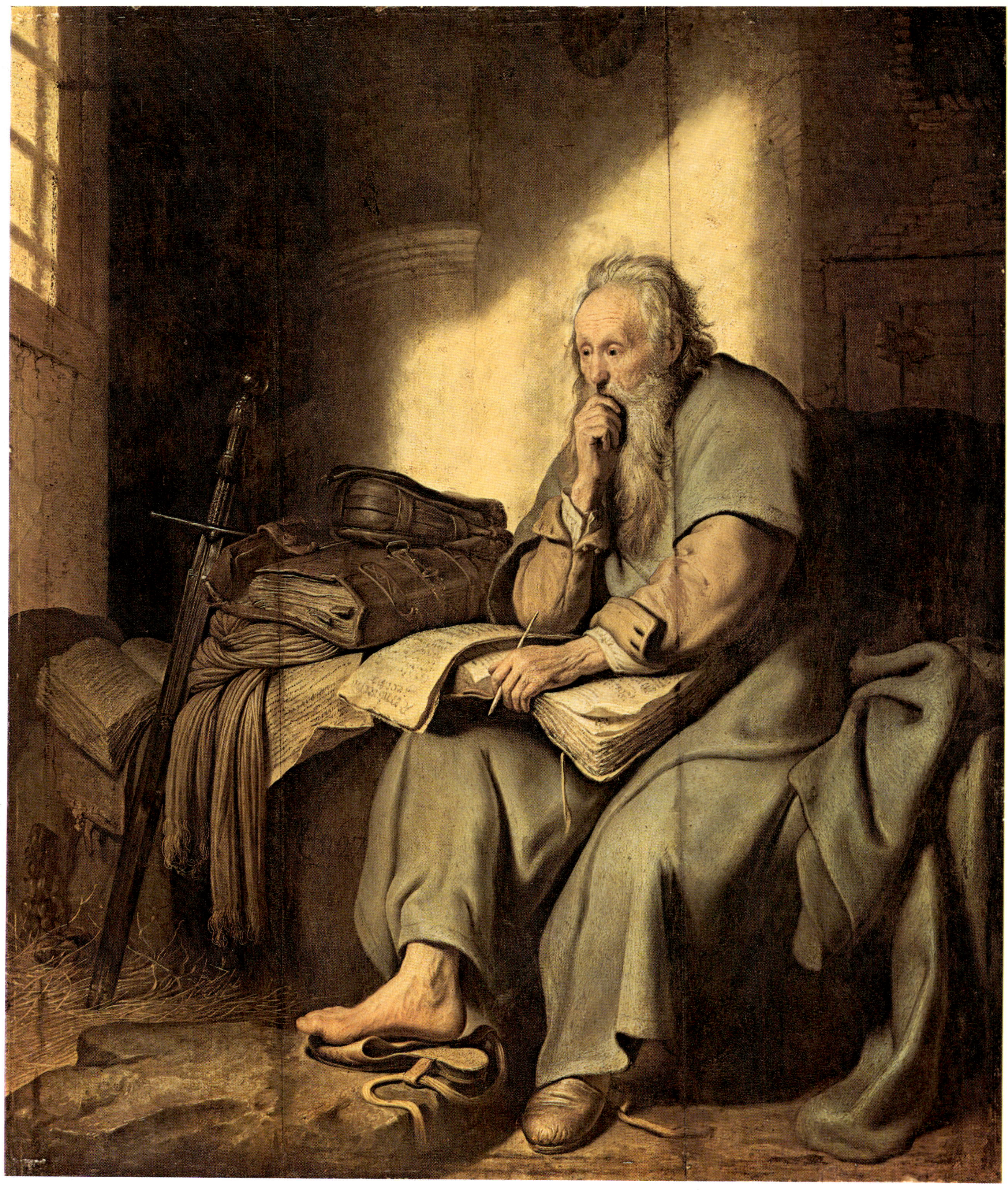

Plate 6
St Paul in Prison
dated 1627
oil on panel
$28\frac{3}{4} \times 23\frac{7}{8}$ in (73 × 60.5 cm)
Staatsgalerie, Stuttgart

In the collection of the Count von Schönborn at Pommersfelden by 1719. Acquired by the museum in 1867.

Plate 7
Self-Portrait
about 1629
oil on panel
$14\frac{3}{4} \times 11\frac{1}{2}$ in (37.5 × 29 cm)
Mauritshuis, The Hague

In the collection of G. von Slingelandt in 1752 and acquired by the Stadtholder William V in 1768. Removed to France in 1795 by the French occupying forces and returned to The Hague after 1815 where it has remained ever since.

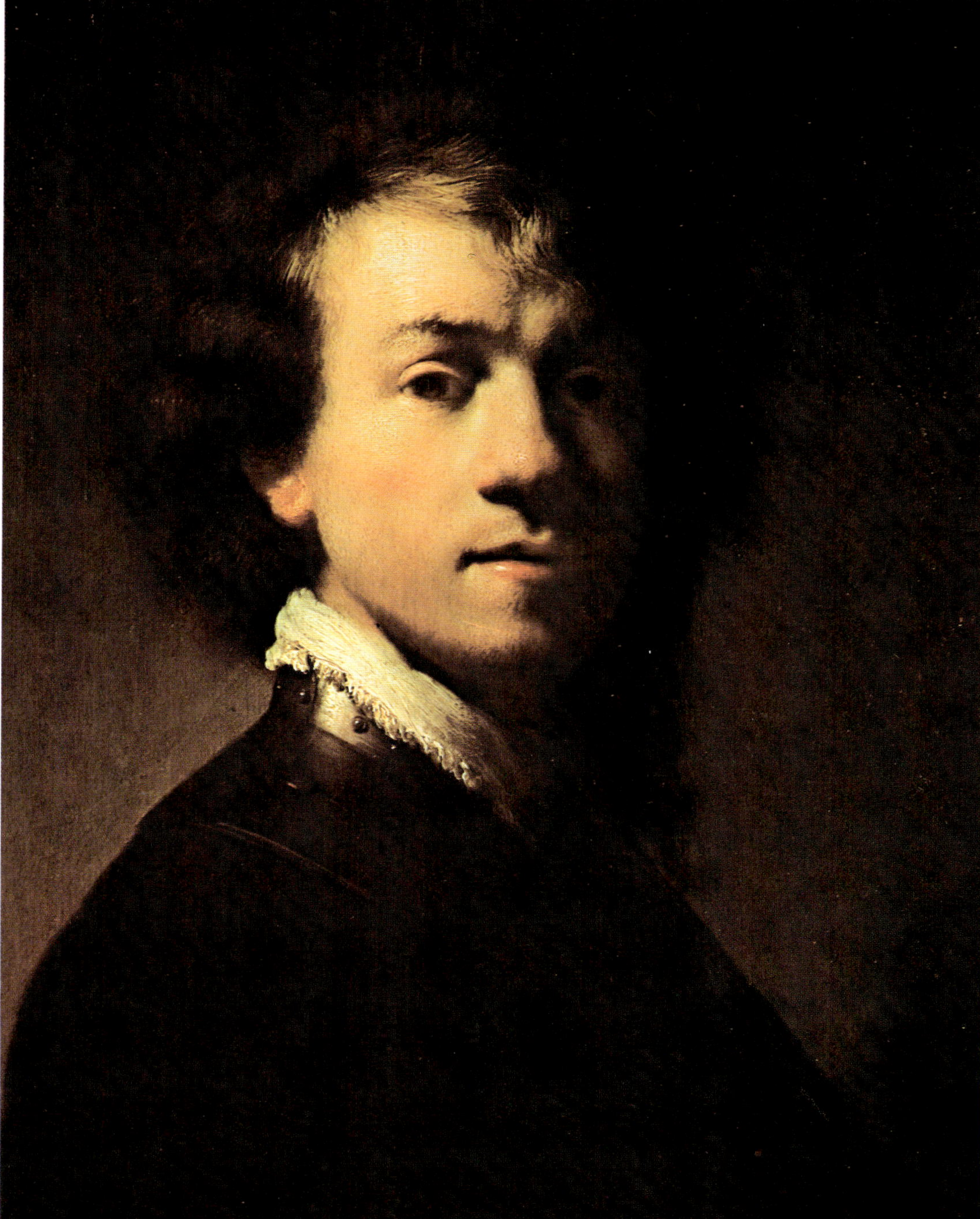

Rembrandt is to take up much later in his career, and which he must have learned from Lievens. We can only surmise all this from the fortunate survival of the picture in Brighton, and it has to be admitted that Rembrandt's greatness is not immediately apparent in these early works.

The *St Paul in Prison* (plate 6) of 1627 in the Staatsgalerie at Stuttgart is a perfect example of the struggle of the young artist (he was only twenty-one) to make sense out of the problems of composition, the handling of light and shade. The latter had taken on a new significance as the influence of that master of light and shade, Caravaggio, was really beginning to make itself felt in Holland at that moment. The saint is shown rather obviously

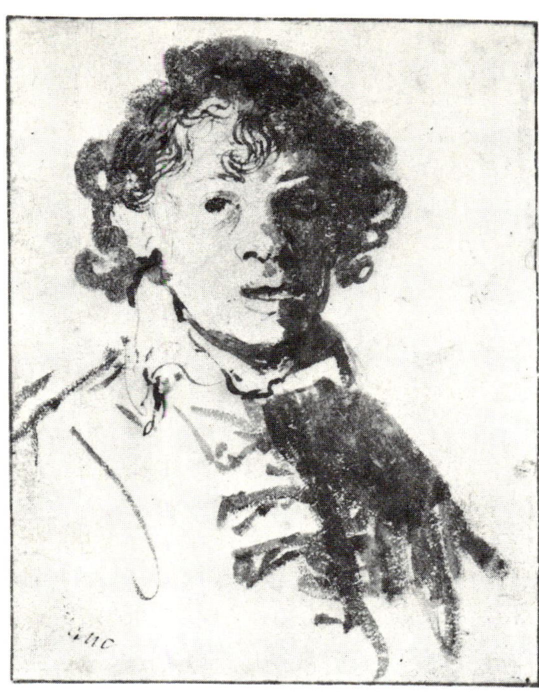

Plate 8
Self-Portrait
about 1627–28
pen and wash
5 × 3¾ in (12.7 × 9.5 cm)
British Museum, London

Formerly in the Gacherode Collection.

Plate 9
Jeremiah Contemplating the Destruction of Jerusalem
dated 1630
oil on panel
22¾ × 18⅛ in (58 × 46 cm)
Rijksmuseum, Amsterdam

Recorded in the Cesar Collection, Berlin, in 1760. Then in the Stroganoff Collection, St Petersburg, and after that in a private collection in Stockholm.
Acquired by the Rijksmuseum from a private collection in 1939.

abstracted in thought with his hand on his chin, and around him is a litter of books as he thinks of what to write next. Even at this stage Rembrandt was in full control of his brush from the point of view of his extraordinary ability to render texture–the books, the saint's hair, the light on the wall; only the penetration of character is lacking.

Also from approximately the same date is the *Self-Portrait* (plate 7) in the Mauritshuis in The Hague. Here the artist has shown himself full-face, a convention which was not often used. In spite of the youth of the sitter there is already a sense of gravity which was to increase many fold in his later pictures. Already there is his passion for fancy dress: he has depicted himself in armour, and his hair is elaborately arranged over his forehead. But it is the treatment of the light and shade which is the most important aspect of the picture. The question of the sources of his peculiar lighting has often been discussed: the influence of Caravaggio can be said to be pervasive in a general sense following the arrival after 1620 of a whole new generation of artists, slightly older than Rembrandt, who had been trained in Italy, and even the arch-Mannerist Bloemaert made a number of quite convincing essays in Caravaggio's manner. The light falling on the right side of Rembrandt's face produces a deliberately dramatic effect–the head appears to emerge from the surrounding darkness, yet the softening of the edges on one side of the shoulder and the careful variation of the tonality of the background assures the three-dimensional quality of the sitter. At this point it is difficult to foresee that Rembrandt was to paint himself over fifty times, and not all of these can have been because he had nothing else to paint. But the number of self-portraits does in fact increase in his last years when commissions were fewer, but even when he seems to be at his busiest, with commissions, with his family and business affairs, he never lost interest in painting himself. One of the artist's early drawings to survive is the very direct *Self-Portrait* (plate 8) in the British Museum, London, which is generally dated to about 1627–28. There is the same dramatic lighting as in the Hague self-portrait (plate 7), but the mood is entirely different in the sense that it is very much less calculated; the half-open mouth gives an impression of liveliness.

The three years which separate the Stuttgart *St Paul* (plate 6) and the *Jeremiah Contemplating the Destruction of Jerusalem* (plate 9) in the Rijksmuseum, Amsterdam, show how far the artist had changed in this comparatively short time. The rather laboured conventions of the *St Paul* have disappeared, and the figure is now completely integrated into the setting. The prophet is seen

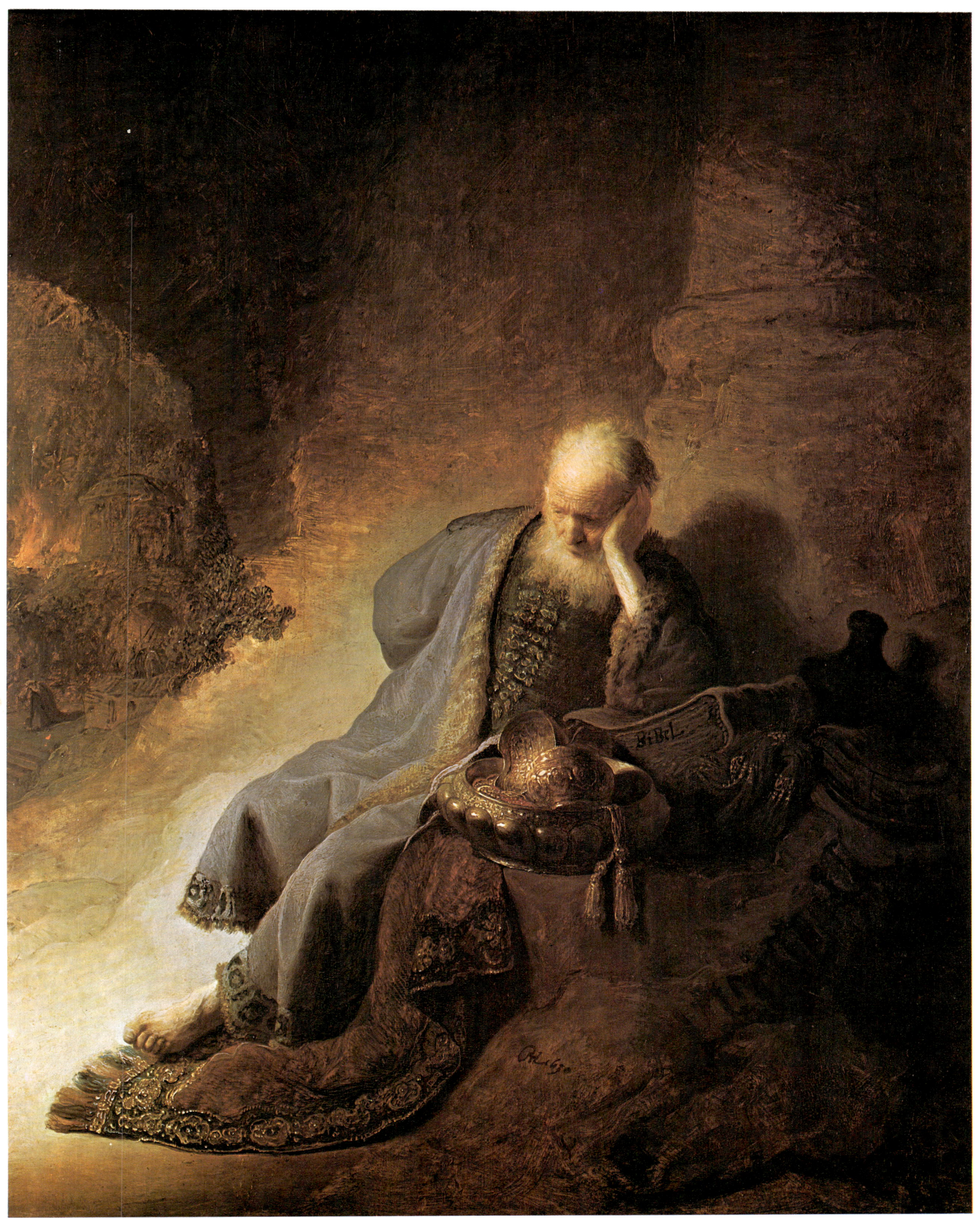
Bibel

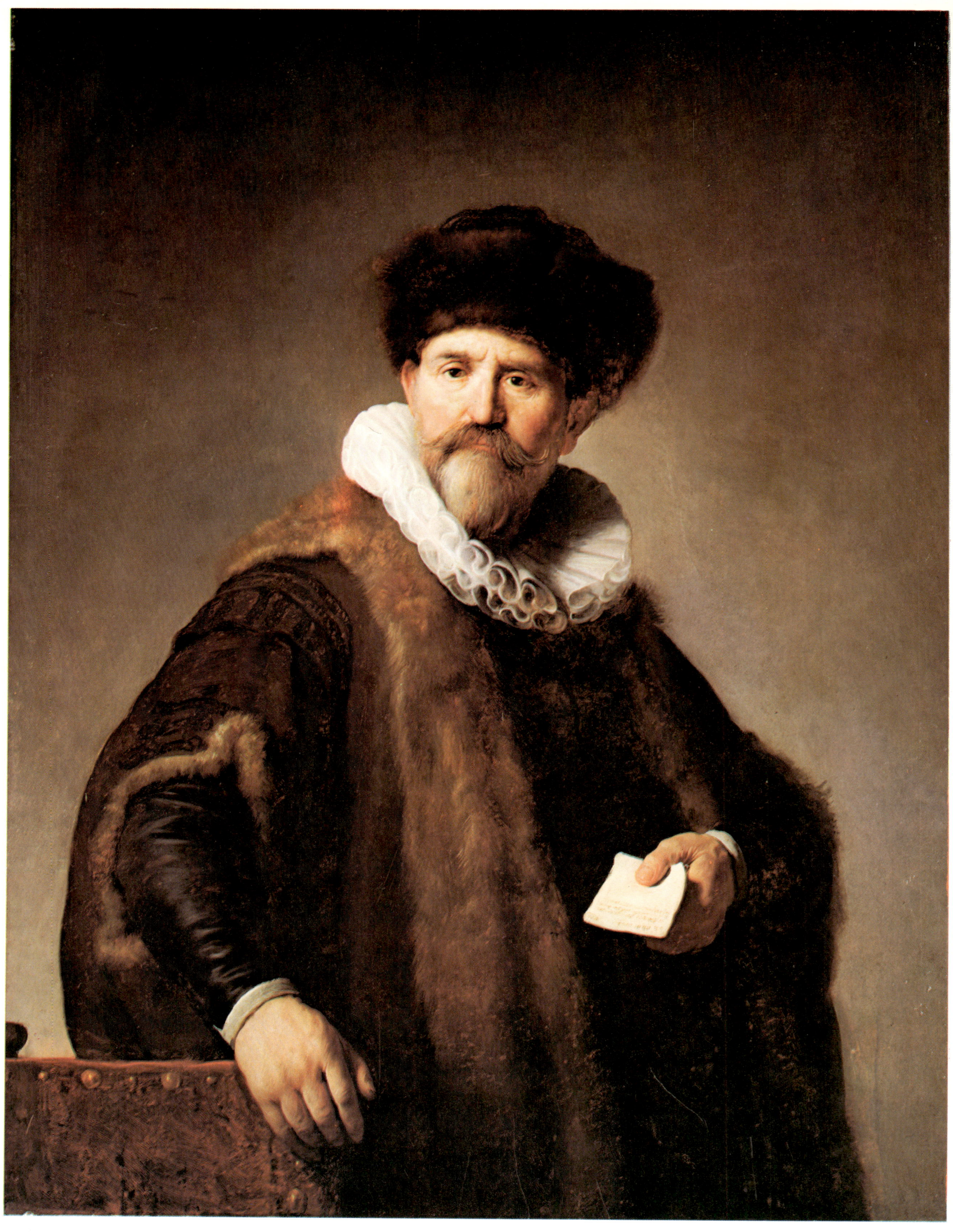

Plate 10
Portrait of the Merchant Nicolaes Ruts
about 1631
oil on panel
$45\frac{1}{4} \times 33\frac{5}{8}$ in (115 × 85.5 cm)
Frick Collection, New York

The picture has a complicated history: it was in the collection of the Stadtholder William II of the Netherlands in the 18th century and in several different collections in England in the 19th century. Acquired by the Frick Collection from Knoedler in 1943.

surrounded by inhospitable rocks, while his beloved Jerusalem burns in the left background. The drama of the fire and the desolation are minimised–the artist is much more interested in Jeremiah himself. The prophet is richly dressed, which contrasts all the more with the gloom around him. He wears a robe of a certain sort of cool blue, which is found in a number of Rembrandt's early pictures, its use being particularly striking in the little *Flight into Egypt* in the Musée des Beaux-Arts at Tours. Jeremiah is leaning his head in his hand in an attitude of contemplative despair. The emotion is subtle, for there is a sense of infinite sadness on the old man's face, the deeply felt regret in the destruction before him.

The Presentation in the Temple (plate 1) in the Mauritshuis in The Hague is a startling advance, again more rapid than that seen between the *St Paul* and the *Jeremiah*. The artist has taken the moment when the aged Simeon takes the infant Jesus in his arms– while the Virgin is seated nearby almost completely surrounded by priests and elders. The setting is dramatic in the extreme. The architecture of the temple is on a grandiose scale: vaguely Gothic, half ruined, half finished, it gives an air of total mystery to the whole scene, while Simeon, who has been promised by the Lord that he should not see Death before he had seen the Lord's Christ, recites the *Nunc Dimittis*.

Rembrandt took his religious subjects very seriously, and his knowledge of the Bible, including the Apocrypha, was exceptional in the sense that he frequently depicted unusual stories. He also has an amazing concern for accuracy to the original text–only rarely does he use artistic licence. It is almost always possible to pin-point the precise source of the subject–in the case of the *Presentation* Luke ii, 25–35. His religious pictures from this early period are relatively numerous, such as the small *St Paul in Meditation* in the Germanisches Nationalmuseum at Nuremberg, the *Tribute Money* in the National Gallery of Canada in Ottawa, and the recently discovered *Crucifixion* in the parish church of Le Mas d'Agenais (Lot-et-Garonne), France.

While the artist was so preoccupied with these religious pictures, his interest in portraiture was not entirely neglected. Many of the sitters have been identified, and most of them were rich merchants or professionals. One of the most important of these is the *Portrait of Nicolaes Ruts* (plate 10) in the Frick Collection, New York, which is dated 1631. It is indeed difficult to believe that this was painted in the same year as the Mauritshuis *Presentation* (plate 1), but already the artist had mastered several different areas of subject-matter and thus was able to change his style depending on the sort of commission required. Ruts was a very rich merchant, then at

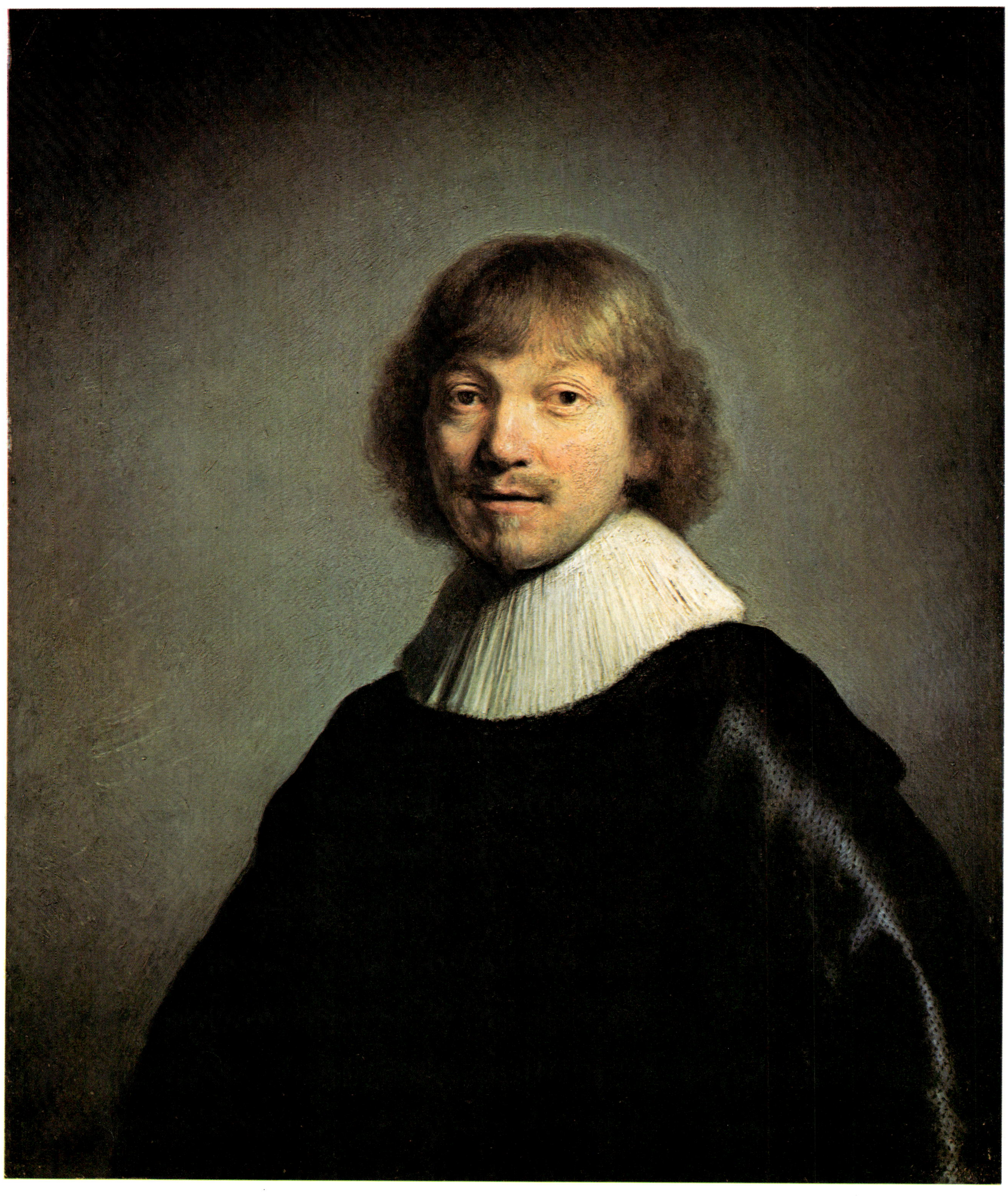

Plate 11
Portrait of Jacob de Gheyn III
dated 1632
oil on panel
$11\frac{3}{4} \times 9\frac{3}{4}$ in (30×25 cm)
Dulwich College Picture Gallery, London

Bequeathed by the sitter to his friend Maurits Huyghens in 1641. There is then a break in the history of the picture until it was sold in Paris in 1804. It was then acquired by the dealer-collector Noel Desenfans who in 1807 bequeathed it to his friend Sir Peter Francis Bourgeois. He in turn bequeathed it, along with 370 other pictures, to Alleyn's College of God's Gift, Dulwich, where it has been since 1811.

the end of his long life, and Rembrandt has depicted him with his intelligent and slightly quizzical face, his hand on the back of a chair. The background is empty, verging on a suggestion of the infinite, and it is painted with a carefully modulated cool tone which makes the fur-trimmed gown of the sitter appear all the more solid and opulent. For sheer technical mastery of the conventional manner of painting as his contemporaries understood it, Rembrandt never surpassed himself. His later experiments in technique were to have the effect of adding a new dimension to painting. Before him only Titian, of whom he was a great admirer, had experimented with the textural qualities of oil paint to such an extent. Here in the Ruts portrait the appurtenances of success, the starched ruff, the fur on the gown, the flesh, slightly puffy from over indulgence, are all recorded in a basically smooth technique, although in the beard there is some vigorous scratching with the end of the brush while the paint was still wet. The general effect of the picture is overwhelming; the dazzle of the fur, the infinitely complex play of subdued light and shade, all of which is subordinated to the character of the man, make mysterious the technique by which the illusion was created. Very much the same is true of the tiny portrait of the Dutch painter and engraver Jacob de Gheyn III (plate 11) in the Dulwich College Picture Gallery. The convention of the slightly hazy background is repeated, and again Rembrandt shows himself to be a master of conventional technique. But the real achievements of this exquisite object is the sense of intimacy and humanity which the artist has given the sitter, who was also an artist. There has been no neccessity for grandeur as in the Nicolaes Ruts portrait.

The year 1632 marks the first major turningpoint in Rembrandt's career. Until this time many of his pictures are seen to be great, simply because they anticipate what is to come, but when he painted *The Anatomy Lesson of Dr Tulp* (plate 12), now in the Mauritshuis in The Hague, it can be said that he had, at the age of twenty-six, achieved the first major masterpiece of his career.

Group portraits had been the stock-in-trade of Dutch painting for almost a hundred years. Even the extreme Mannerist Cornelis van Haarlem had tried it with conspicuous success, as Frans Hals had seen fit to use the Cornelis composition when painting one of his own group portraits. Coupled with the tradition of the customary group portraits of militia companies and boards of governors (this survives today in the form of the school or team photograph and the board-room portrait) there was the convention of painting anatomy lessons.

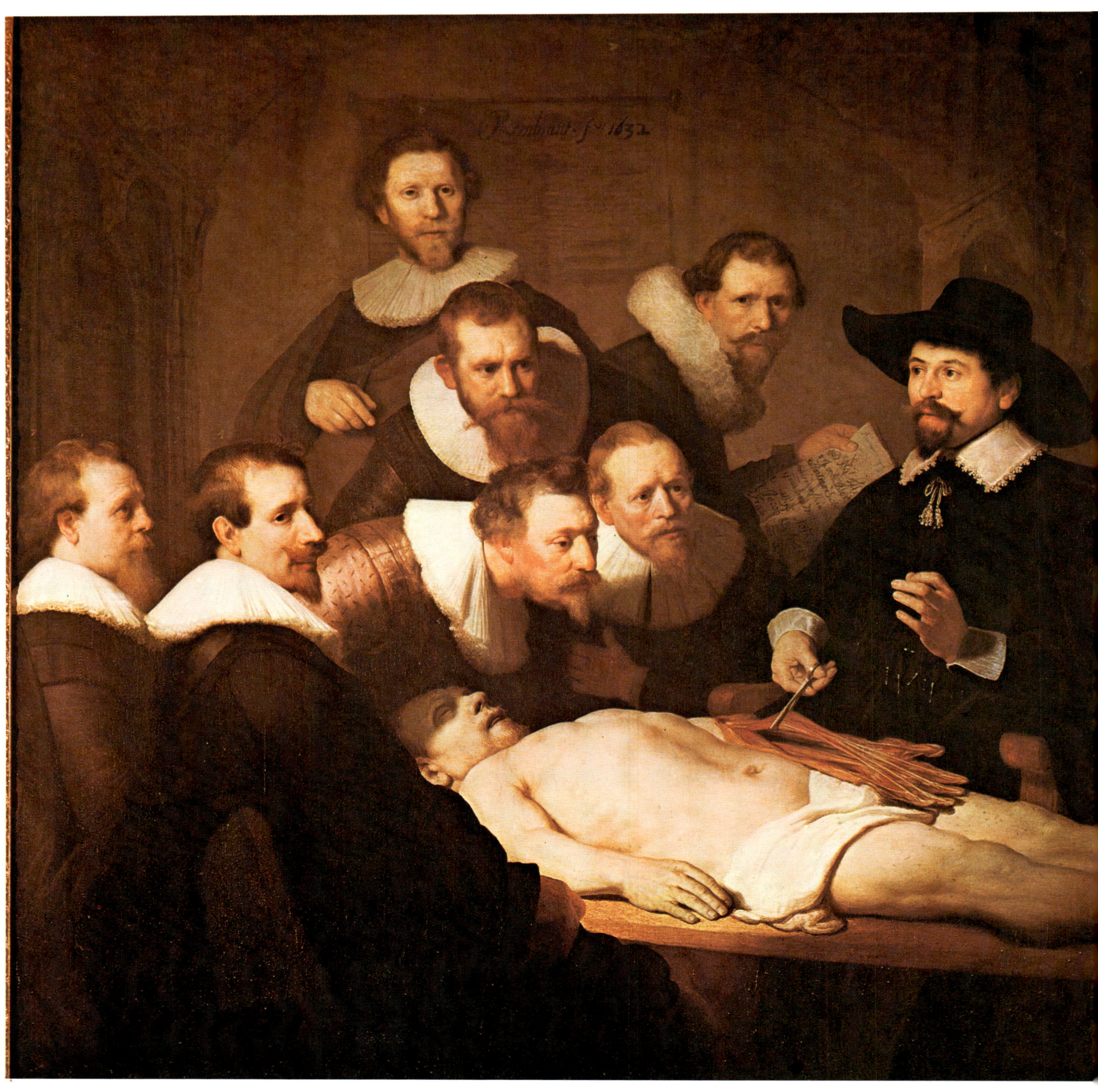

Plate 12 *see page 24*

It was the custom in Holland for learned physicians to dissect the human body in public, the corpses of convicted criminals being used for the purpose. When it is realised that the discovery of the circulation of the blood, with the consequent increase of surgical knowledge, had fairly recently been made, the excitement and interest that these grisly operations stimulated is easily understood.

Rembrandt has shown the learned Dr Tulp at the moment when he is demonstrating the anatomy of the arm. Dr Tulp himself appears almost indifferent to the excitement and curiosity he is causing in his audience, who also in some cases have an air of slight unease. As a composition the picture is not altogether successful,as for instance the artist must have been required to produce a careful likeness of all those present, which means that the dramatic quality of the picture is sacrificed to this end. Seen in isolation Dr Tulp could almost be a straight portrait, and the relationship between the other figures is awkward and sometimes impossible. The position of the corpse straight along the front of the canvas has the effect of drawing the eye towards the right-hand side of the picture, which involved the artist in attempting to close the composition with the large anatomy book at which nobody seems to be looking. Such a picture satisfied the demands of the most philistine of patrons–all was seen to be there. In spite of criticisms, however, the picture has a grave presence, the characters come to life on the canvas and there is a feeling that the whole scene is being enacted right in front of the spectator.

Rembrandt did not attempt any more elaborate compositions of this type for some years to come, but seen in retrospect such large pictures form a thread through his career culminating in *The Syndics* (plate 92) thirty years later. Occasionally Rembrandt departed so completely from his own conventions, let alone those of his contemporaries, and produces something so totally unexpected that had the particular picture not survived, its existence could not possibly be deduced. Such a picture is the *Christ and His Disciples on the Sea of Galilee* (plate 13), dated 1633, in the Isabella Stewart Gardner Museum, Boston. The artist has painted the storm with an astonishing bravura, not to say dramatic exaggeration. In order to give the impression of the maximum confusion the boat has been tipped at an angle of almost forty-five degrees, while some of the rigging, which has broken loose, flies helplessly in the wind. The picture is an interesting example of the artist's eternal versatility: whatever genre he attempted there is the same accomplishment. Obviously he was not really interested in the sea, as this is the only picture of this type to survive from the whole of his career, but he painted it with a mastery which would

Plate 12
The Anatomy Lesson of Dr Tulp
dated 1632
oil on canvas
$66\frac{3}{4} \times 85\frac{1}{4}$ in (169.5 × 216.5 cm)
Mauritshuis, The Hague

Painted for the Corporation of Surgeons of Amsterdam and placed in the Anatomy Theatre there. Put up for sale by the administrators of the Company of Surgeons in 1828 and bought, before the sale, by King William I of Holland for 32,000 florins, and given to the Mauritshuis.

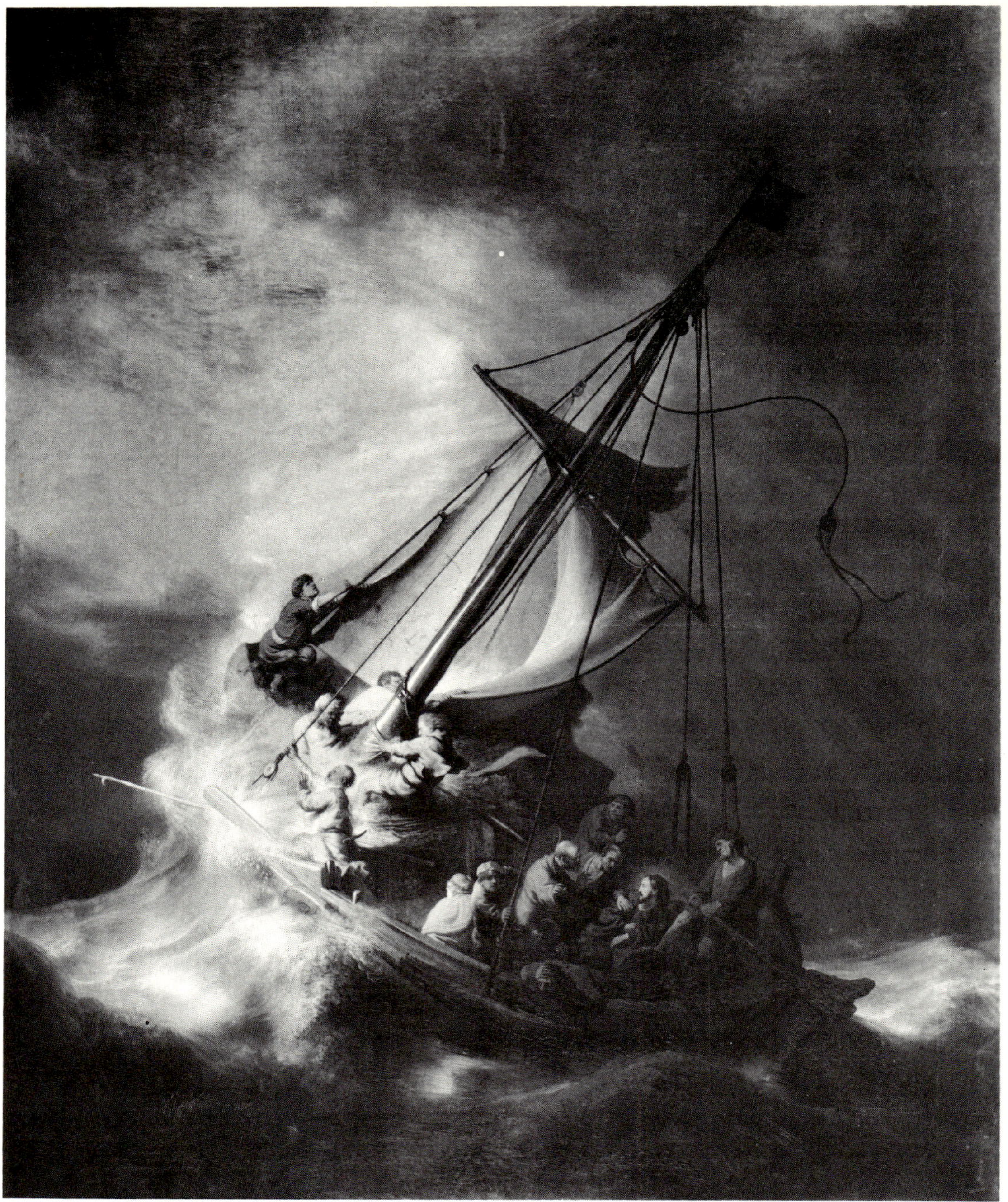

Plate 13
Christ and His Disciples on the Sea of Galilee
dated 1633
oil on panel
63 × 50 in (160 × 127 cm)
Isabella Stewart Gardner Museum, Boston

First recorded in the 17th century as having belonged to the Burgomaster Jan Jacobsz. Hinloopen in Amsterdam. Then in the collection of King Augustus III of Poland in 1765. Sold in Amsterdam in 1771 when it was bought by Henry Thomas Hope. By descent from him the picture eventually became the property of the 6th Duke of Newcastle. Sold by him to Colnaghi, London, in 1898 and acquired in the same year by Isabella Stewart Gardner through Bernard Berenson.

lead the uninformed to think that he was a specialist in this field.

The oval *Self-Portrait* (plate 2) in the Louvre, Paris, dated 1633, when the artist was 27 years of age, makes it clear that Rembrandt was already losing the first flush of youth and settling down to what seems, from the fifty or so self-portraits, to be a long middle age. He has the same slightly worried face as the spectators in the recently completed *Anatomy Lesson*. His use of colour is much more subdued at this point. It has, however, to be admitted that there is no general trend as far as his use of colour is concerned in the sense that he may paint a series of virtually monochrome pictures and then suddenly use those brilliant reds and golds which make *The Jewish Bride* (plate 97) so unforgettable. The only relief in the Louvre picture is the gold chain the artist is wearing–

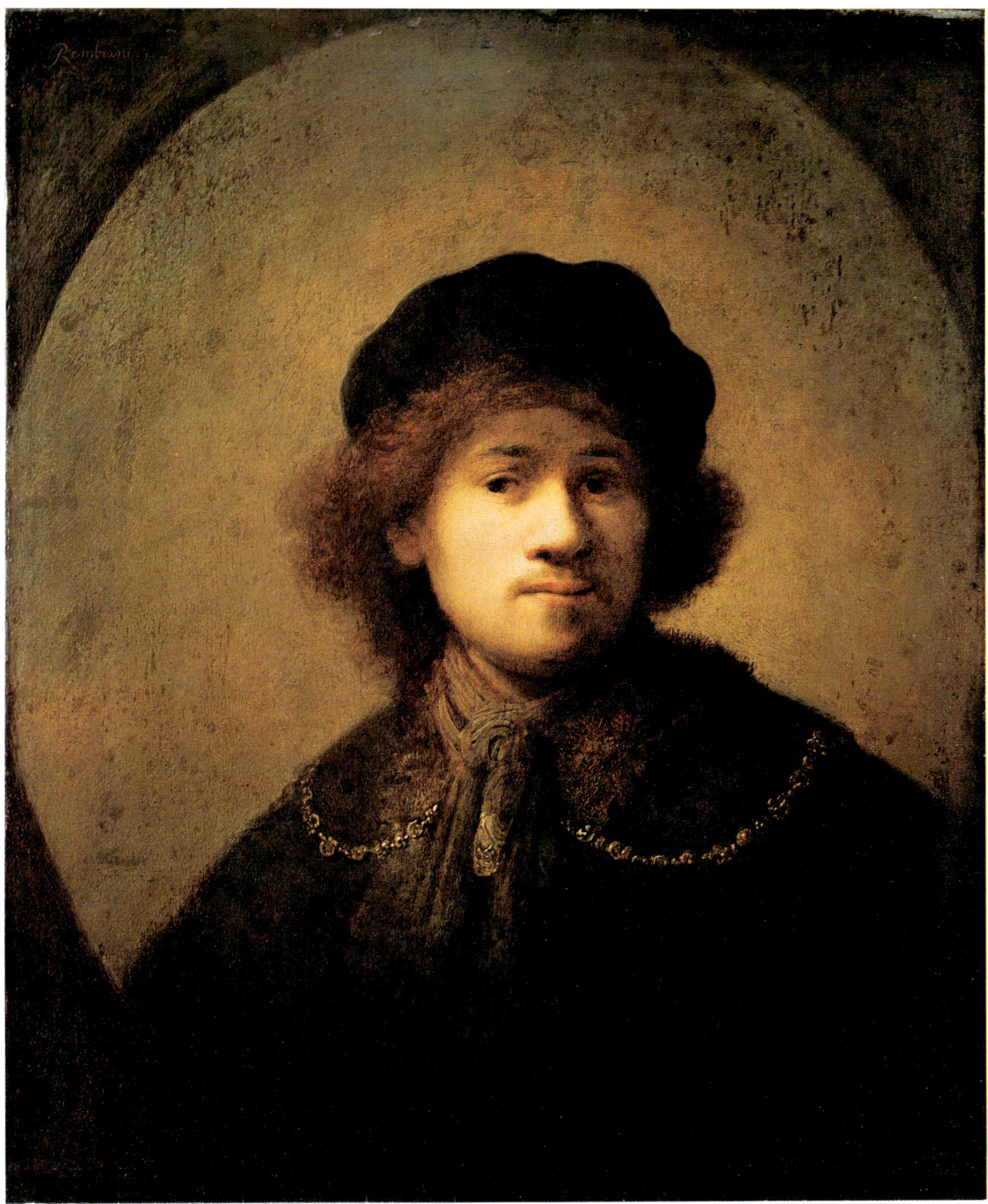

Plate 14
Self-Portrait
late 1620s
oil on panel
$28\frac{3}{4} \times 22\frac{3}{4}$ in (72.5 × 58 cm)
Walker Art Gallery, Liverpool

Given to Lord Ancram by the Stadtholder Frederick in 1629. The former gave it to Charles I of England in 1633. It is described in the inventory of Charles I's collection drawn up by Van der Doort as 'Item above my Lo: Ankrom's doore the picture done by Rembrandt being his owne picture done by himself in a black cap and furred habbitt with a little goulden chaine uppon both his shouldrs. In an oval and square black frame.' Sold by the Commonwealth in 1651. The picture was then untraced for almost two centuries. It appeared in the collection of the Lord de l'Isle and Dudley at Penshurst Place, Kent, and was sold at Sotheby's in 1948. Bought at the sale by Mrs Borthwick Norton from whom it was acquired in 1953 and presented to the Walker Art Gallery by Alfred Holt & Co.

the same chain appears in the moody *Self-Portrait* (plate 14) now in the Walker Art Gallery, Liverpool. This Liverpool picture has been dated as early as about 1629–it can hardly be very much later, as it is virtually certain that it belonged to Charles I of England in 1632, thus being one of the few pictures by Rembrandt to leave Holland at this early date. Doubts have been cast on the Liverpool portrait, as it seems to be painted in a style that Rembrandt took up later in his career, but a careful examination of most of his early pictures reveals that he constantly changed his style of painting to suit his mood or the commission. Only when he became older did he settle down and produce the 'typical' Rembrandt beloved by us all.

An example of this highly successful type of society portraiture

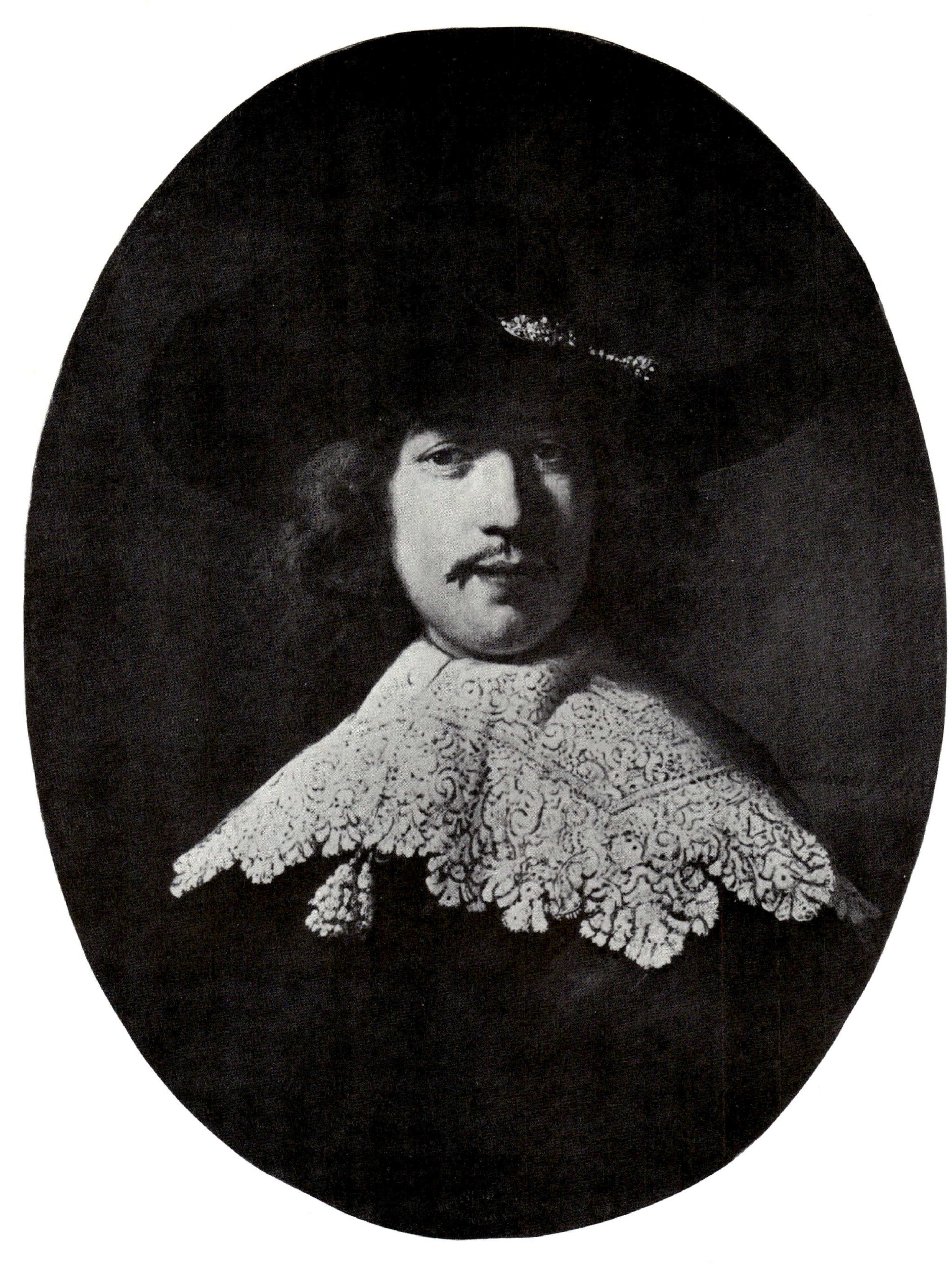

Plate 15
Portrait of an Unknown Man
dated 1634
oil on panel
$27\frac{1}{2} \times 20\frac{1}{2}$ in (70×52 cm)
Hermitage, Leningrad

is the pair of pictures now divided between the Hermitage in Leningrad (plate 15) and the collection of the Duke of Sutherland, which is on loan to the National Gallery of Scotland at Edinburgh. The lady at Edinburgh (plate 16) is shown in all her finery and with flowers in her hair. For the Dutch, flowers always had a deep

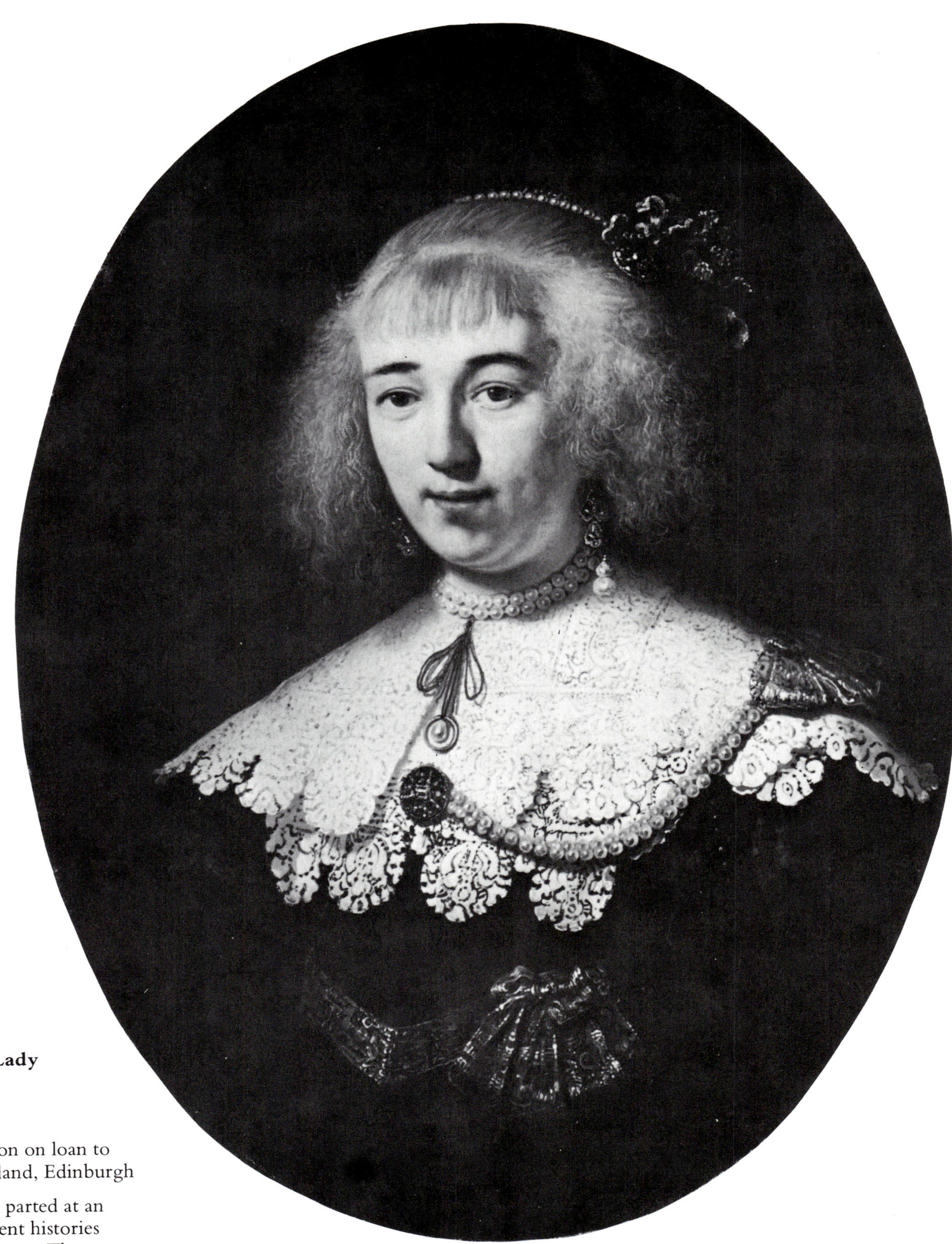

Plate 16
Portrait of an Unknown Lady
dated 1634
oil on panel
28 × 20⅞ in (71 × 53.5 cm)
Duke of Sutherland Collection on loan to the National Gallery of Scotland, Edinburgh

The pictures must have been parted at an early date as they have different histories from the end of the 18th century. The Leningrad picture was acquired from the Duchesse de St-Leu in 1829, while that in the collection of the Duke of Sutherland was bought by the Marquess of Stafford sometime before 1808. It passed by descent to the present Duke of Sutherland who has lent it to the National Gallery of Scotland since 1946.

allegorical significance. Some of this tradition survives today in the sense that lilies, for instance, are connected with Easter or funerals, but in the 17th century every flower was associated with some emotion or was thought to have medicinal properties. Thus we cannot now explain just what was meant by each flower in the

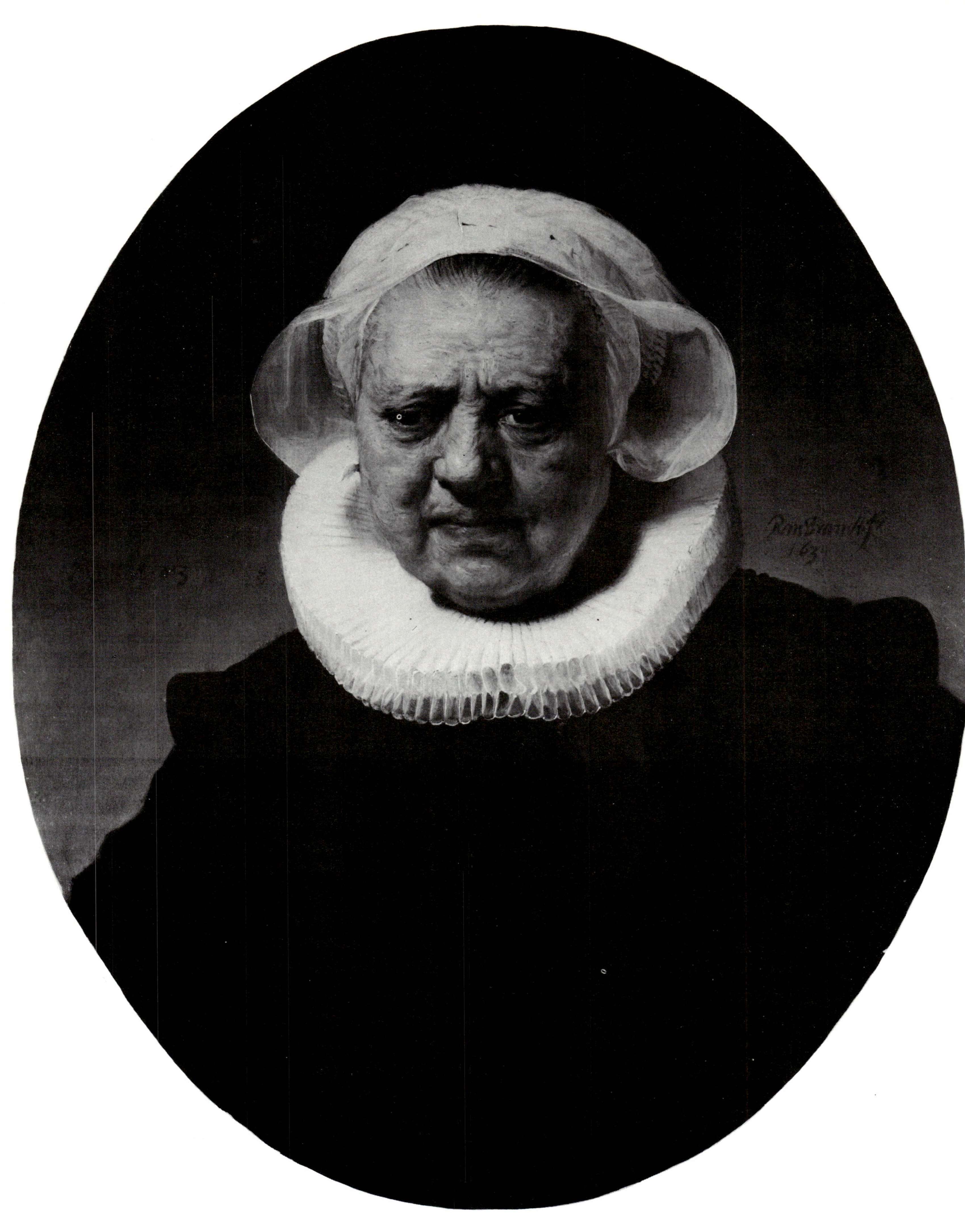

Plate 17
Portrait of an 83-year-old Woman
dated 1634
oil on panel
27 × 21⅛ in (68.5 × 53.5 cm)
National Gallery, London

Appeared in several sales in Holland in the late 18th and early 19th centuries. In England by 1835 in which year it was exhibited at the British Institution. Acquired by Sir Charles Eastlake, then director of the National Gallery, London, for his own collection. Bequeathed to the gallery by his widow in 1867.

Plate 18
The Raising of the Cross
about 1634
oil on canvas
37¾ × 28⅜ in (96 × 72 cm)
Alte Pinakothek, Munich

The whole series was in the collection of Prince Frederick Henry of Orange in 1647 and was also mentioned in the inventory of the Noordeinde Palace at The Hague in 1667. For the rest of the 17th century the history of the series is unknown, but the pictures appeared in 1719 as part of the famous gallery at Düsseldorf. Transferred to Mannheim for a time in the 18th century and brought in 1806 from Düsseldorf to Munich where the series has remained ever since.

Plate 19
The Slaughtered Ox
about 1640
oil on panel
36¼ × 26⅜ in (92 × 67 cm)
Art Gallery, Glasgow

Bequeathed to the Glasgow Art Gallery by Mrs John Graham Gilbert in 1877. Earlier the picture had belonged to Samuel Woodburn and had also been recorded in the J. van Dijk sale, Amsterdam, in 1791.

lady's hair, but it is virtually certain that they had a purpose as well as being decorative. The lady herself is no beauty by today's standards, but the artist has recorded her overdressed and podgy features with an unerring eye which neither criticises nor flatters. The handling of the paint is unusually minute, but by this method the artist achieved a sense of the real, which was bound to please his not altogether agreeable sitter. The man is painted with equal intensity–he too wears elaborate lace, and his hat is trimmed with decoration. Both portraits succeed in penetrating the character of the sitters through minute observation rather than that broad understanding of the feel of the person which was to be Rembrandt's forte in his later years.

The above is also true of the *Portrait of an 83-year-old Woman* (plate 17) in the National Gallery, London. It is not the ultimate statement about old age–that was to come thirty years later–but a minute and brilliant observation of the texture of an old woman's skin looked at almost exclusively from a surface point of view. The humanity of the sitter is just visible because Rembrandt observed so carefully.

But one is painfully aware that at this stage he lacked the understanding which makes the Trip portraits (plates 88, 89) in the same gallery so memorable. Rembrandt was still the money-conscious bourgeois intent on the good living his painting was undoubtedly bringing him. This is not a criticism, but it has to be accepted that worldly failure, or at least adversity, brought Rembrandt, who had a unique mastery of technique as a young man, into another world. This process was almost imperceptible at first, but the financial crises in the 1650s completed the metamorphosis of his spirit.

In the mid 1630s Rembrandt painted a series of pictures depicting the Passion of Christ. They are now all together in the Alte Pinakothek, Munich. They were commissioned by Prince Frederick Henry of Orange through the good offices of Rembrandt's intellectual friend Constantin Huyghens, whose portrait by Jan Lievens is in the Musée de La Chartreuse at Douai. As the whole series, although probably executed over a period of years, is very similar in mood and execution, only *The Raising of the Cross* (plate 18) has been reproduced here. Another high point has been reached in the development of the artist's sense of drama. He achieves this partly by the relatively obvious method of lighting and partly by the composition. The Cross is seen on the point of being raised to the vertical, and thus it makes a violent and uncompromising angle right across the picture. The soldier at the left serves to continue this line, creating a mood of disquiet in the

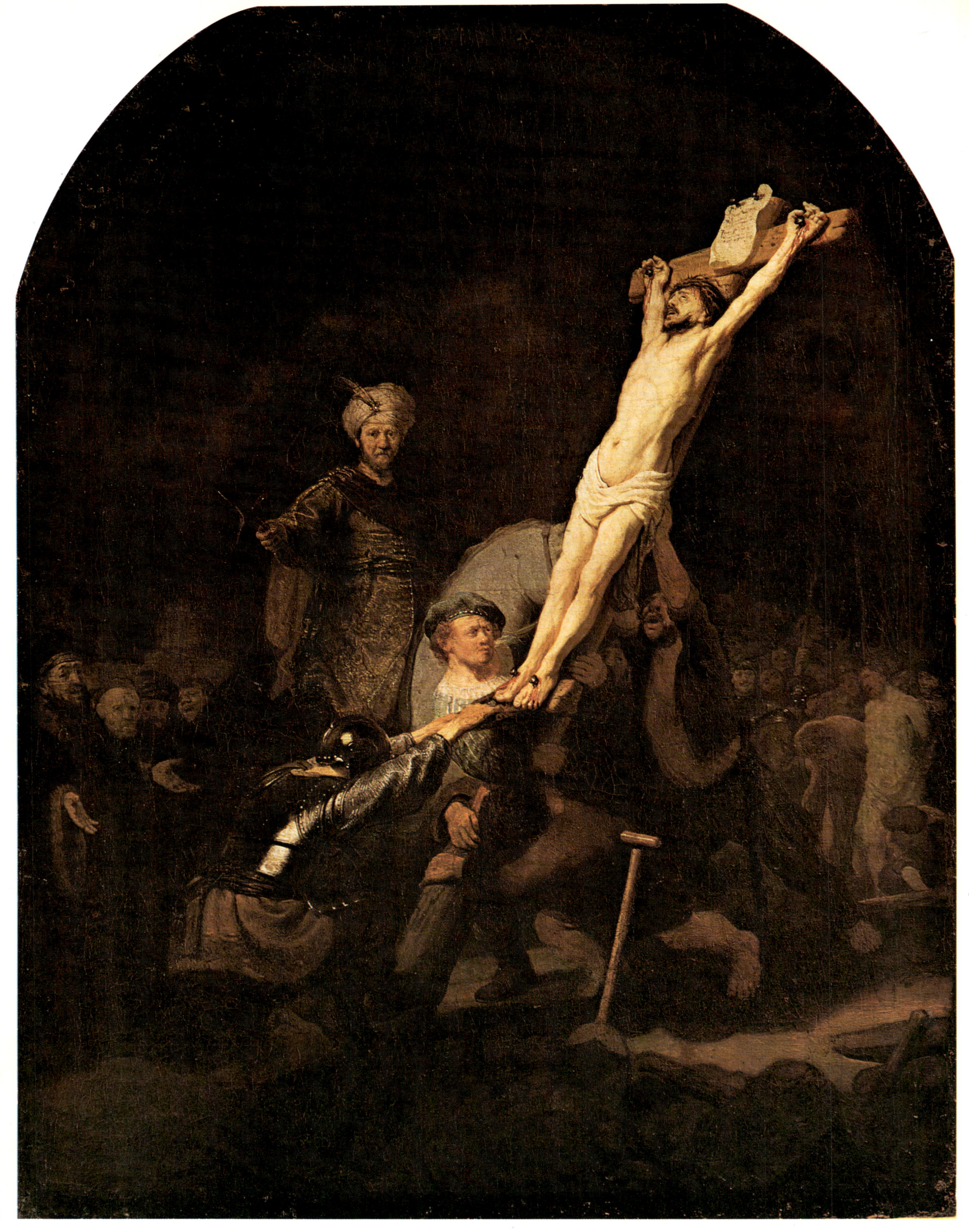

Plate 18 *see page 29*

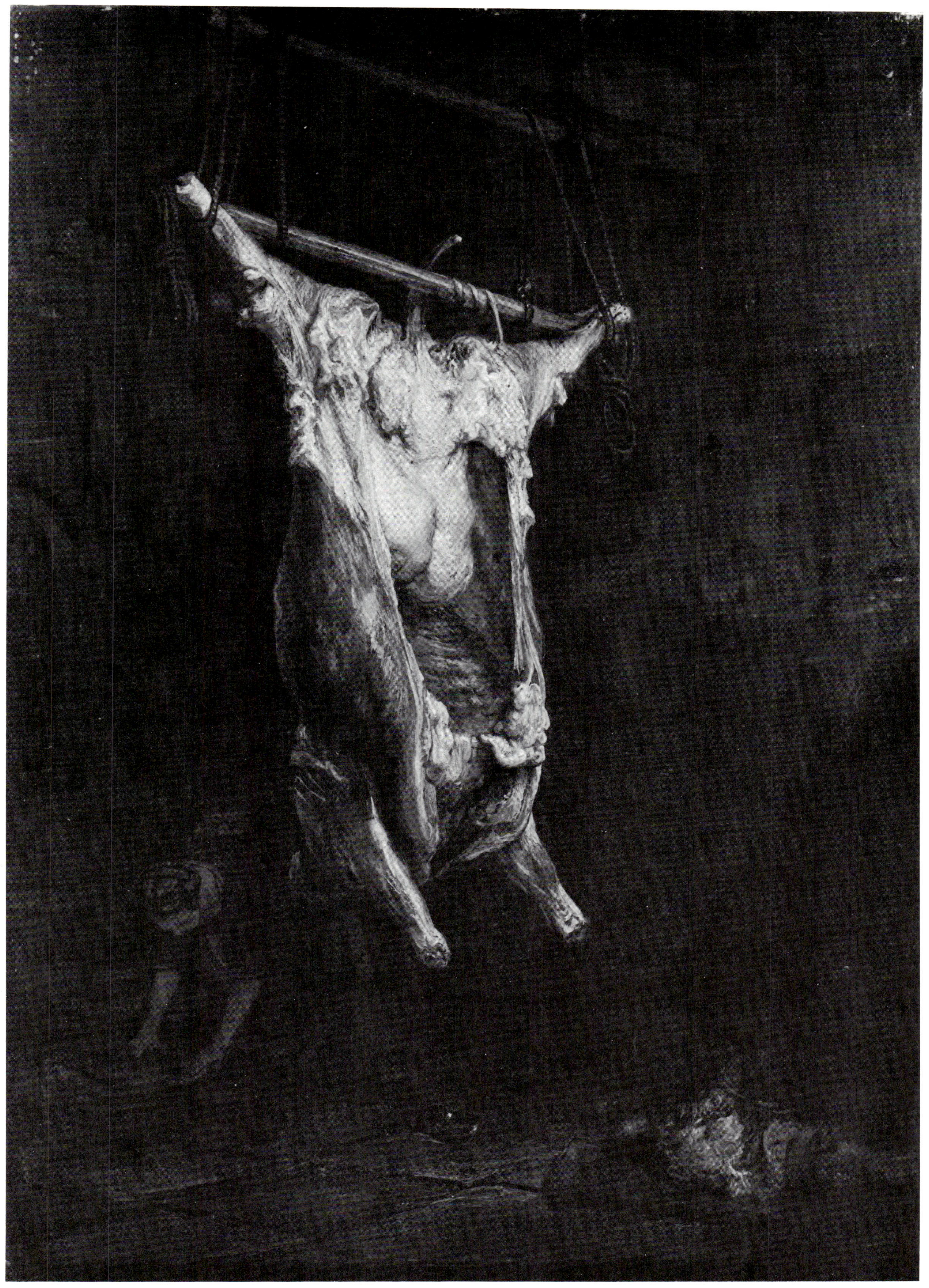

Plate 19 *see page 29*

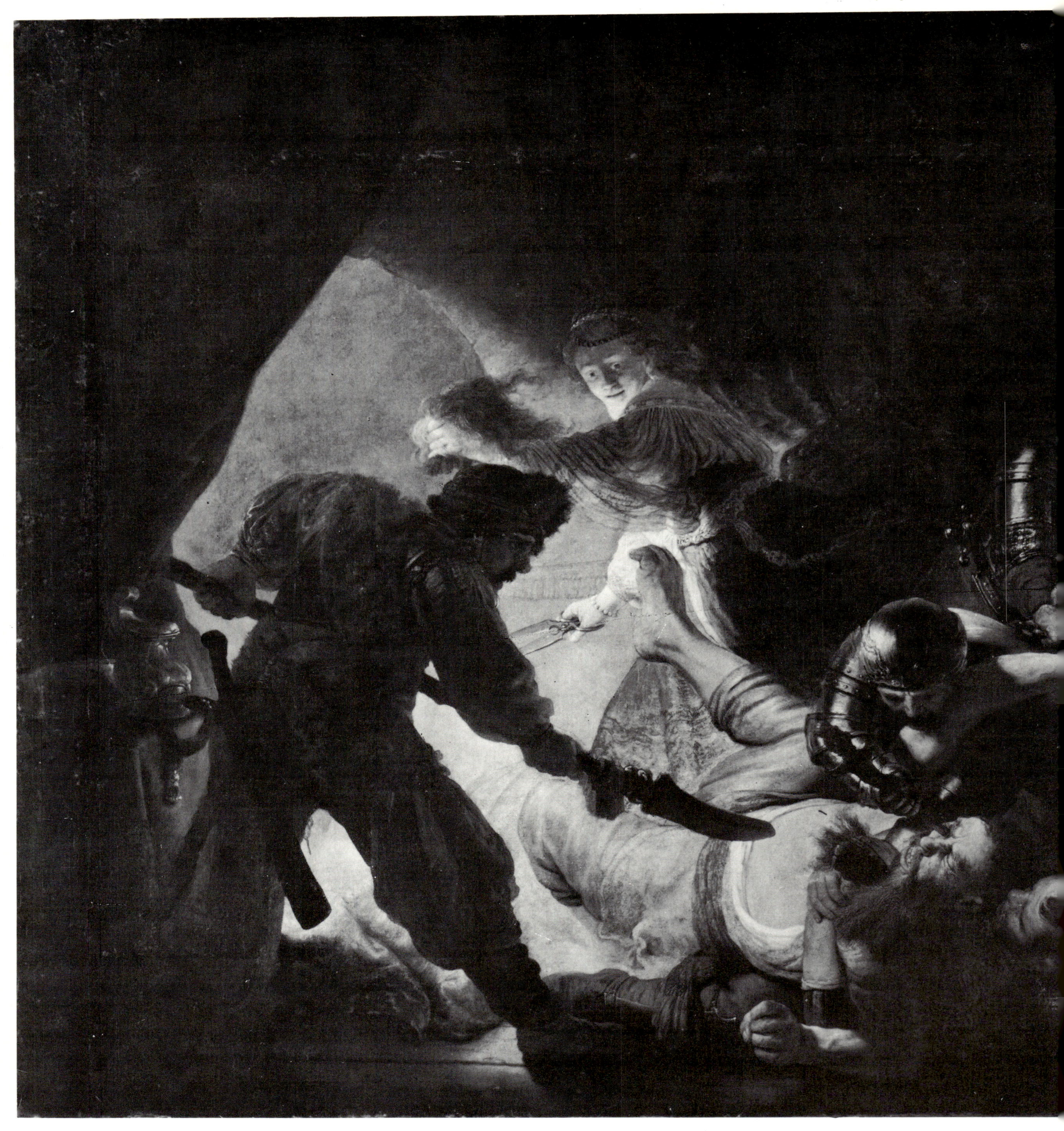

Plate 20 *see page 35*

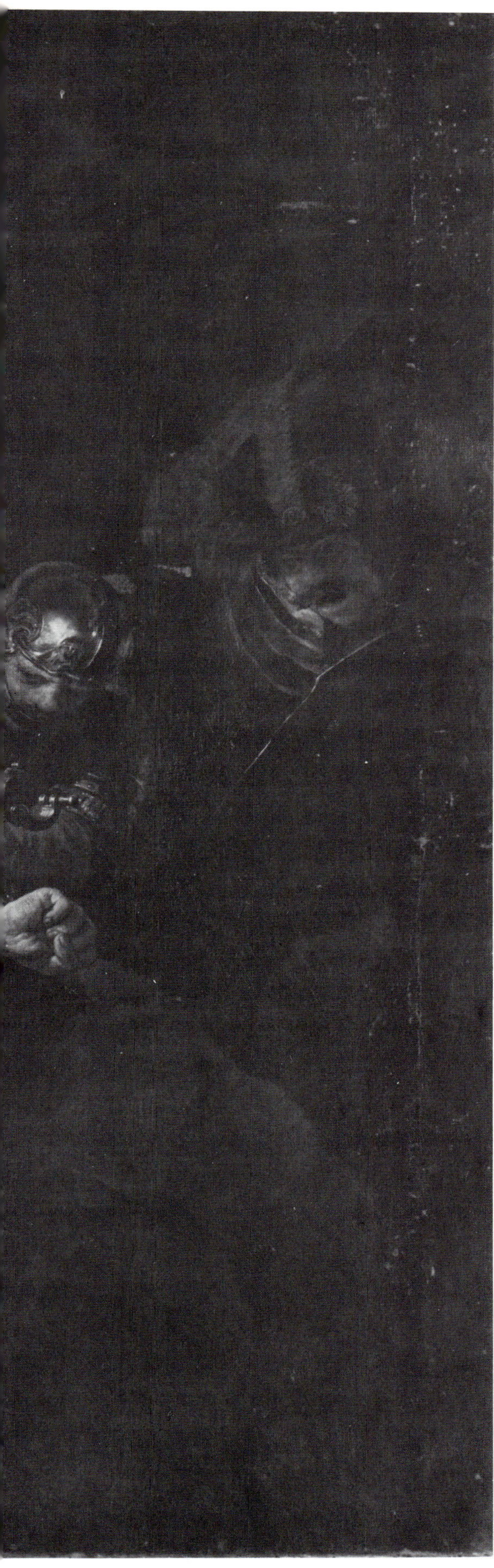

spectator even before the subject has been fully taken in. The head of the man at Christ's feet, which is in fact a self-portrait is one of the rare occasions where the artist has depicted himself in action, and he has succeeded in making himself so much part of the scene that we are hardly aware that it is Rembrandt himself who is occupying a key position in the picture.

The artist never shrank from depicting the horrific when the necessity arose, and it is seen here in the utterly convincing trickle of blood from Christ's feet. Such elements of horror appear in the celebrated *Slaughtered Ox* of twenty years later. The best version is in the Louvre, but that in the Art Gallery at Glasgow (plate 19), which must date from about 1640, is equally bloodthirsty, whilst being less satisfying as a picture. The ultimate extreme of this type of painting is *The Blinding of Samson* (plate 20) in the Städelsches Kunstinstitut at Frankfurt where the only reaction can be a deeply felt shudder, so grim is the action of putting the helpless Samson's eyes out.

Rembrandt's interest in the greatest of the old masters is proved by the spirited drawing in Berlin, dated 1635, of *The Last Supper* (plate 21) after Leonardo da Vinci. Rembrandt must have known the Leonardo fresco in Milan, either from an engraving, or possibly from one of the painted copies, which would have been available. The measured solemnity of the original has been transformed by Rembrandt into something very much more agitated. Although the Leonardo is full of movement, Rembrandt has exaggerated it and altered all the facial expressions to form a composition which gives a tremendous feeling of excitement.

Also in this vein of drama is the *Ganymede Carried away by the Eagle of Zeus* (plate 22) at Dresden. Here the 'horror' is transformed into a sense of humour which verges on the ridiculous. Ganymede was carried off by an eagle, in order to be a serving boy for the gods, on account of his inordinate beauty. Rembrandt has not

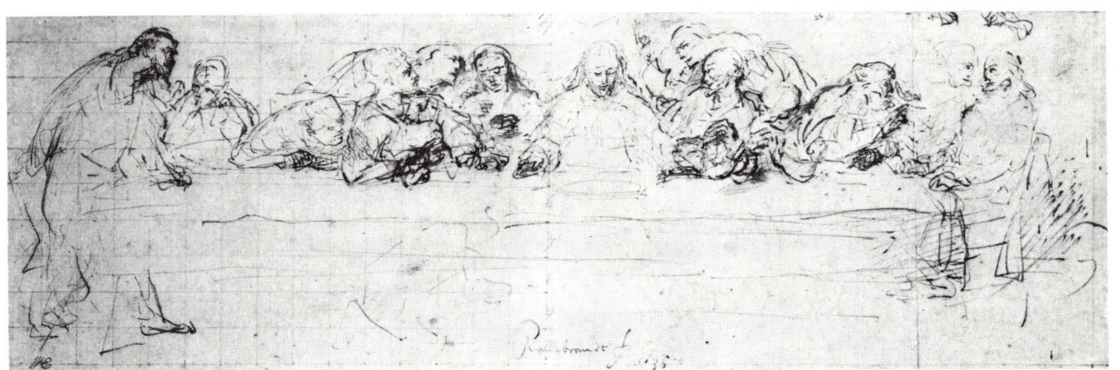

Plate 21 *see page 35*

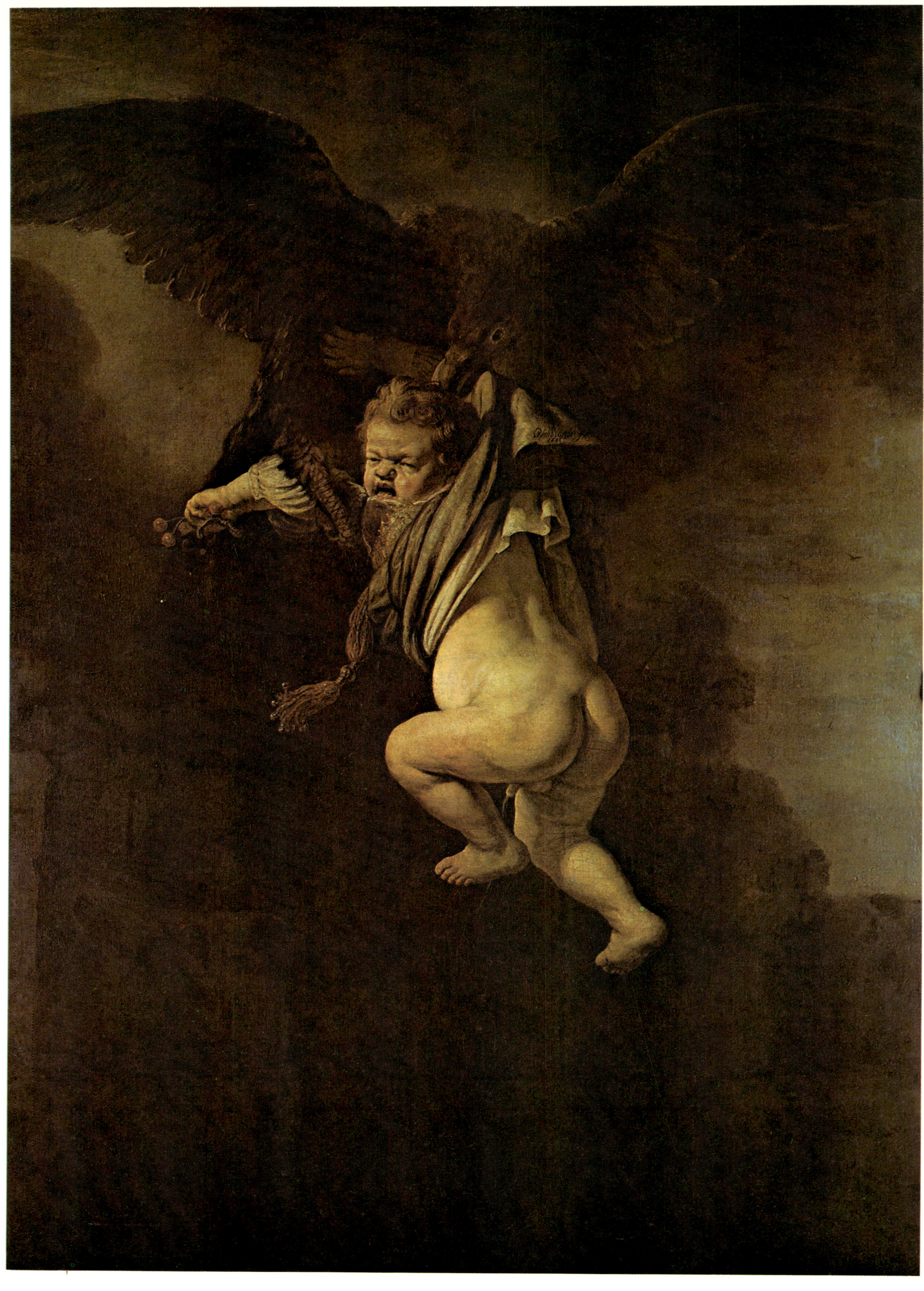

Plate 20
The Blinding of Samson
dated 1636
oil on canvas
93 × 118⅞ in (236 × 302 cm)
Städelsches Kunstinstitut, Frankfurt

Formerly in the collection of the Counts von Schönborn at Vienna and bought from them by the Städelsches Kunstinstitut in 1905.

Plate 21
Rembrandt after Leonardo da Vinci
The Last Supper
dated 1635
pen
5 × 15⅛ in (12.8 × 38.5 cm)
Kupferstichkabinett, Berlin

Like so many Rembrandt drawings, before being acquired by the Berlin Print Room, this drawing was in the collection of Sir Thomas Lawrence and then in the collection of William Esdaile.

Plate 22
Ganymede Carried away by the Eagle of Zeus
dated 1635
oil on canvas
67¼ × 51¼ in (171 × 130 cm)
Gemäldegalerie, Dresden

Recorded in an Amsterdam sale in 1716. At Dresden since 1751.

Plate 23
Ganymede Carried away by the Eagle of Zeus
about 1635
pen and wash heightened with white
7¼ × 6¼ in (18.3 × 16 cm)
Kupferstichkabinett, Dresden

The earlier history of this drawing seems unknown as it was not mentioned by Benesch.

chosen to interpret the story in a conventional way; Ganymede is in fact a grossly proportioned infant who is held in the grip of the eagle, and most of his clothes have been removed, or are in disarray, because of the struggle. As the eagle lifts the unfortunate child from the ground he urinates in fear. It seems clear that the picture was intended to raise a smile; the eagle is both monstrous and endearing–he will not hurt Ganymede too much, but just enough to give him a nasty fright. Ganymede's expression is exactly that of a fractious child in a moment of tantrum–a theme which the artist used to effect in several of his drawings. Rembrandt has thus given the story a totally human content; all the ideal elements have been removed to the point where Ganymede's over-ample posterior thrusts itself at the spectator in a manner whose parallel is easily found in Chaucer or Rabelais.

The drawing for the Dresden *Ganymede* (plate 23) also survives in the same collection, and it can be seen how the artist refined the original bold conception into the very carefully composed canvas. This would seem to have been his working method–that is, to have many different ideas put down rapidly on paper, and then to choose the most felicitous composition to turn into the finished

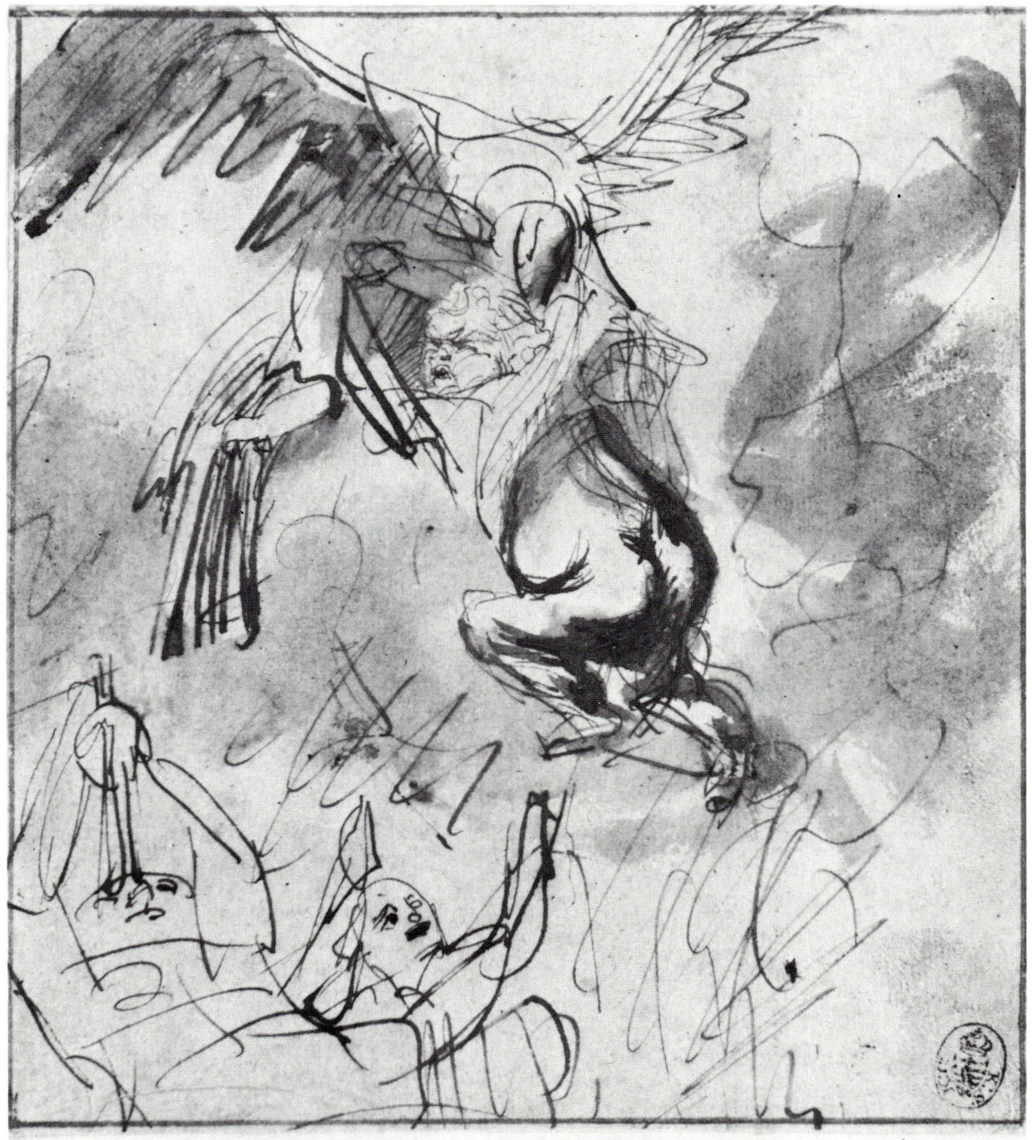

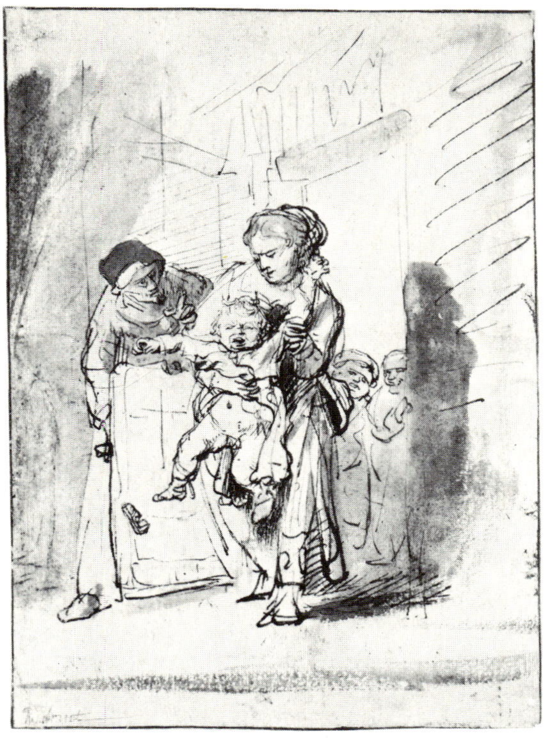

Plate 24
The Naughty Child
about 1635
pen and wash
$8\frac{1}{8} \times 5\frac{5}{8}$ in (20.6 × 14.3 cm)
Kupferstichkabinett, Berlin

Recorded in several different sales in the 18th century. Last sold in 1851 and subsequently acquired by the Berlin Print Room.

Plate 25
Belshazzar's Feast
early 1630s
oil on canvas
$66 \times 82\frac{1}{4}$ in (167.5 × 209 cm)
National Gallery, London

Long in the collection of the Earls of Derby at Knowsley Hall near Liverpool, the picture was bought from the Earl in 1964 by the National Gallery.

Plate 26
The Sacrifice of Isaac
dated 1635
oil on canvas
$76 \times 52\frac{3}{8}$ in (193 × 133 cm)
Hermitage, Leningrad

Formed part of the fabled collection of Sir Robert Walpole from whose descendants it was acquired in 1778 by Catherine the Great of Russia.
The whole collection was placed in the Hermitage where it has remained ever since.

painting. The expression on the child's face is particularly striking, but the drawing has much less humour than the finished picture.

Rembrandt's preoccupation with naughty children is well illustrated in the drawing in Berlin (plate 24). How many unwilling parents have suffered from a small child in a tantrum? The artist has caught this mood exactly. The vexed expression of the mother is contrasted with the hardened face of the old woman on the right and the grinning faces of the other children, not in the unfortunate predicament of being the centre of attraction. The same dramatic manner from the same year is found in *The Sacrifice of Isaac* (plate 26) in the Hermitage, Leningrad. Abraham was required to sacrifice his beloved son Isaac and was stopped at the last moment by the Angel of the Lord, who is in the act of making Abraham drop the knife, with which he is about to end the life of Isaac. Abraham's heavy hand is covering Isaac's face with a suffocating gesture. The whole picture gives an almost miraculous impression of an exact moment in time frozen in the manner which today we expect from a film still. A further fraction of a second and Isaac would have been dead. It is not often realised that the ideal of many artists of the 17th century was the complete generalisation. The search was for the most perfect mode of expression rather than an attempt to freeze a moment in time in the casual manner with which we are now so familiar because of the camera. Rembrandt was trying to do just the opposite. For instance Nicolas Poussin spent his whole life in the search for how to depict a scene where every gesture and emotion was a

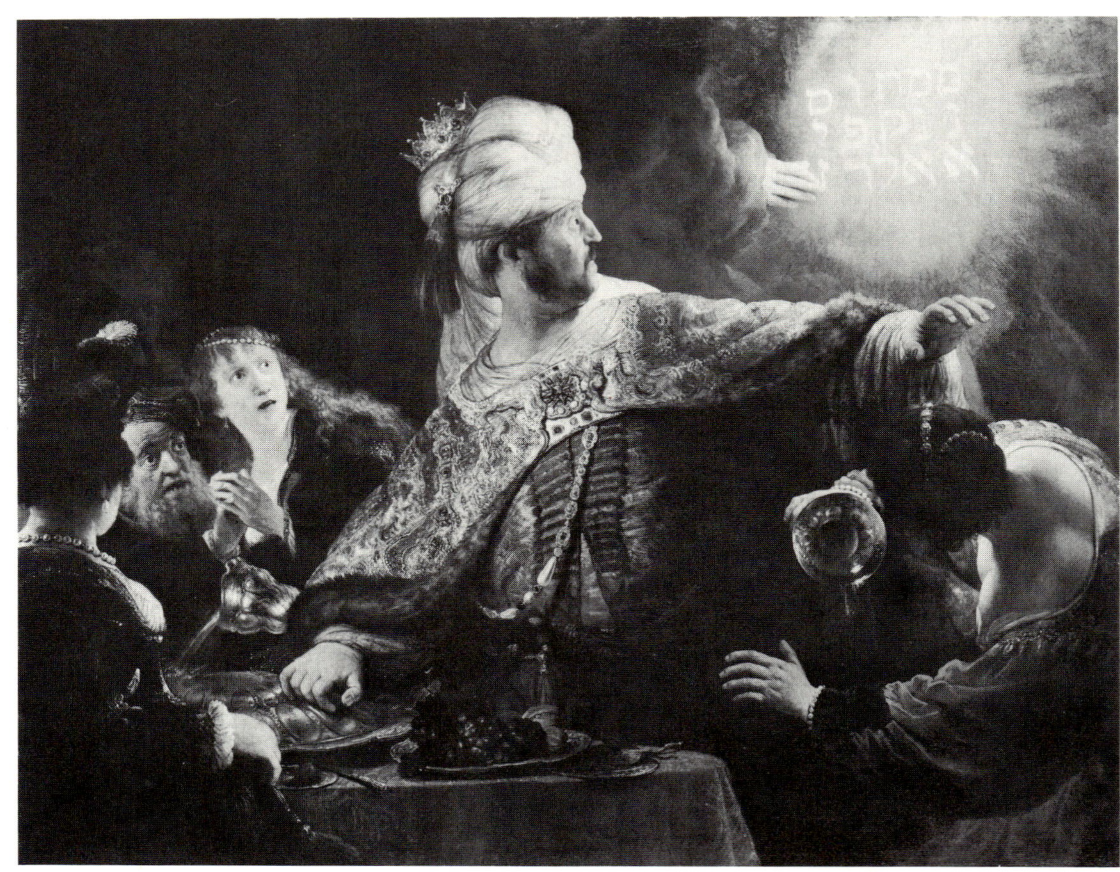

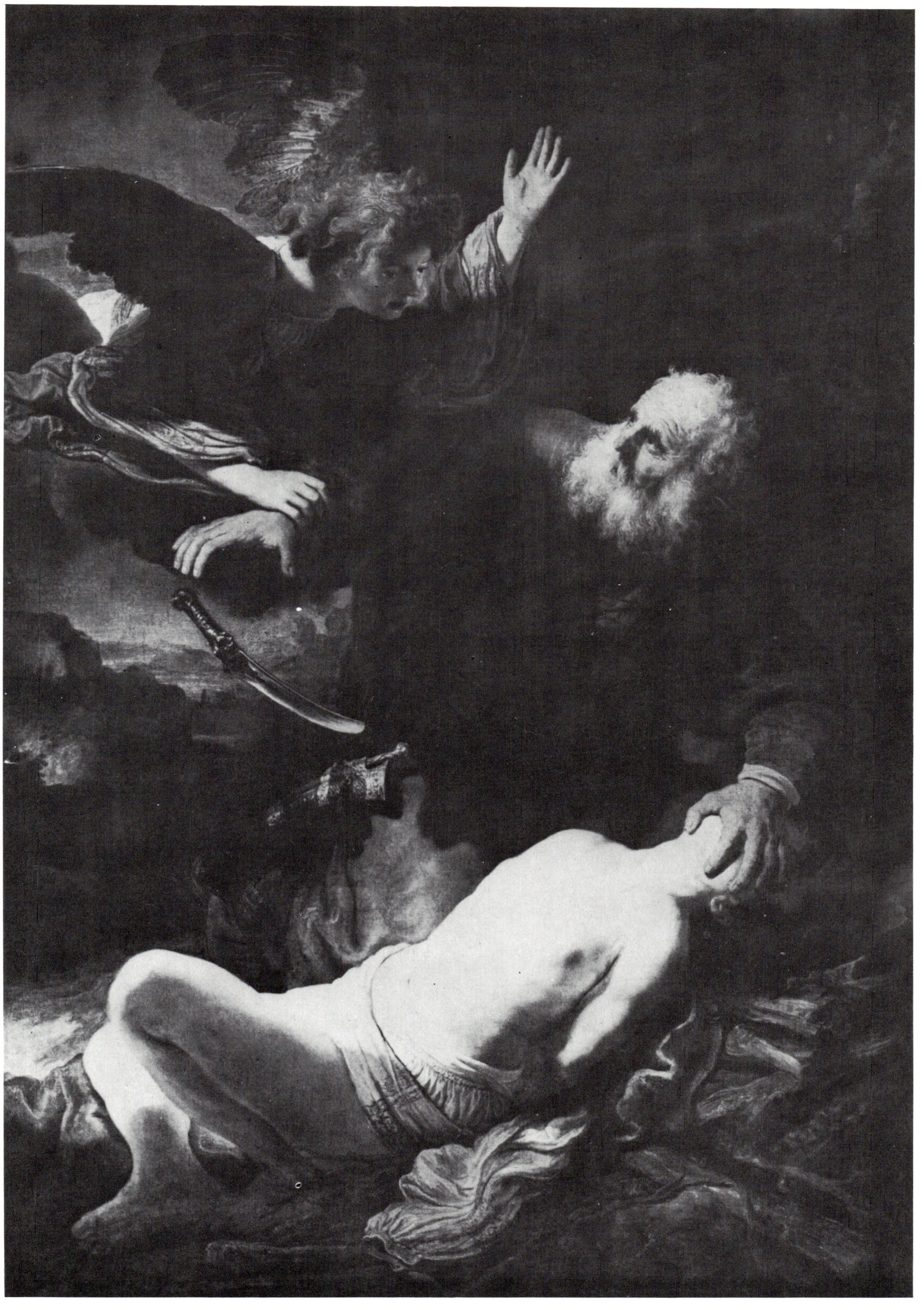

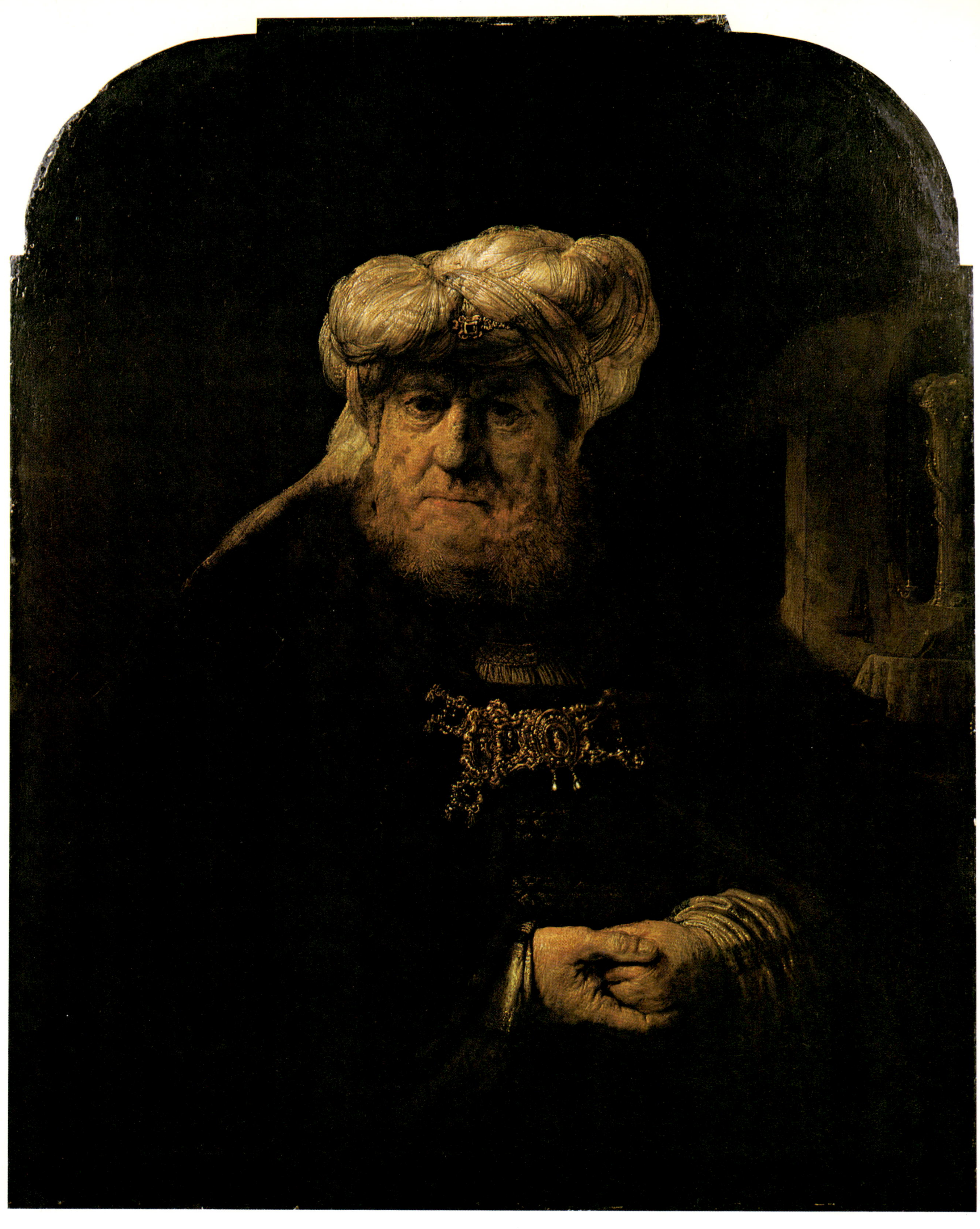

Plate 27
Head of an Oriental
King Uzziah Stricken with Leprosy (?)
dated 1635
oil on panel
40 × 30¼ in (101.5 × 77 cm)

Devonshire Collection, Chatsworth, Derbyshire

This picture has been for a long time in the collection of the Dukes of Devonshire at Chatsworth.

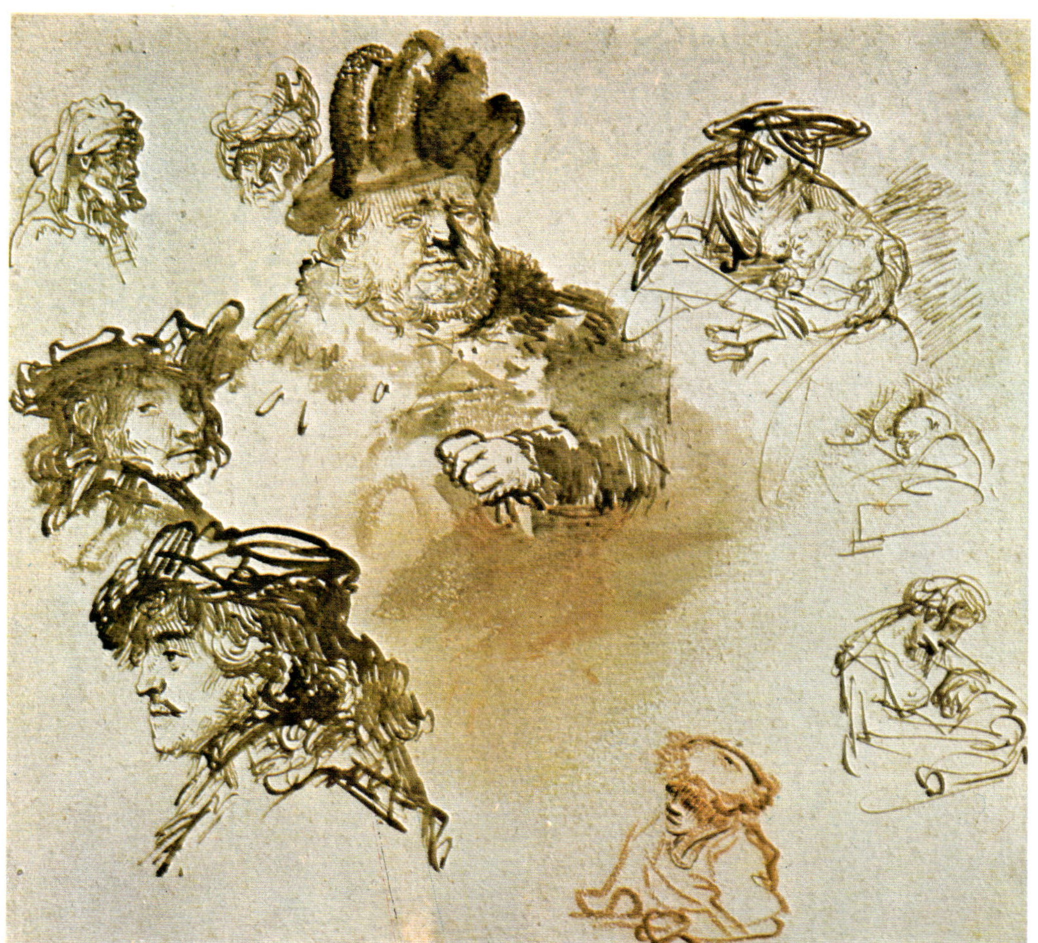

Plate 28
Sheet of studies
latter half of 1630s
pen and wash with red chalk
8¾ × 9¼ in (22 × 23.3 cm)
Barber Institute of Fine Arts, Birmingham University

Bought by the distinguished Rembrandt collector J. P. Heseltine at the Roupell sale at Christie's in 1887. Then in the collection of Henry Oppenheimer. Bought by Thomas Bodkin for the Barber Institute at the sale of Henry Oppenheimer's brother (Christie's, June 1949).

distillation of the specific to the general. Rembrandt's preoccupations in this direction, curiously enough, develop much later in his life, but in the 1630s Poussin and Rembrandt represent opposite extremes.

A similar moment of drama is found in the overwhelming, but disagreeable, *Belshazzar's Feast* (plate 25) in the National Gallery, London. The hand of God is actually putting the famous writing on the wall much to the discomfiture of Belshazzar. It has to be admitted that in attempting to present a scene of confusion the artist has failed to pull the whole picture together, the eye roves over the composition, registering surprise and confusion. In other words from a dramatic point of view the artist has succeeded, but as a work of art the picture is one of the most difficult to contemplate in his whole oeuvre.

In a much quieter mood, but still in the tradition of this whole group of biblical and mythological pictures is the *Head of an Oriental* (plate 27) in the collection of the Duke of Devonshire at Chatsworth. The picture is now generally believed to represent King Uzziah. Uzziah 'transgressed against the Lord' although the nature of his sins are not specifically stated. When he tried to burn incense to the Lord in the temple he was stricken with leprosy on the forehead. Notwithstanding the problematic interpretation of the subject the picture emerges as one of the artist's many

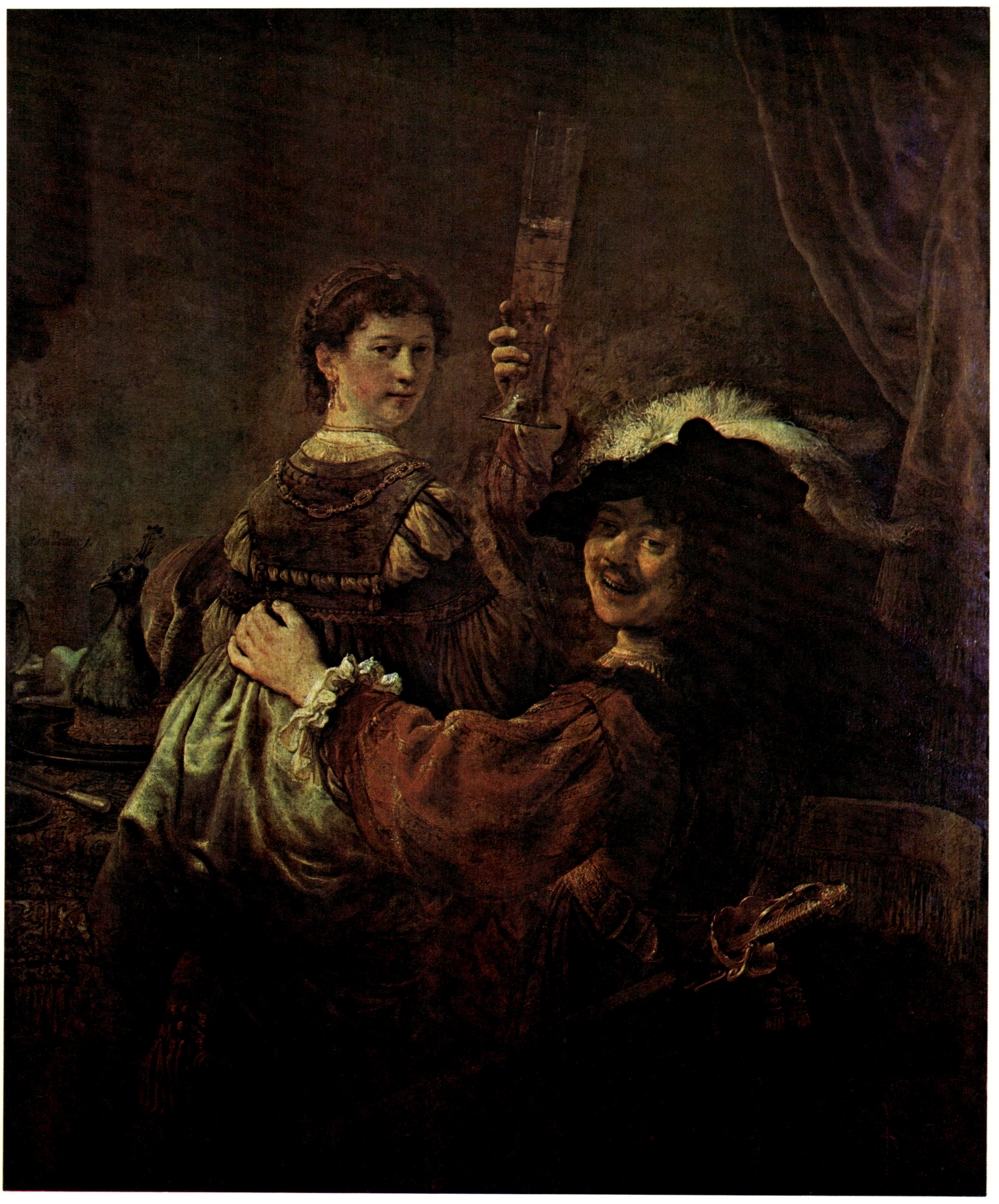

Plate 29
Self-Portrait with Saskia on His Knee
about 1635
oil on canvas
$63\frac{3}{8} \times 51\frac{1}{2}$ in (161 × 131 cm)
Gemäldegalerie, Dresden

From the Le Leu Collection in Paris. Acquired by the Dresden Gallery after 1751.

statements about the dignity of old age. The man is solemnly and richly dressed, but the artist has concentrated on the elaborate clasp which holds the cloak and on the turban. All this is then subordinated to the rather flaccid face. He appears near to death. He bears with a quiet dignity the feeling that the decay of the flesh has already set in.

The sheet of studies (plate 28) in the Barber Institute at Birmingham is not only an excellent example of Rembrandt's versatility, as he has used several different styles of drawing on the one sheet, but also gives a clear insight into his ability to depict character. Probably dating from the latter half of the 1630s, the enormous head of the old man with the plume is familiar, as he is related to the type found in the Chatsworth painting (plate 27), while the two striking studies of the same head at the lower left have something of the artist's own features in them.

The *Self-Portrait with Saskia on His Knee* (plate 29), at Dresden, comes almost as a shock at this point in his artistic career. There has been a general increase in solemnity, a heightening of the drama, not always by obvious means, and then he paints this incredibly rumbustious, swashbuckling portrait which has recently been interpreted as *The Prodigal Son in a Tavern*. Considering the happy quality of the picture, and how Saskia appears confident and elegant–she is just this in the *Portrait of Saskia in a Red Hat* at Kassel–the conclusion that Rembrandt was going through a happy and successful period of his life can hardly be avoided. Extravagant, almost flamboyant, the artist has completely dispelled the introspective character of the prematurely aged man we have been coming to expect already. The 1633 *Self-Portrait* (plate 2) in the Louvre is a warning to us of what is to come, but in this Dresden picture we are reminded that Rembrandt still has a long way to travel towards the ultimate self-analysis. Saskia is perched saucily on her husband's knee, he holds an enormous glass, two-thirds full, while a roast peacock (this bird, now thought to be unpalatable, was then considered to be a great delicacy) is ready to eat on the table at the side. Nothing could be further from the tragic melancholy which is to saturate his art so soon, and yet, even in this overtly suggestive picture, the artist was able to give precisely the right emphasis to the appropriate expressions which lifts it from the level of the banal.

If the Dresden picture is regarded as somewhat of an exception, *The Angel Leaving Tobias and His Family* (plate 30) of 1637 in the Louvre comes as no surprise. The Archangel Raphael is rushing back to Heaven, having delivered his message which has left Tobias and his family terror-stricken on the ground. The expressions on

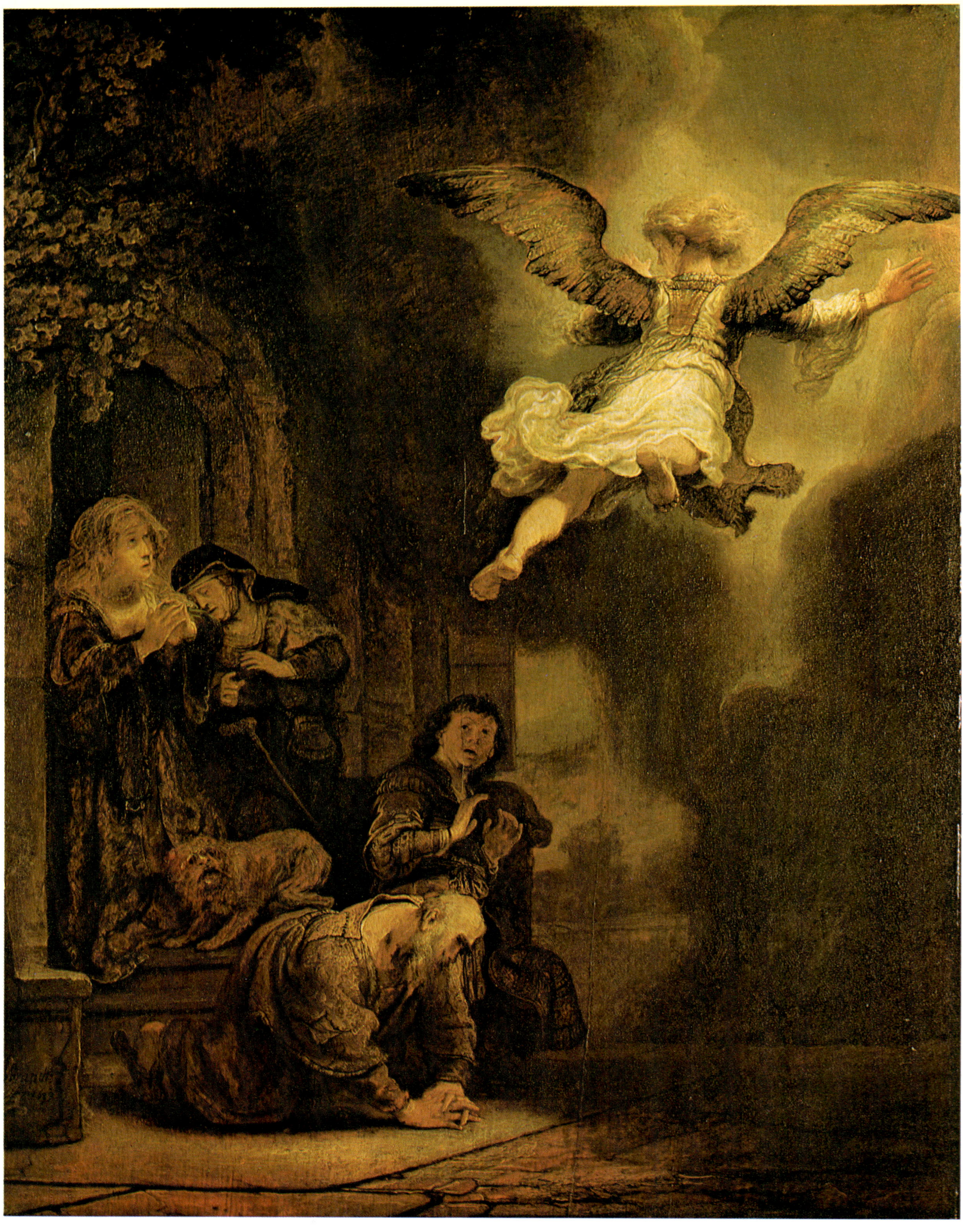

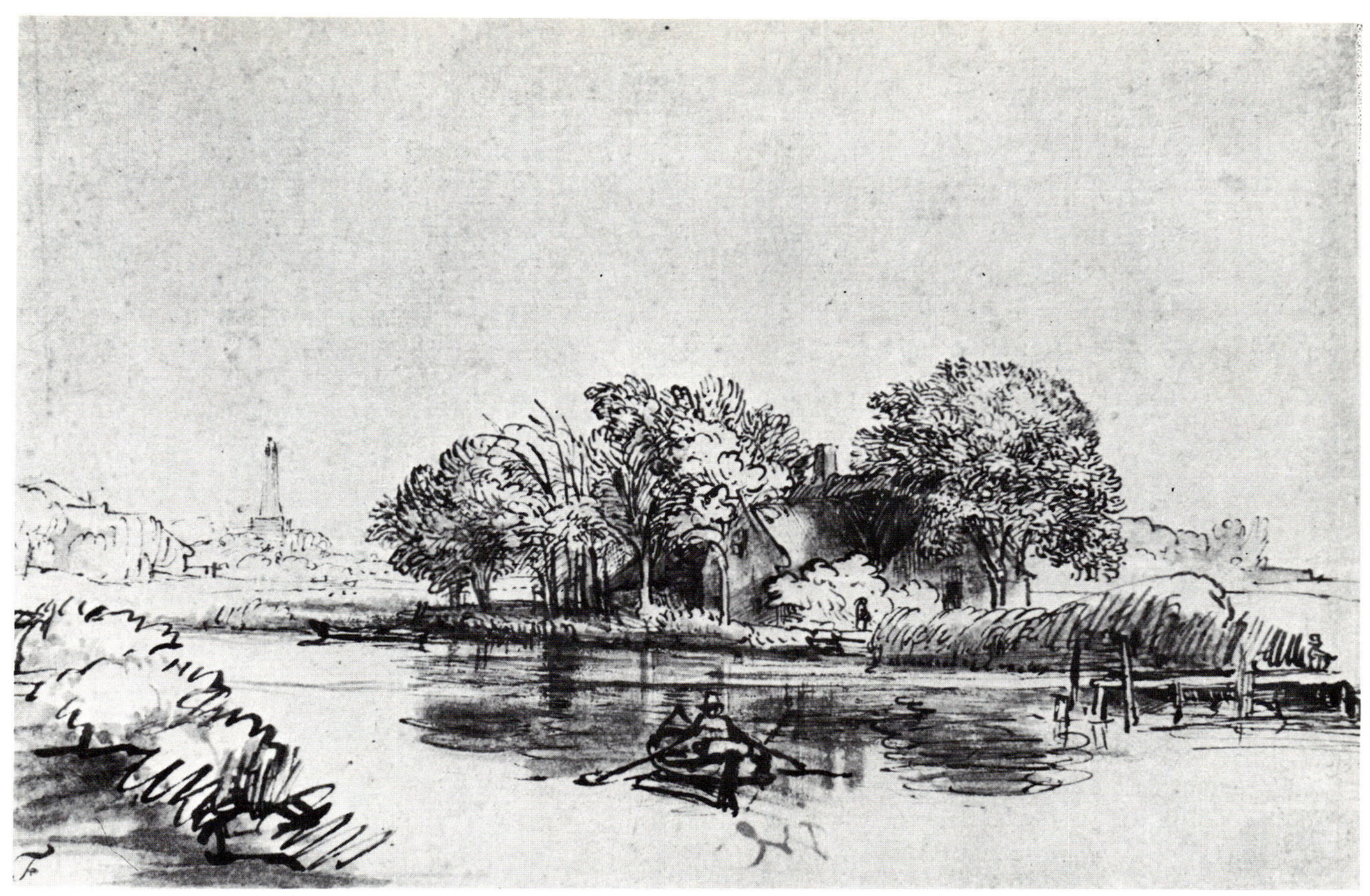

Plate 30
The Angel Leaving Tobias and His Family
dated 1637
oil on panel
$26\frac{3}{4} \times 20\frac{1}{2}$ in (68 × 52 cm)
Musée du Louvre, Paris

Sold in Brussels in 1738 and acquired in 1742 at the sale of the Prince de Carignan in Paris, for the collection of Louis XV of France. Placed in the Luxembourg Palace in 1750 and in 1785 transferred to the Louvre.

Plate 31
View on the Bullewijk near Amsterdam
early 1650s
pen and wash
$5\frac{1}{4} \times 7\frac{7}{8}$ in (13.3 × 20 cm)
Devonshire Collection, Chatsworth, Derbyshire

Formerly in the Flinck Collection before being acquired early in the 18th century by the Duke of Devonshire for Chatsworth.

the faces of the figures and the dog are interesting studies in the various aspects of terror. Tobias is on the ground in an attitude of complete subjugation, while the dog cowers in fear. As is usual with Rembrandt the Angel is no heavenly apparition, but a very solid being who is miraculously airborne.

In the 1630s Rembrandt was very much preoccupied with the painting of landscape. This was no new thing in the Holland of his time; very many of the younger generation of artists had begun to specialise exclusively in landscapes for which there seems to have been a ready market. Broadly they fell into two types. Those which depicted more or less exactly the terrain of Holland or the nearby Rhine country. The other type was the fantastic or romantic foreign landscape which had its roots in the Flemish tradition. In some ways Rembrandt seems to have combined these two traditions. He was obviously very responsive to the surrounding countryside of Amsterdam, as many of his studies survive in the form of careful, but rapid drawings. Most of them are at Chatsworth. They show an interest in recording the scene both accurately and atmospherically. There is no attempt in most of the drawings to make them conform to the conventions of the time as they were understood.

This is especially obvious when a comparison is made with the landscapes of Salomon van Ruisdael and Jan van Goyen. Both

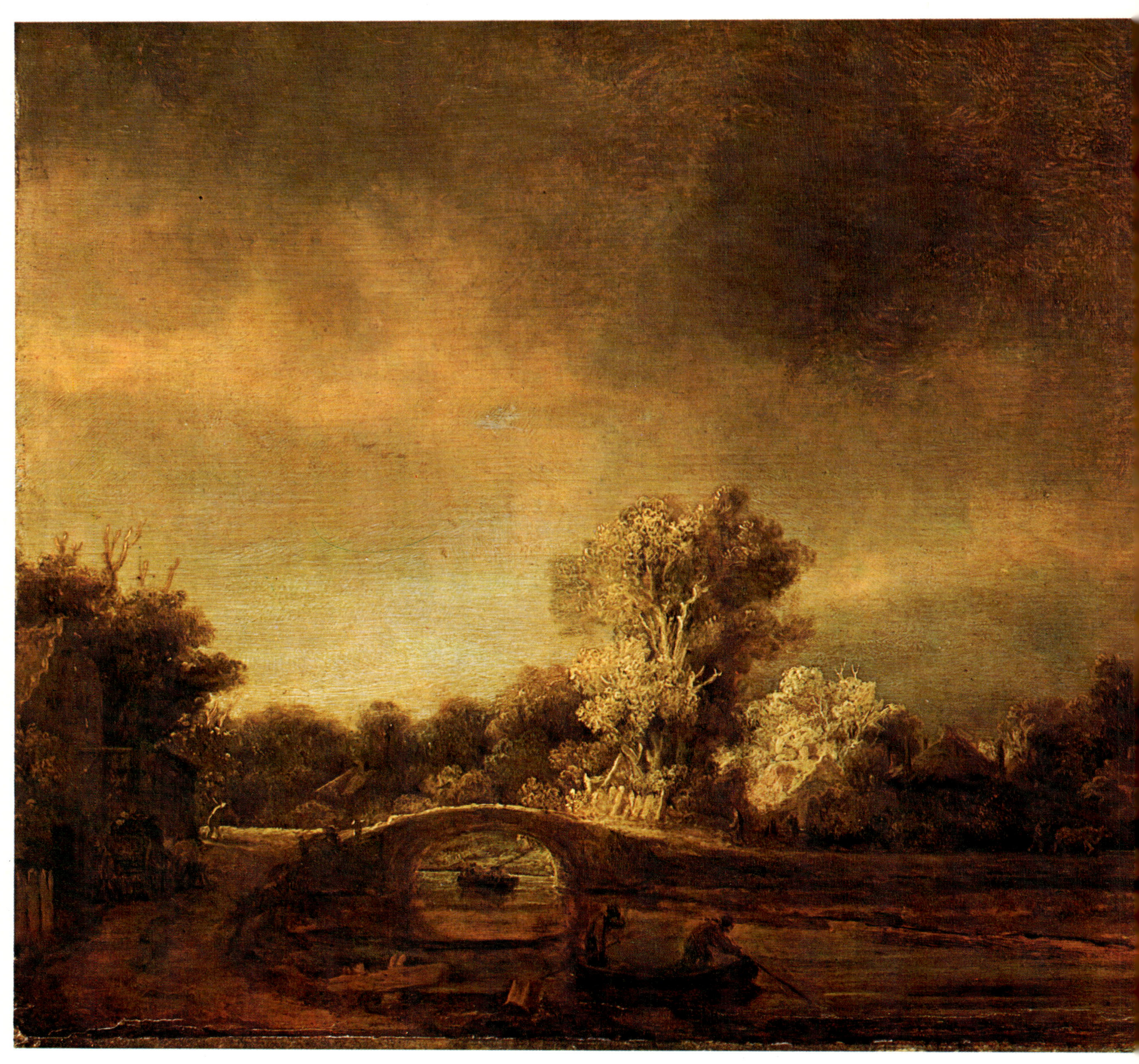

Plate 32
Landscape with a Bridge
about 1637
oil on panel
$11\frac{5}{8} \times 16\frac{3}{4}$ in (29.5×42.5 cm)
Rijksmuseum, Amsterdam

In the Lapeyrière Collection in Paris in 1817. Then in the collection of the Marquess of Lansdowne at Bowood, Wiltshire, in 1883. Acquired by the Rijksmuseum from James Reiss of London in 1900.

these artists were singularly unimaginative once they had evolved an agreeable composition. Their experiments were concentrated in achieving a distilled charm, a characteristic which Rembrandt eschewed throughout his life. In his drawings he was very much concerned with the atmosphere produced by the tranquil day. It is difficult to know whether they were intended as notes for a series of landscape paintings of which only a few were executed or survive, or whether they were spontaneous responses to nature with no further motive. A typical, and beautiful, example of this type of drawing, although it probably dates from the 1650s, is the *View on the Bullewijk near Amsterdam* (plate 31) at Chatsworth, where there is a solitary figure in a boat rowing on the quiet water. Rembrandt was not the only artist of his time to react to nature in this way–in distant Rome the Frenchman, Claude Lorraine, who produced very carefully finished and idealised painted landscapes, had a totally different and very free style when he drew from nature in the countryside surrounding Rome. Indeed it is often not realised that the spirit of a particular age may produce very similar results in artists who never knew one another.

When we turn to the landscape paintings there is a very different feeling. There is a solemn brooding quality in the *Landscape with a Bridge* (plate 32) in the Rijksmuseum, Amsterdam. A little wan golden light falls on the trees in the centre, while the clouds gather on the right denoting the impending storm. Every element in the landscape is subordinated to this end–even though it represents an actual scene on the outskirts of Amsterdam, for the spire of the Oudekerk is in the background. Another, even more dramatic example of this type is the *Landscape with an Obelisk* (plate 33) in the Isabella Stewart Gardner Museum, Boston, where the landscape is not Dutch in inspiration at all. It is not known whether Rembrandt left Holland, but if he did it was for a very short time. The only real evidence relates to a possible short visit to England. Several drawings of English subjects exist, notably of old St Paul's cathedral in London and Windsor Castle. Both of these could have been derived from engravings, or even the sketches of another artist, but the magnificent drawing of the great tower of *St Albans Abbey, Hertfordshire* (plate 34), in the Teyler Museum, Haarlem, is more difficult to explain. Both St Albans and Windsor are relatively near London and, should some actual proof turn up that Rembrandt was here for a short time about 1640, it would come as no surprise. With regard to the inspiration of the Boston picture it is easily explained by the immense popularity of landscape views of the Rhine country, especially of its more dramatic upper reaches. So many pictures of this type were being bought and sold

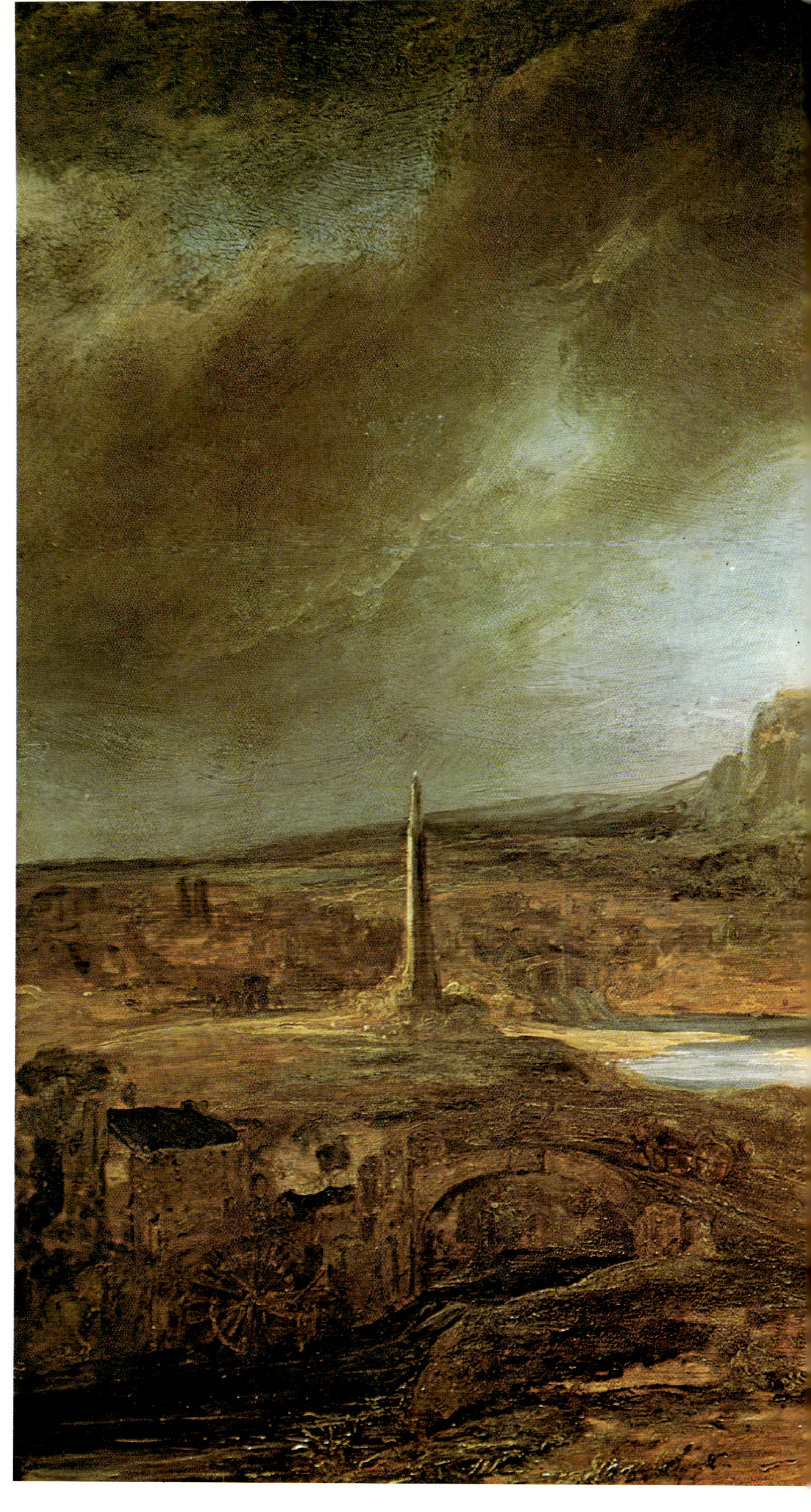

Plate 33
Landscape with an Obelisk
dated 1638
oil on panel
$21\frac{5}{8} \times 28\frac{1}{8}$ in (55×71.5 cm)
Isabella Stewart Gardner Museum, Boston

The history of this picture is relatively recent as it was first recorded in the Paris salerooms in the 1880s when it appeared several times. It then passed to a collection in Vienna and from there to the Rath Collection in Budapest. Acquired by Colnaghi of London who sold it in 1900 to Isabella Stewart Gardner through Berenson.

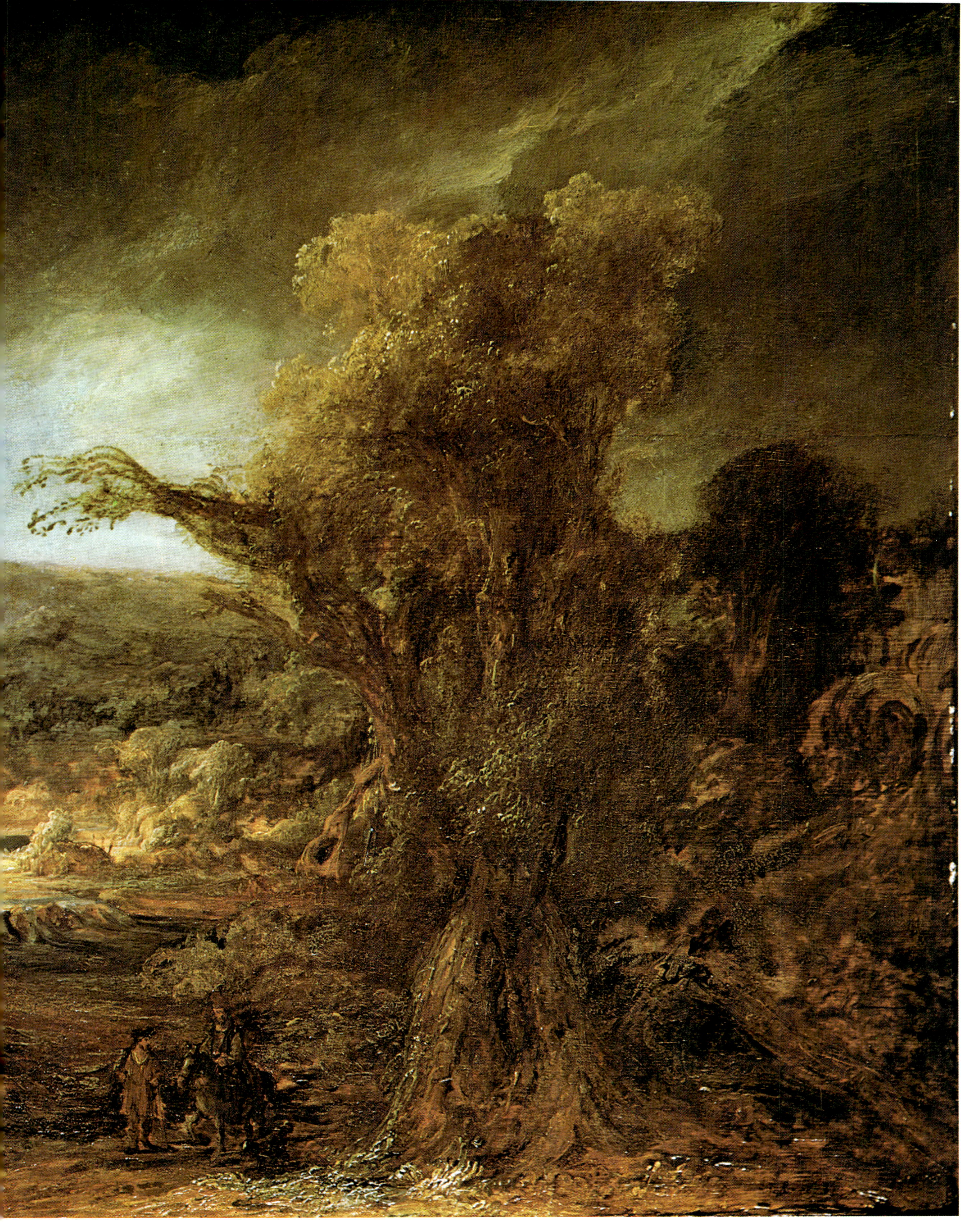

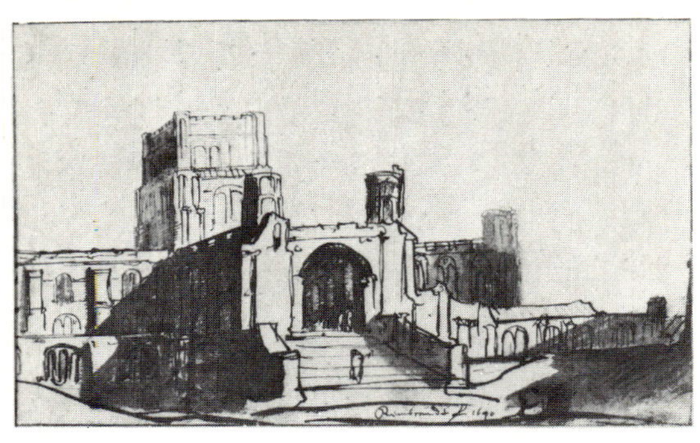

Plate 34
St Albans Abbey, Hertfordshire
dated 1642
pen and bistre wash with slight washes of white
$7\frac{1}{4} \times 11\frac{1}{2}$ in (18.5 × 29.3 cm)
Teyler Museum, Haarlem

Benesch assumed that this drawing was a copy made by Rembrandt after another drawing or engraving. This would explain why Rembrandt need not have visited England to make the drawing. Before going to Haarlem the drawing belonged to the famous scholar and connoisseur Cornelis Hofstede de Groot.

Plate 35
The Departure of the Shunamite Wife
dated 1640
oil on panel
$15\frac{3}{8} \times 20\frac{7}{8}$ in (39 × 53 cm)
Victoria and Albert Museum, London

Sold in Haarlem in 1749 and brought to England soon after. Changed hands several times in the succeeding century and acquired about 1885 by Constantine Alexander Ionides, who bequeathed it to the museum in 1900.

in Amsterdam that Rembrandt could hardly have avoided contact with such works of art. Thus he imagined a huge vista with a truly enormous mountain in the distance and an obelisk, which, when its great distance from the spectator is considered, must have been several hundred feet high. The whole picture is rather bluish in tone as if he had been looking at one of the conventional landscapes of such Flemish artists as Paul Bril or Joos de Momper, who used a brown/green/blue colour scheme for the foreground, middle ground and distance respectively. Tiny figures appear in the background of the Boston picture, which serve to emphasise the scale and the distance.

Although Rembrandt's preoccupations in the latter half of the 1630s has been with the large, dramatic and even sensational pictures, he occasionally painted small works which unfortunately are often overlooked in books of this type, as they do not readily fit into a general pattern. Some of these little works have all the grace and intimacy of so many of his contemporaries. Metsu and Terborch have been adored for these qualities, the ability to record the trivial with such charm that the spectator accepts without question the banal subject-matter. A picture of this type, but inevitably with Rembrandt of interesting or curious subject-matter, is the little figure on a horse accompanied by two other figures, in the Victoria and Albert Museum, London. It has recently been considered to represent *The Departure of the Shunamite Wife* (plate 35). The whole is rather dark; it is painted largely with a range of browns and a certain amount of red. The woman on the donkey has all the sad air of a reluctant departure, while the old man makes a gesture in the direction in which the woman is to go. Perhaps it is looking too far ahead to suggest that even on this tiny scale there is an inkling of *The Night Watch* (plate 41), which was to be painted only two years later.

Ever since Dr Hunter bequeathed *The Entombment* (plate 36) to the university of Glasgow in the late 18th century, this dazzling little sketch has been in the museum there. Accepted and reproduced in all the standard works on Rembrandt, it has rarely been seen except by the intrepid. On a very small scale, the picture gives the impression from a few feet away of being a carefully considered modello for a much grander composition. But on approaching closer the spectator is suddenly aware that the painting is in fact made up of a series of broad strokes which define the figures and only suggest the expressions. It is quite astonishing that the faces which peer in at the dead Christ through the gloom are painted with the merest hint of their form, yet the whole hangs together and does not appear in the slightest to be unfinished. The

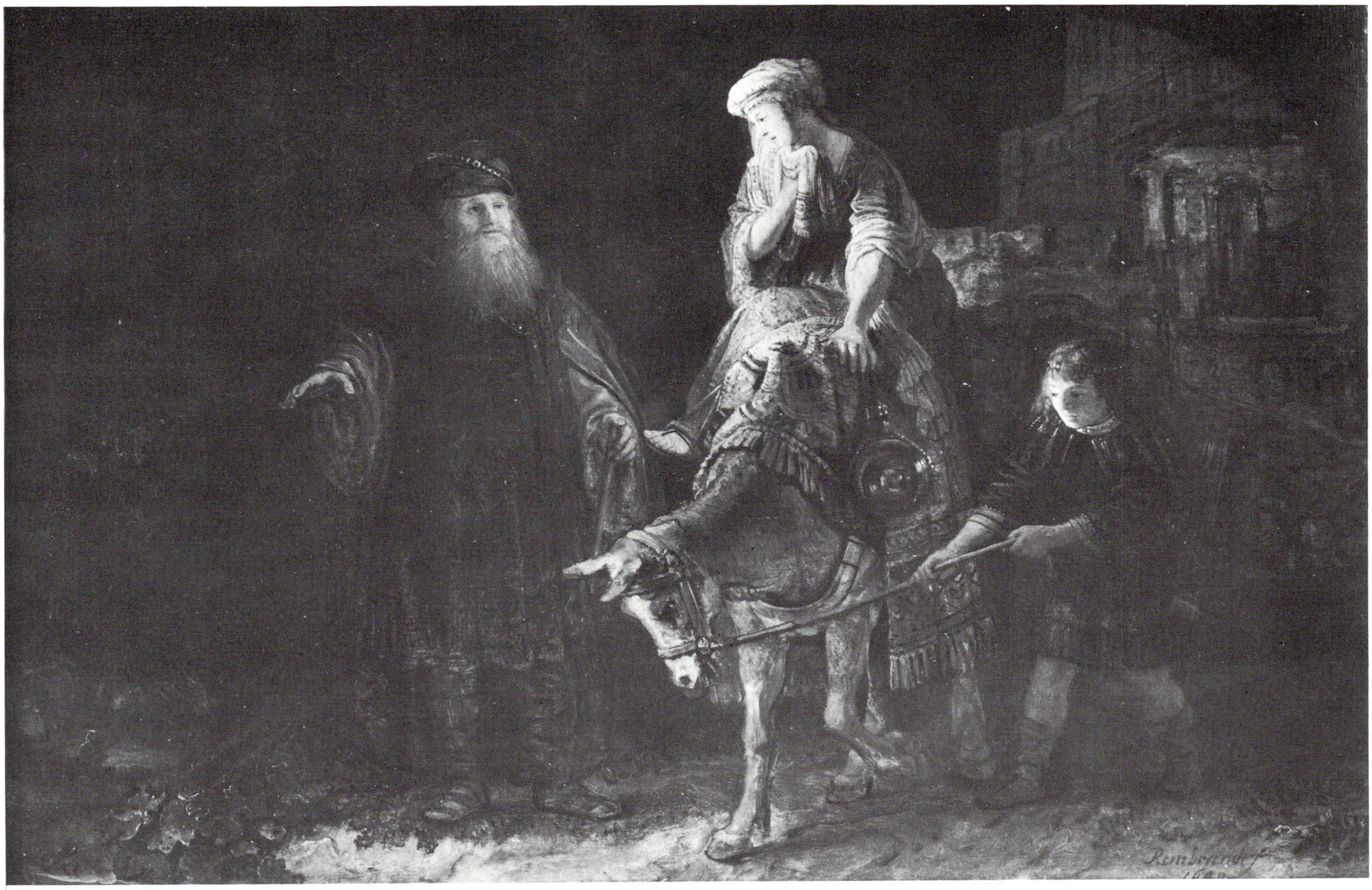

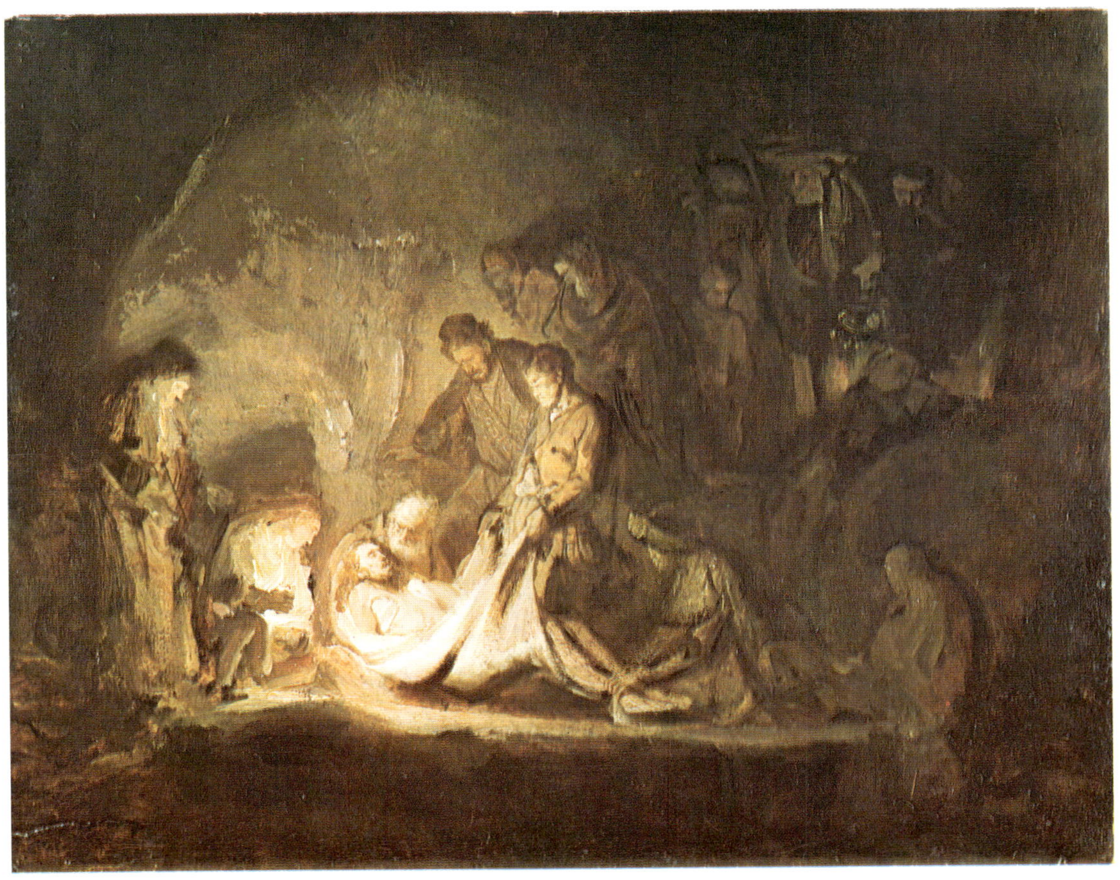

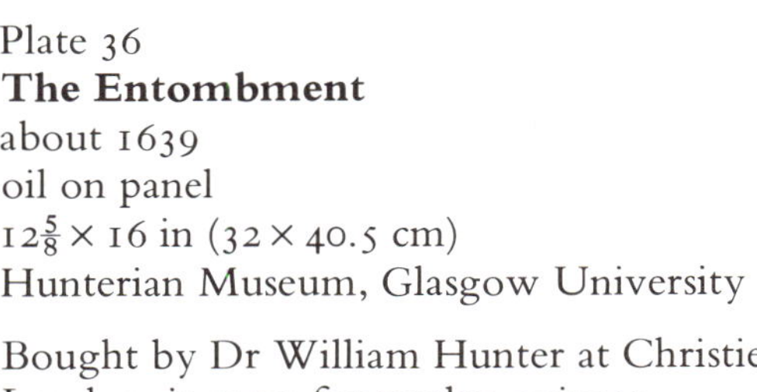

Plate 36
The Entombment
about 1639
oil on panel
12$\frac{5}{8}$ × 16 in (32 × 40.5 cm)
Hunterian Museum, Glasgow University

Bought by Dr William Hunter at Christie's, London, in 1771 for twelve guineas. Bequeathed by Dr Hunter to the University of Glasgow in 1783 and on permanent exhibition there, in the museum which bears his name, since 1808.

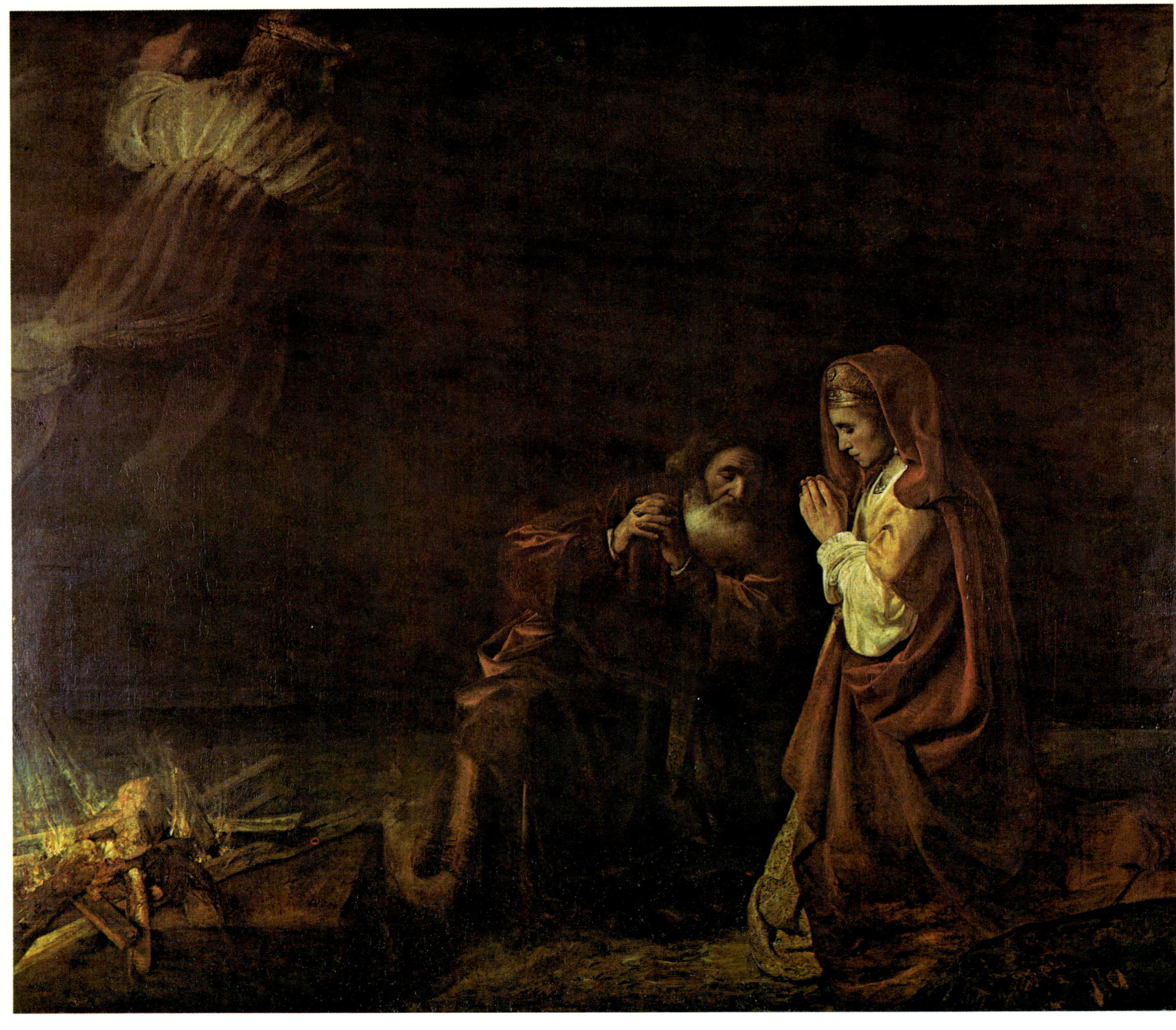

Plate 37
Rembrandt and an assistant (?)
The Angel Ascending in the Flames of Manoah's Sacrifice
dated 1641
oil on canvas
$95\frac{1}{4} \times 111\frac{1}{2}$ in (242 × 283 cm)
Gemäldegalerie, Dresden

At Dresden since the 18th century. The doubts cast on the picture's authenticity are of recent origin.

usual dating is about 1639, but slightly later would also seem sensible bearing in mind that the same broad brushstrokes, on a slightly larger scale, are found in the *Woman Bathing* (plate 63) in the National Gallery, London.

The Angel Ascending in the Flames of Manoah's Sacrifice (plate 37) in Dresden, although on a large scale, has much of the fragile and intimate quality of *The Departure of the Shunamite Wife* (plate 35). In such a picture Rembrandt shows a certain sort of tenderness, an emotion which he was largely to reserve for the portraits of his son Titus. Modern scholarship has come round to the view that Rembrandt did not paint this picture at all, it merely being the masterpiece of one of his pupils, Jan Victoors. Such an interpretation is difficult to accept on account of the originality of the conception. Jan Victoors was more competent than imaginative; only Jan Lievens in his work of about 1630 was capable of exceeding Rembrandt in the quality of his invention. Typical of Rembrandt is the way that the angel appears in the flames of the sacrifice, solid yet evanescent. It is unfortunately true that too little is known about the way Rembrandt retouched his pupils' pictures, but we would prefer to believe that such a category is reserved for that vast number of pictures of variable execution which are clearly derived from known pictures by the master.

The drawing of *Manoah's Sacrifice* (plate 38) of 1639 in Berlin, which is related to the Dresden *Manoah*, is very instructive as it shows the artist's mind at an earlier stage of the composition. The angel is a very different creature from the one seen in the painting, as are the relationships between the figures. Indeed the composition is closely related to the Louvre *Angel Leaving Tobias and His Family* (plate 30). Obviously the artist experimented with the theme before evolving the final statement seen in the Dresden

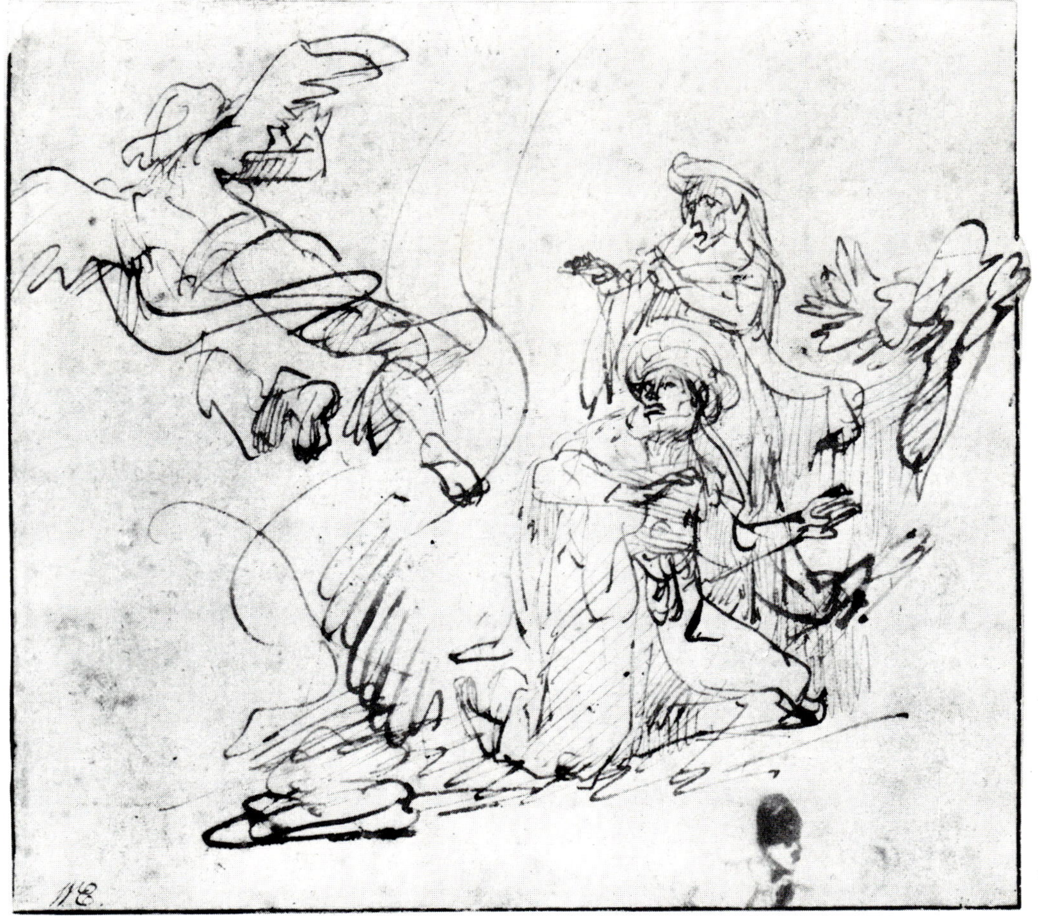

Plate 38
The Angel Ascending in the Flames of Manoah's Sacrifice
about 1639
pen
$6\frac{7}{8} \times 7\frac{1}{2}$ in (17.5 × 19 cm)
Kupferstichkabinett, Berlin

In the collections of Sir Thomas Lawrence, and then of William Esdaile, both of whom were noted collectors of drawings. Later in the 19th century acquired for the Berlin Print Room.

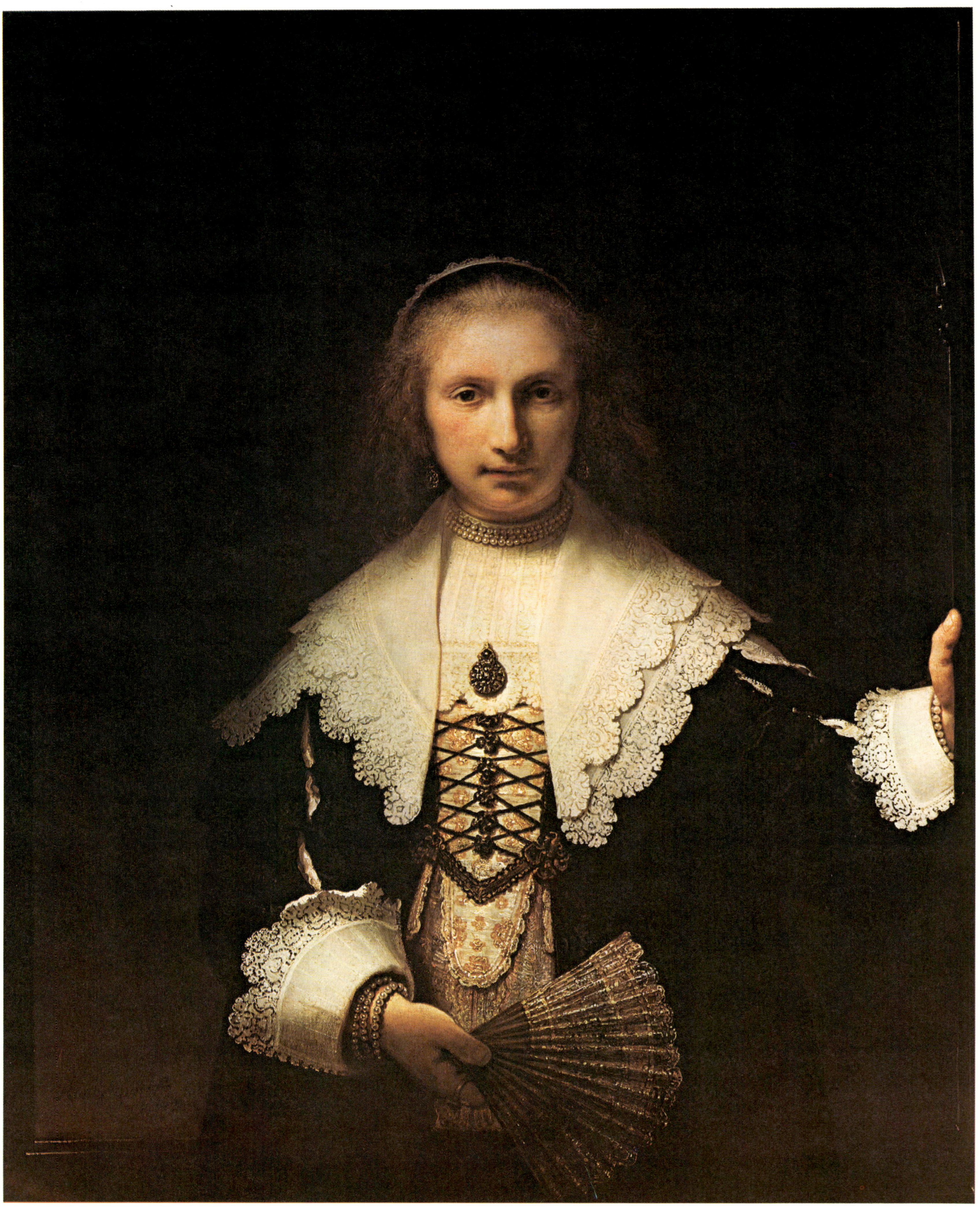

picture. Indeed, the artist must have been preoccupied by the theme, because there is a drawing in Stockholm of the same subject which is much closer to the Dresden composition, but which is dated rather later (about 1655), and a further drawing in the collection of Dr O. Reinhart at Winterthur, which Dr Otto Benesch suggested was a project for the alteration of the Dresden picture also to be dated about 1655.

From the same year 1641 there is the striking portrait of Agatha Bas, usually known as *The Lady with the Fan* (plate 38), in the Royal Collection at Buckingham Palace. Repeating his earlier conventions he has chosen the direct frontal view – it has even been suggested that he took this idea from the famous Holbein of *King Edward VI when Prince of Wales*, now in Washington.

Plate 39
Portrait of Agatha Bas
The Lady with the Fan
dated 1641
oil on canvas
$41\frac{5}{8} \times 33$ in (105.5 × 84 cm)
Royal Collection

Bought by the Prince Regent in 1819 at the sale of Lord Charles Townsend. The history of the picture is not known before it arrived in England in 1814.

Plate 40
Saskia in Bed, with a Nurse
about 1635 or slightly later
pen and wash
$12\frac{7}{8} \times 6\frac{1}{2}$ in (32.8 × 16.5 cm)
Staatliche Graphische Sammlung, Munich

Before entering the collection at Munich this drawing belonged to the Counts Palatine.

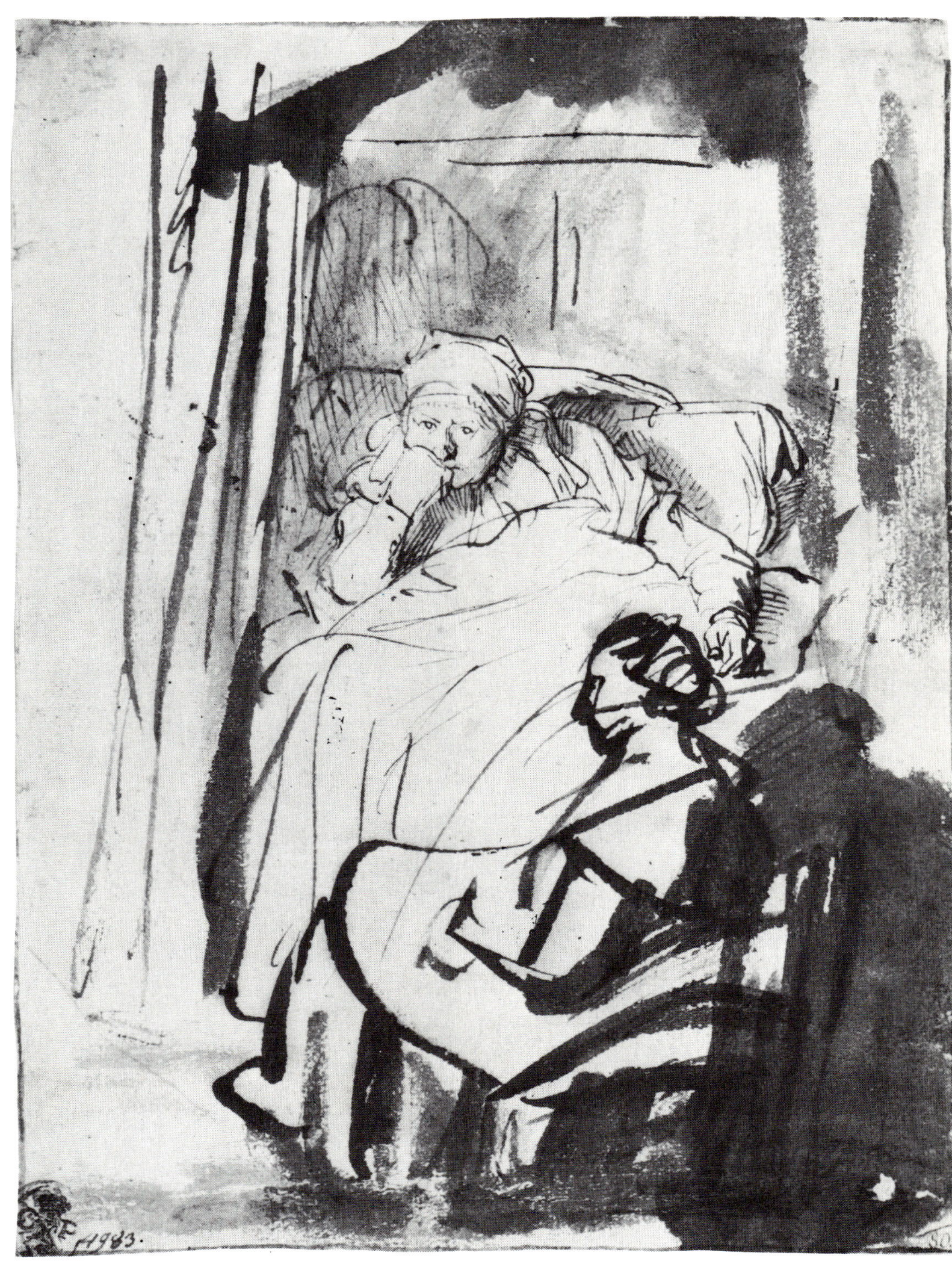

Plate 41
The Militia Company of Captain Frans Banning Cocq
The Night Watch
dated 1642
oil on canvas
$141\frac{1}{4} \times 172\frac{1}{2}$ in (359 × 438 cm)
Rijksmuseum, Amsterdam

First hung in the large hall of the 'Doelen' of the Arquebusiers and transferred in 1712 to one of the small court rooms of the Town Hall. Removed to the Trippenhuis in 1815. Since the early 19th century lent by the City of Amsterdam to the Rijksmuseum.

Rembrandt has produced a *tour de force* of straightforward portraiture in the same way that Vermeer was to produce a *tour de force* of straightforward landscape with his *View of Delft*, in the Mauritshius, The Hague.

Again the picture has a gentle quality, the sitter is shown in all her finery, but a quick look back at the Edinburgh *Portrait of a Woman* (plate 16) shows how during the decade between them the artist has gained more control over his subject-matter. The early directness remains, but this is tempered with an ever-increasing compassion. The sitter's dark eyes are looking straight in front of her, but they are not focussed on the spectator. In this largely monochromatic painting a sense of opulence is achieved by the simplest possible means, the use of colour being limited to the natural ones of the flesh tones and hair. Not until Vermeer, whose first faltering steps were taken ten years later than this picture, was there to be such a direct approach to the visual world where the eye is focussed on the object for its own sake.

All through his life Rembrandt's work as a draughtsman had a boldness which was coupled with a sense of refinement. In the drawing in Munich of *Saskia in Bed with a Nurse* (plate 40), usually dated 1635 or rather later, both these characteristics are present. Saskia appears old and ill, which is the reason for suspecting that the drawing is rather nearer 1642, the date of her death. Great sweeps of the brush define the bed and the silhouetted figure of the nurse, while Saskia herself is drawn with great delicacy.

Like so many of the very greatest creations of man, Rembrandt's *Night Watch* (plate 41), in the Rijksmuseum, Amsterdam, is unexpected at this stage in his career. The artist has already shown himself to be infinitely curious about the world around him, experimenting in almost every genre of painting and cutting across local traditions. His reputation in Amsterdam must already have been considerable, although it would be wrong to suppose that he dominated the artistic life of the city. Many of those who tramp round the Rijksmuseum in order to see *The Militia Company of Captain Frans Banning Cocq* (as *The Night Watch* is properly called) are more than a little disappointed when they arrive in front of this vast canvas which is mostly very dark. How can it be that the Dutch regard it as their greatest national treasure of painting? It is easy to be critical of the very famous, the *Mona Lisa*, *The Laughing Cavalier*, *The Blue Boy* and *The Hay Wain*, partly because we are too familiar with them, and partly because their very fame and popularity often means that they have inspired the banal. *The Night Watch* falls into this category; there is a suspicion that we look at the reputation and not at the picture.

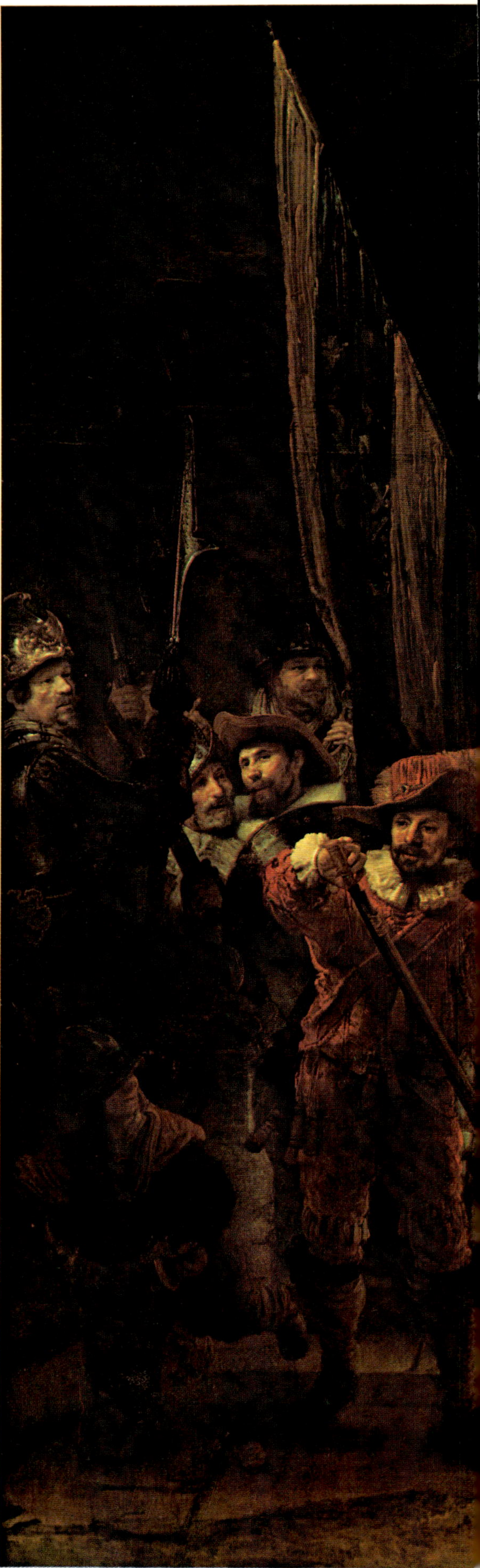

Plate 41 *see page 53*

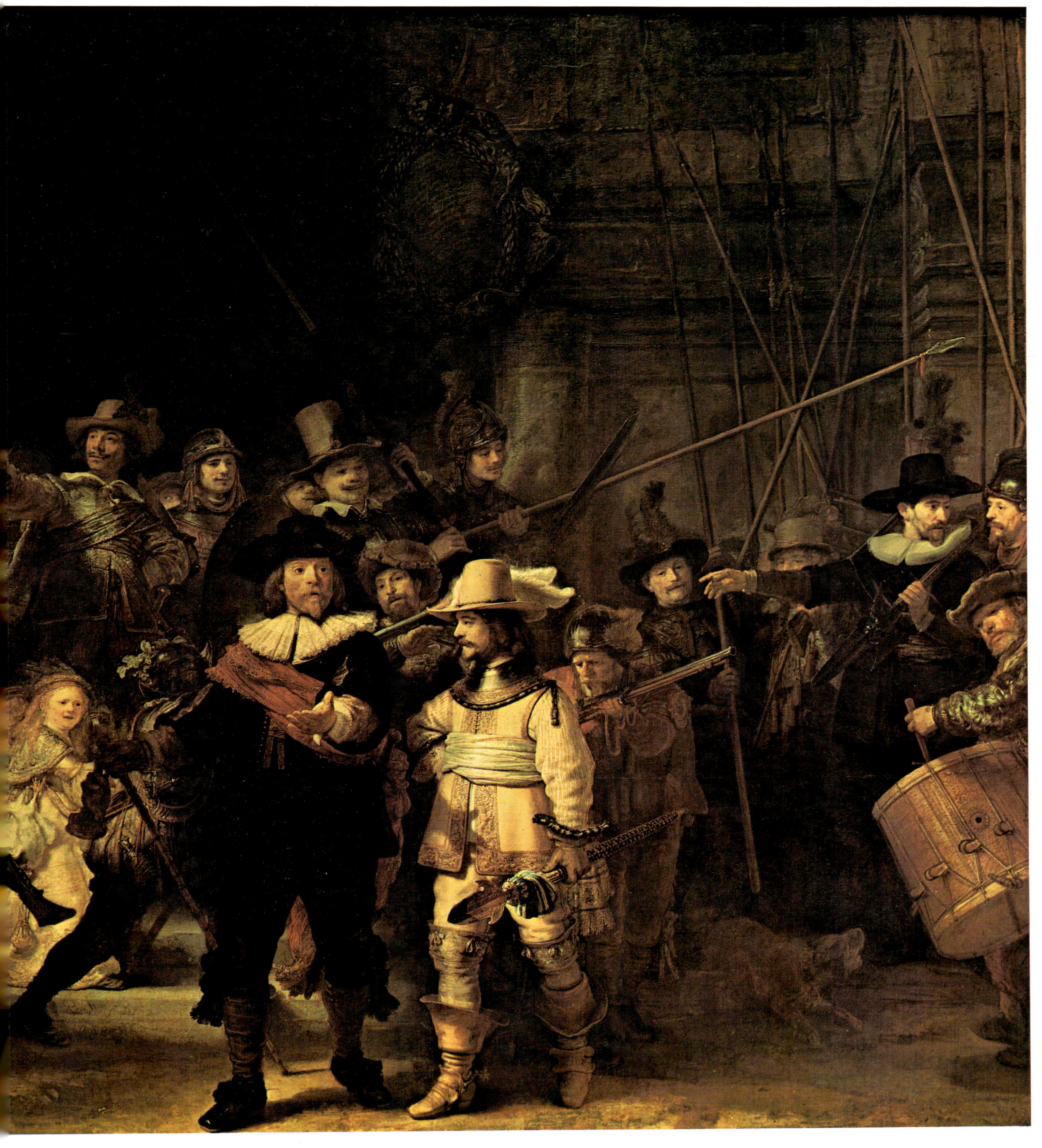

If one can think away the crowds, the picture gives the impression of the utmost seriousness and solemnity, although nothing very important is actually going on. Each member of the militia company was required to pay a considerable sum of money for the privilege of appearing in the picture, although the amount varied according to how clearly they were represented. They are shown in front of a large gate and seem to be making a kind of exit, although this may be pictorial licence on the artist's part. If the whole company posed outside the gate rather like a present-day football team photograph, what more natural than for the artist to insist that they appeared to be coming forward out of the gate in order to give some movement to an otherwise dreary line of dignitaries. In nearby Haarlem Frans Hals got round the problem by turning the militia companies' portraits into drinking scenes, which, in spite of their brilliance of execution and insight into the individual characters of the sitters, wear a little thin on account of his failure, until the end of his long career, to vary the somewhat alcoholic atmosphere.

Until Rembrandt created *The Night Watch* no Dutchman had produced so large and complicated a picture: that was an Italian prerogative. The fact that he succeeded so brilliantly makes it all the more admirable. Although there is no proof of this it is not unlikely that he was influenced, through the medium of engravings, by the large pictures of Titian and Veronese, which are so full of life and action, not in a nervous Northern sense, but in a rounded, relaxed way. Some of this seems to have filtered through to Rembrandt when he was painting *The Night Watch*. How different it all is from the charming awkwardness of *The Anatomy Lesson of Dr Tulp* (plate 12). The groups of figures are in fact very carefully composed in much the same way that Titian himself would have approached such a problem, but the feeling of excitement, even confusion, is caused by the elaborate system of lighting. Even the lances on the right, which seem in disarray, form a carefully calculated part of the composition. *The Night Watch*, for all its subsequent fame, was not a great success in Rembrandt's lifetime: it did not make him famous, and quite understandably some of the sitters grumbled about their lack of prominence. Such a picture was soon to lose its topical nature, and it survived as a curiosity, recording the faces of a group of long dead militia men.

Following *The Night Watch* Rembrandt produced in the 1640s a series of rather intricate religious pictures which include the ever-popular *Adoration of the Shepherds* of which there are two similar interpretations in the National Gallery, London, and the

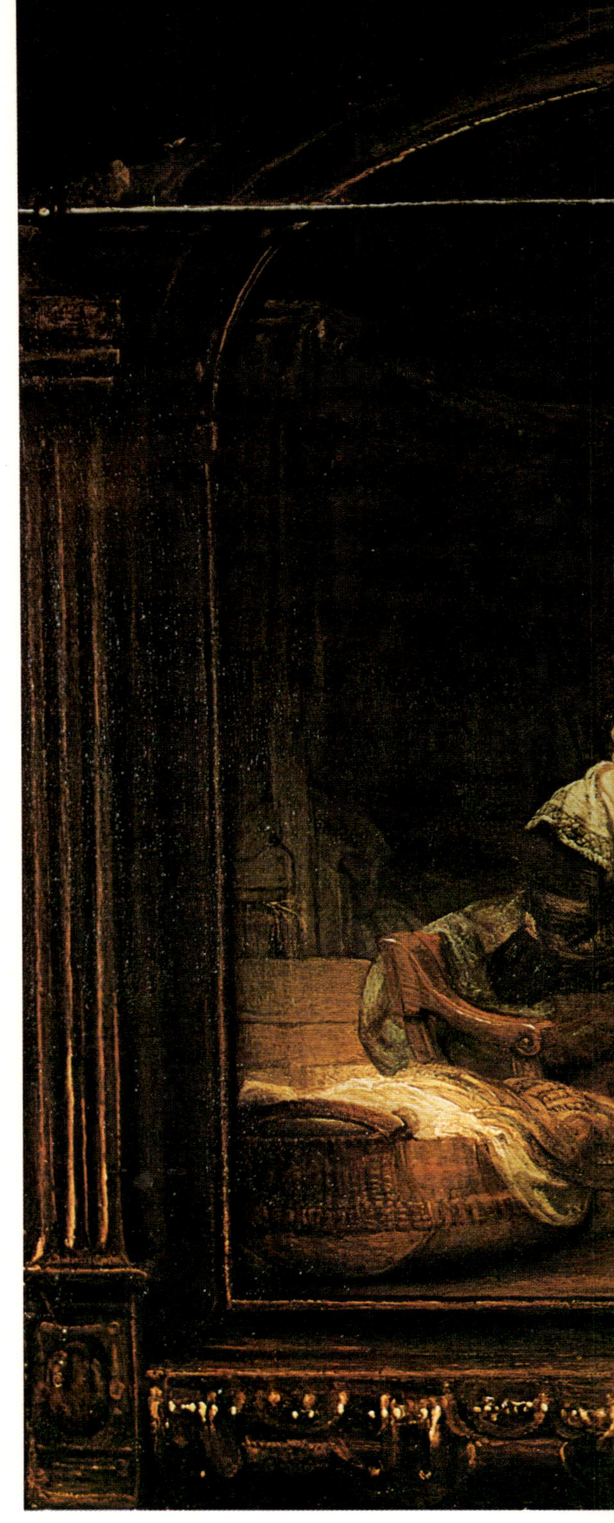

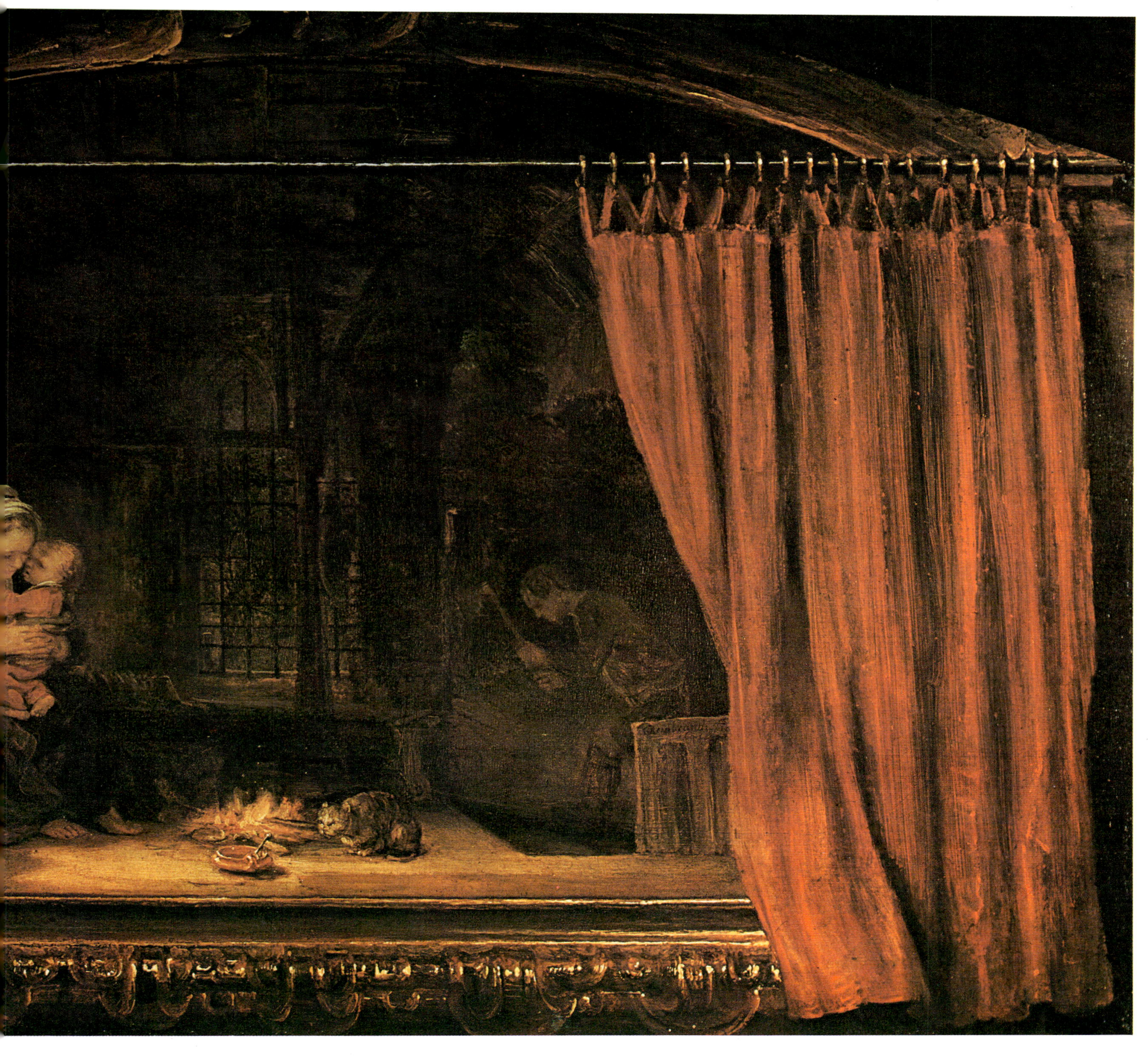

Plate 42
The Holy Family
dated 1646
oil on panel
$18\frac{1}{4} \times 27\frac{1}{4}$ in (46.5 × 69 cm)
Staatliche Gemäldegalerie, Kassel

At Kassel since the middle of the 18th century. Taken to Paris in 1806 by the Napoleonic troops and returned to Kassel in 1815.

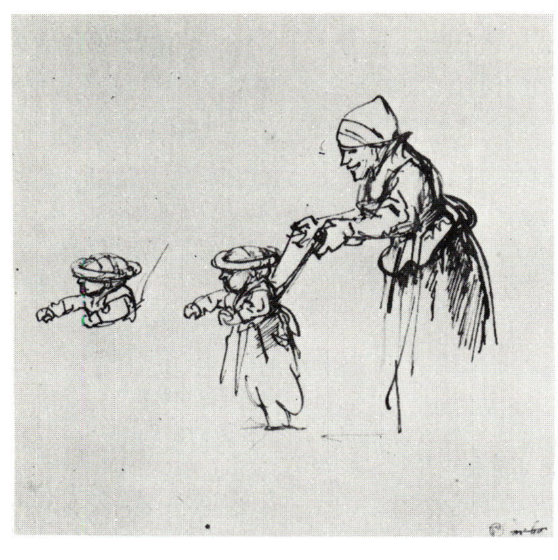

Plate 43
An Old Woman Holding a Child by Reins
about 1645
pen and wash
$6\frac{1}{4} \times 6\frac{1}{2}$ in (16 × 16.5 cm)
Nationalmuseum, Stockholm

From the Crozat Collection. Then in the famous Tessin Collection in the 18th century and since in the Nationalmuseum, Stockholm.

Pinakothek, Munich. The most endearing picture of this type is *The Holy Family* (plate 42) at Kassel. Such pictorial capriciousness, the *trompe l'oeil*, the curtain drawn across the picture, a painting of a painting, is common in Dutch art at the time but rare in the work of Rembrandt himself. The whole picture is very small, with a painted frame and then a painted curtain, which is partially drawn across the picture. This may seem a curious convention today, but it was common in Holland at the time. Collectors liked to place little curtains in front of their pictures, which must have increased the charm and pleasure of showing a collection to friends, rather than bringing them into a cluttered room where the eye is distracted with so many interesting pictures.

The artist has created the archetypal happy family at home. The infant Christ clings to his mother with typical gesture as if he had

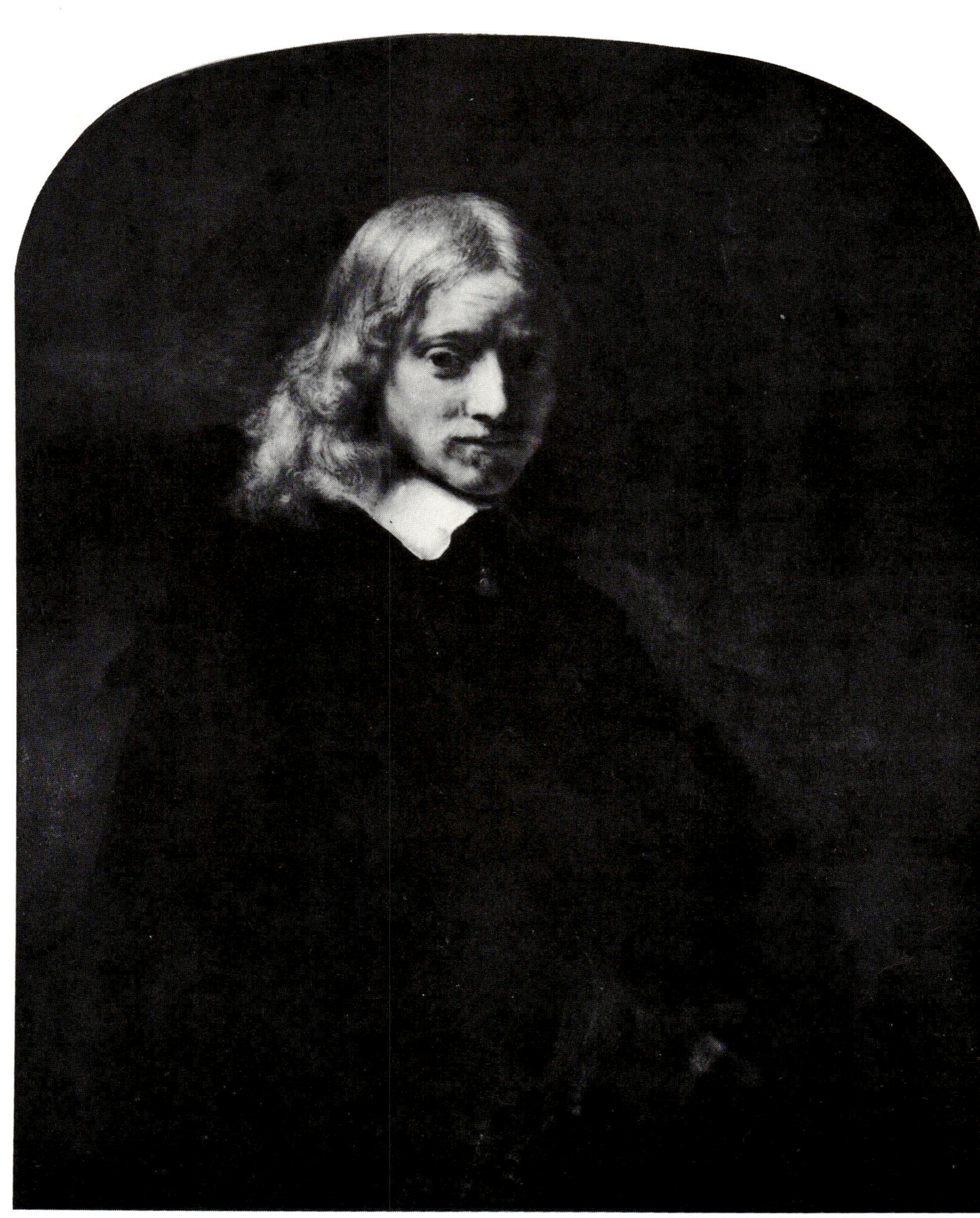

Plate 44
Portrait of a Young Man
about 1644
oil on panel
$36\frac{3}{8} \times 28\frac{1}{2}$ in (92.5 × 73.5 cm)
Private collection

Brought to England by Samuel Woodburn. Afterwards in Lord Dover's collection and bought by Alexander Henderson, later 1st Lord Faringdon, from Agnew in 1894.

been crying and his mother has just picked him up from the cradle for the sake of peace and quiet, while Joseph works away at his carpentry in the background. The artist's delight in children has already been noted in the drawing of *The Naughty Child* (plate 24) and it also appears in the drawing of *An Old Woman Holding a Child by Reins* (plate 43). There is a feeling of infinite tenderness in the delight of the grandparent or nurse in the first faltering steps of the child guided by the reins. To the left is another study of the child's face with a slightly different expression and his tiny arms outstretched to aid his balance. The drawing is generally dated about 1645.

The *Portrait of a Young Man* (plate 44) of about 1644 in a private collection in England is included here for no other reason than the fact that it is one of Rembrandt's most successful portraits of the conventional type. The flaxen hair of the sitter is inimitable; it hangs in great locks on the black gown and white collar of the man. He has a withdrawn, almost sad, face with wide eyes. The placing of the figure on the canvas is a perfect example of the apparent ease with which Rembrandt tackled this most difficult of problems. He was able to fill the canvas so that it appeared quite natural; only when he wanted to disturb the spectator, as in the Munich *Raising of the Cross* (plate 18) did he break the rules and introduce discordant elements.

It is a truism to say that Rembrandt's debt to other artists is manifold; this applies to his contemporaries, to the earlier tradition of painting in the North, and also to much Italian painting as well. Indeed Lord Clark has devoted a whole book (*Rembrandt and the Italian Renaissance*) enquiring into Rembrandt's relationship with the art of the Italian Renaissance. Many of his borrowings are subtly disguised and changed; he simply made the most of what other forms of art could teach him.

It is perhaps worthwhile to analyse one specific case of this to see how the ideas are changed and developed. The story begins in Rome with the German artist Adam Elsheimer, who came from Frankfurt. Almost all his pictures were on a tiny scale; but they often introduced new subject-matter and ways of seeing and were influential all over Europe, mostly through the medium of engraving. Two of Elsheimer's pictures were of paramount importance for Rembrandt. The first was his *Tobias and the Angel in a Landscape* of which the best version is in the National Gallery, London. This composition, or one very closely related to it, was engraved by Hendrick Goudt (plate 45), and thus spread rapidly to the North. Rubens himself collected several pictures by Elsheimer, and his fame spread far and wide. The Goudt engraving was then

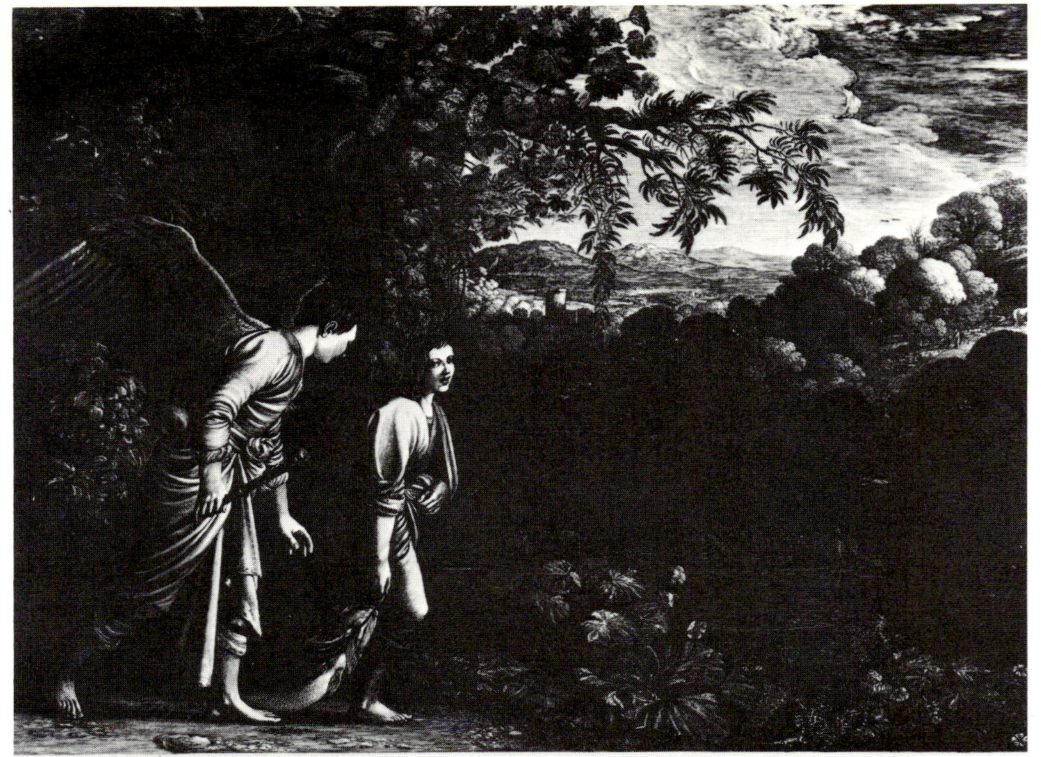

Plate 45
Hendrick Goudt after Adam Elsheimer
Tobias
dated 1613
etching
$7\frac{3}{4} \times 10$ in (19.7×25.5 cm)
Städelsches Kunstinstitut, Frankfurt

Usually known as the *Large Tobias*. As was usual with prints after paintings, the composition is reversed.

Plate 46
Hercules Seghers
Tobias
before 1635
etching
$8\frac{1}{4} \times 11\frac{1}{8}$ in (20.7×28.4 cm)
Rijksprentenkabinet, Amsterdam

This print is exceptionally rare and is found in only a few of the major print rooms of Europe. Seghers' print is reversed from the original print by Goudt and therefore ends up the same way round as Elsheimer's painting.

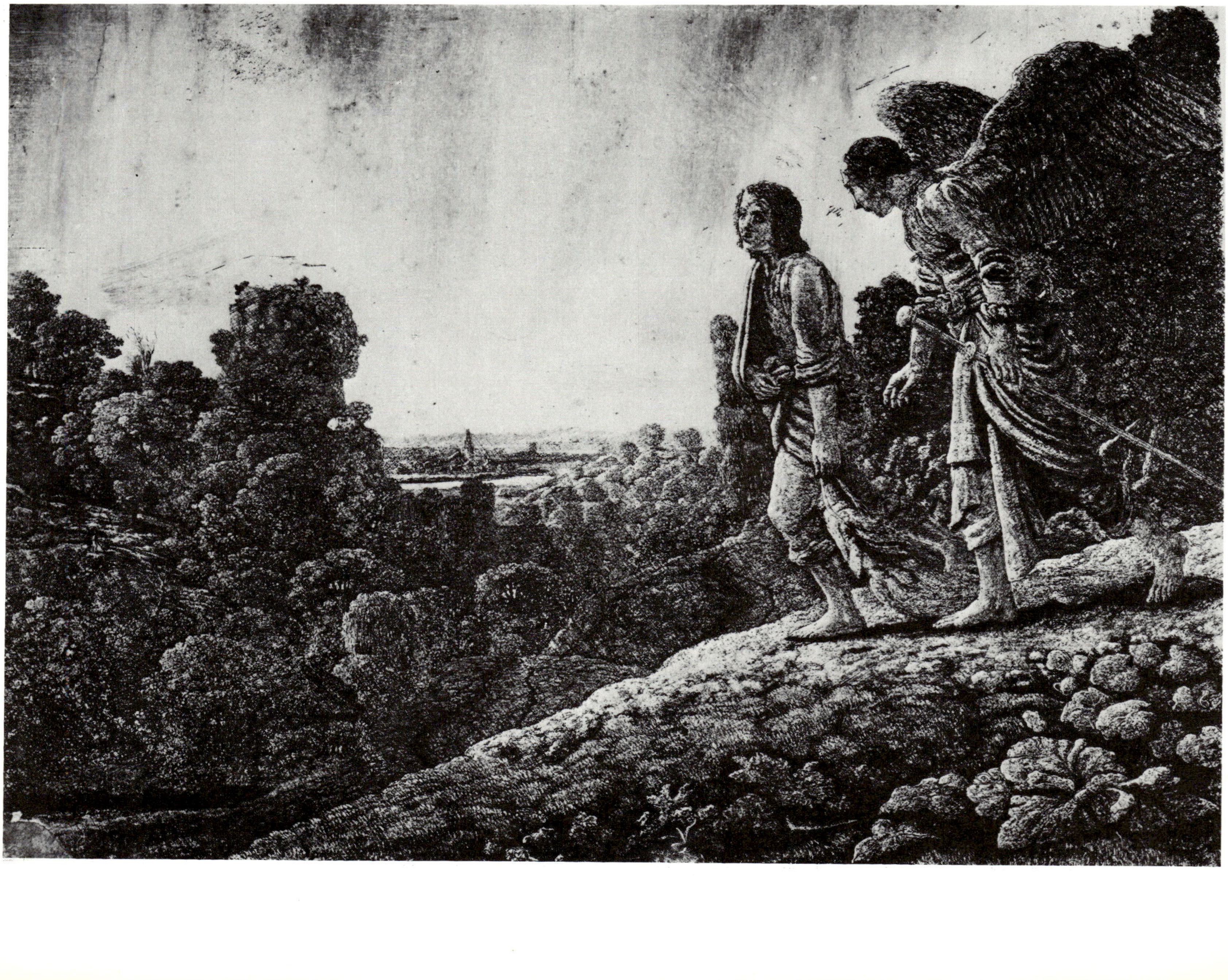

Plate 47
Rembrandt and Hercules Seghers
The Flight into Egypt
about 1653
etching
$8\frac{3}{8} \times 11\frac{1}{8}$ in (21.2×28.4 cm)
Städelsches Kunstinstitut, Frankfurt

It is easy to see where Rembrandt erased the figures of Tobias and the Angel and substituted the Holy Family on their way to Egypt.

copied by one of Rembrandt's contemporaries, Hercules Seghers, who etched the composition (plate 46) making it slightly more atmospheric. This etching (plate 47), indeed the actual copper plate, was then acquired by Rembrandt, and he then reworked the Seghers, after Goudt, after Elsheimer, largely removing the figures of Tobias and the Angel, adding further atmosphere and substituting the Holy Family. When Elsheimer painted his minuscule *Rest on the Flight into Egypt* (plate 48), now in the Alte Pinakothek, Munich, he created a picture which was unique in Western art at that time. It was a perfectly observed moonlit landscape, Milky Way included, with a large moon and distant dark trees. In the foreground there is a diminutive Holy Family resting by the light and warmth of a small bonfire. The whole picture is very precise; although subtle, all the edges are very sharp. It is difficult to believe that Rembrandt did not know this picture, a good copy of it, or Goudt's engraving, as his own interpretation, *Landscape with the Rest on the Flight* (plate 49) in the National

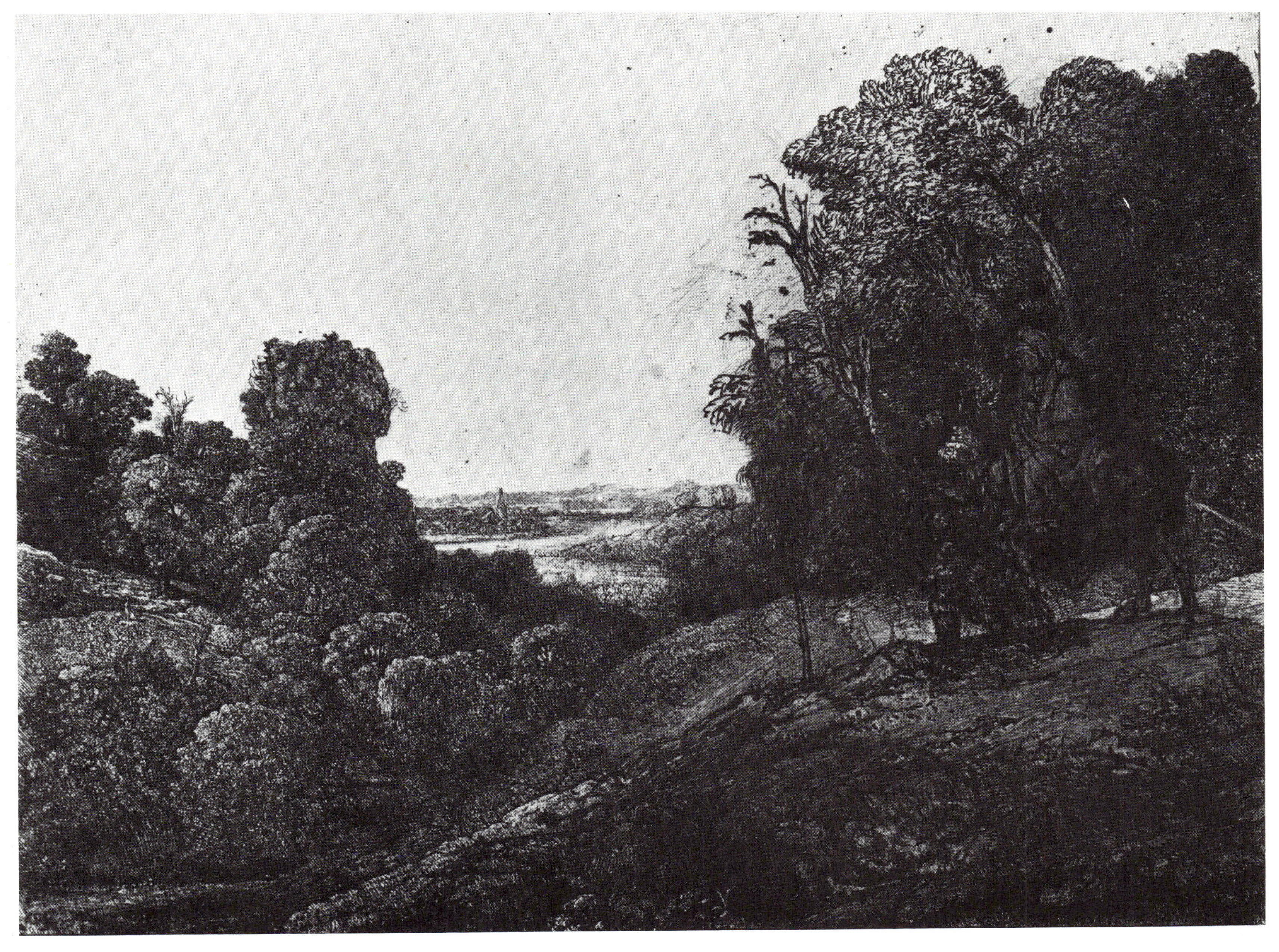

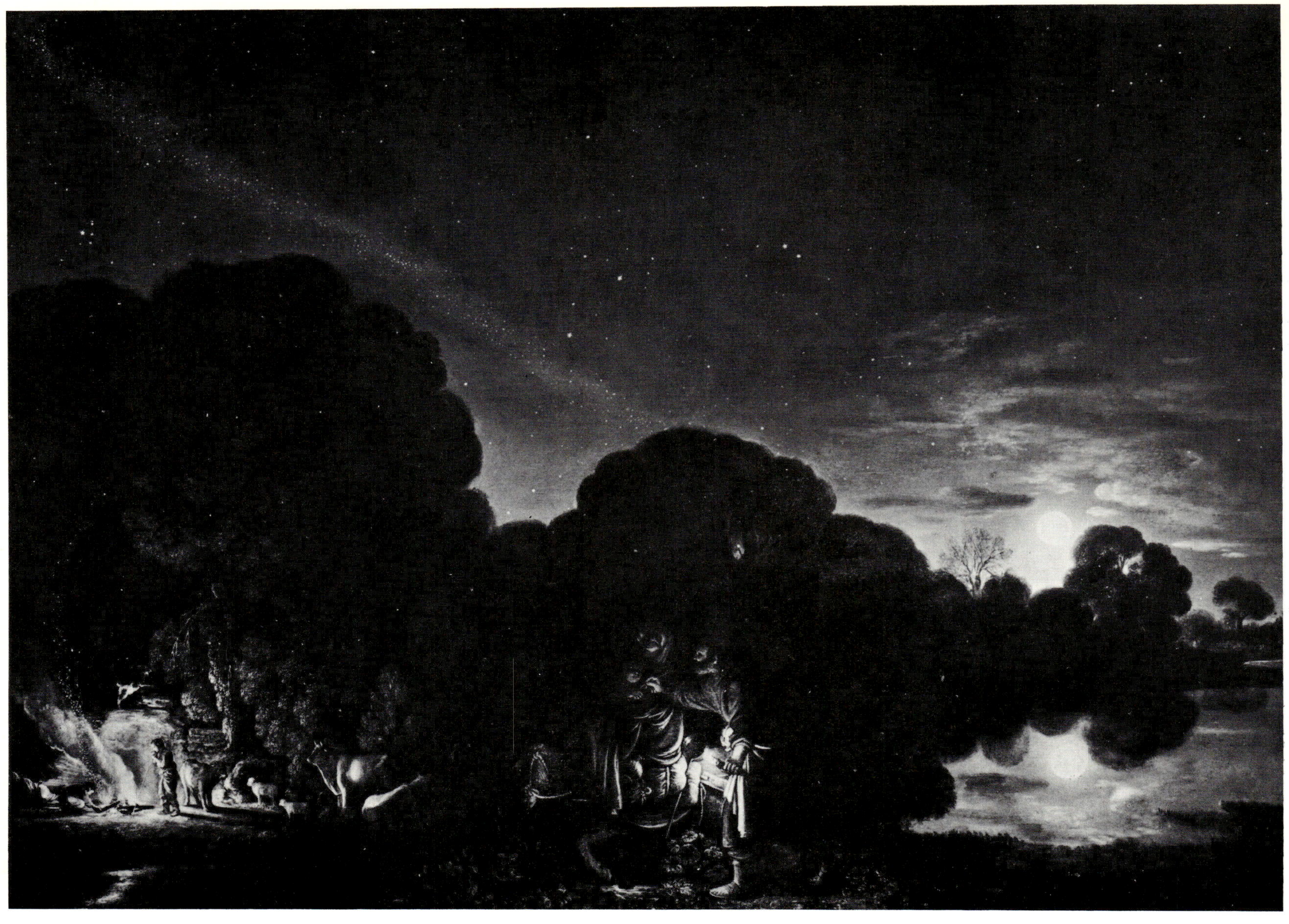

Plate 48
Adam Elsheimer
The Rest on the Flight into Egypt
dated 1609
oil on copper
$12\frac{1}{4} \times 16\frac{1}{4}$ in (31 × 41 cm)
Alte Pinakothek, Munich

Engraved in 1613 by Hendrick Goudt who presumably owned the picture. In the company of Rembrandt's 'Passion' series (see plate 18) in the Picture Gallery at Düsseldorf in the 18th century. For a time at Mannheim and transferred to Munich in 1806.

Gallery of Ireland, Dublin, is so close in spirit to its prototype.

This picture too is small. The artist assimilated everything he could learn from Elsheimer, the composition, the way of lighting a night scene out of doors, and then he transposed it into something magical of his own. There is a bluish haze not found in the Elsheimer, the ethereal quality of the air of the late evening mixing with the slowly rising smoke from the fire. The tiny pricks of light which Elsheimer used for the stars are here used to denote lights in the distant and almost indefinable buildings. It is easy to forget that in this painting Rembrandt produced one of the most enchanting works of the 17th century in the North of Europe.

From the same year, 1647, is the *Susanna Surprised by the Elders* (plate 50) in Berlin, which is a supreme example of the artist's ability to integrate his figures into a landscape setting, the culmination of this being of course *The Polish Rider* (plate 69) of a few years later. The unfortunate chaste Susanna is about to take her bath when she is surprised by two prying elders who catch her in a

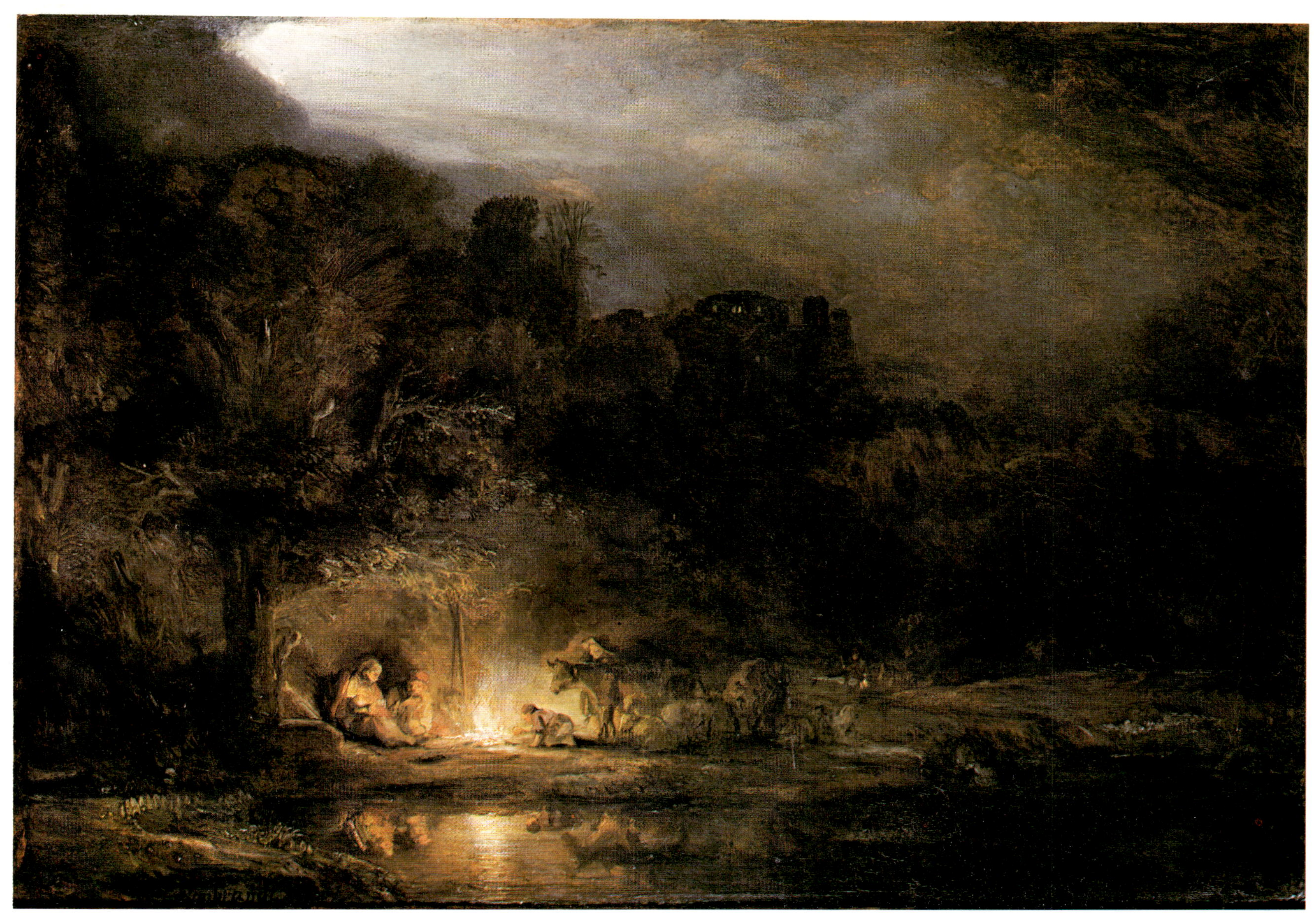

Plate 49
Landscape with the Rest on the Flight into Egypt
dated 1647
oil on panel
$13\frac{3}{8} \times 18\frac{7}{8}$ in (34×48 cm)
National Gallery of Ireland, Dublin

For a long time at Stourhead Park, Wiltshire, and purchased by the National Gallery of Ireland at the sale of the Stourhead heirlooms in 1883.

very awkward position. One of these lascivious old men is in the act of removing Susanna's shift which would reveal her nakedness completely, while the other, less sprightly, hurries along to join in the impending rape. Rembrandt has succeeded in painting that most difficult of emotions, embarrassment. Usually his naked figures have an immense dignity so characteristic of Venetian painting, but here Susanna is full of shame and fright.

In the years around 1650 the problem of exactly dating the pictures increases, and they have to be grouped together stylistically. Thus it is usually possible to be accurate to within five years or so by looking very carefully at a dated picture and grouping round it all the obviously similar undated ones. The artist concentrated on a series of heads of different types of people. Many versions of the *Head of Christ* (plate 51) exist, the one chosen here being the excellent example in the Metropolitan Museum, New York. There is a certain element of sentimentality in this series of heads – the sad eyes and the handsome bearded face.

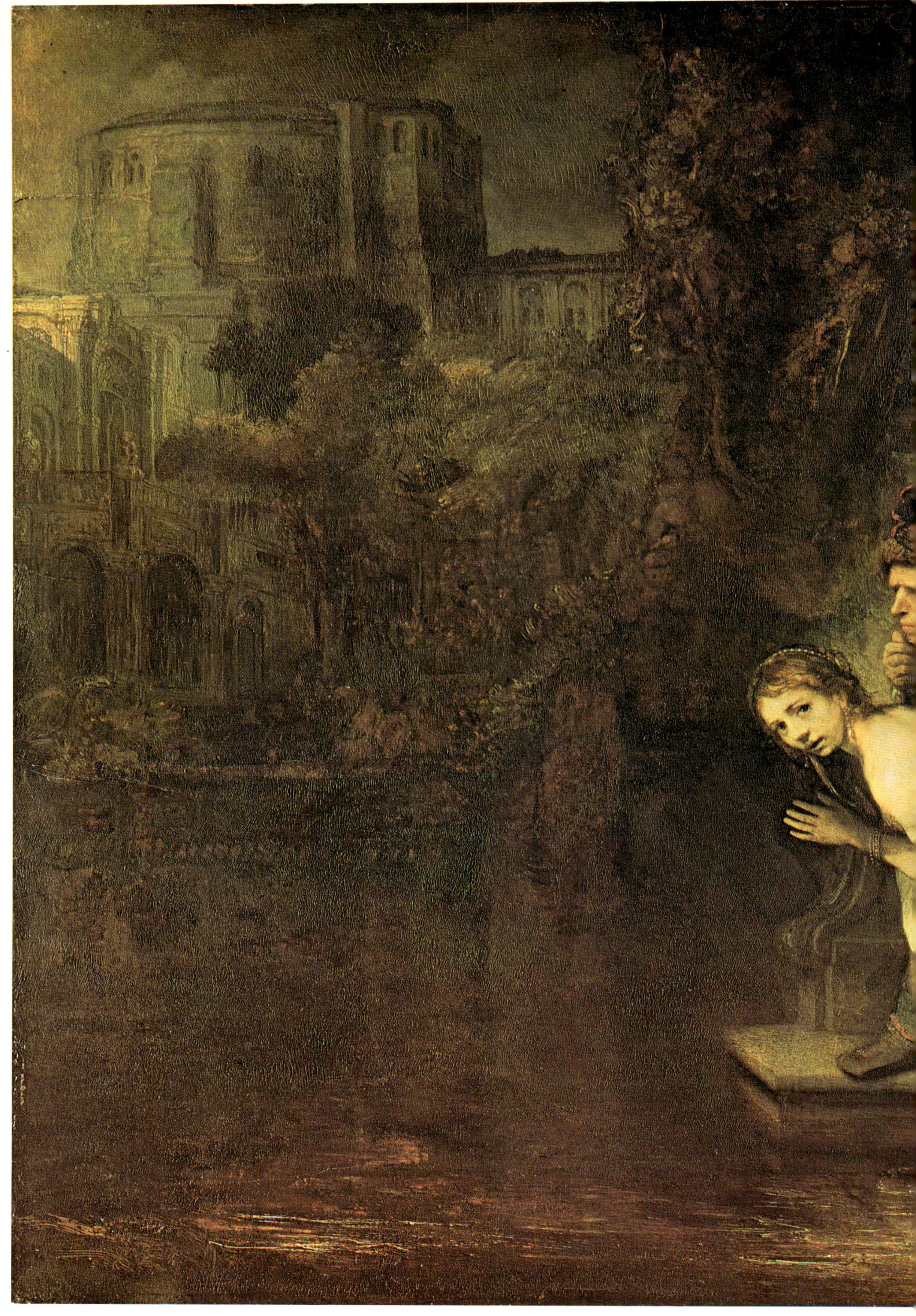

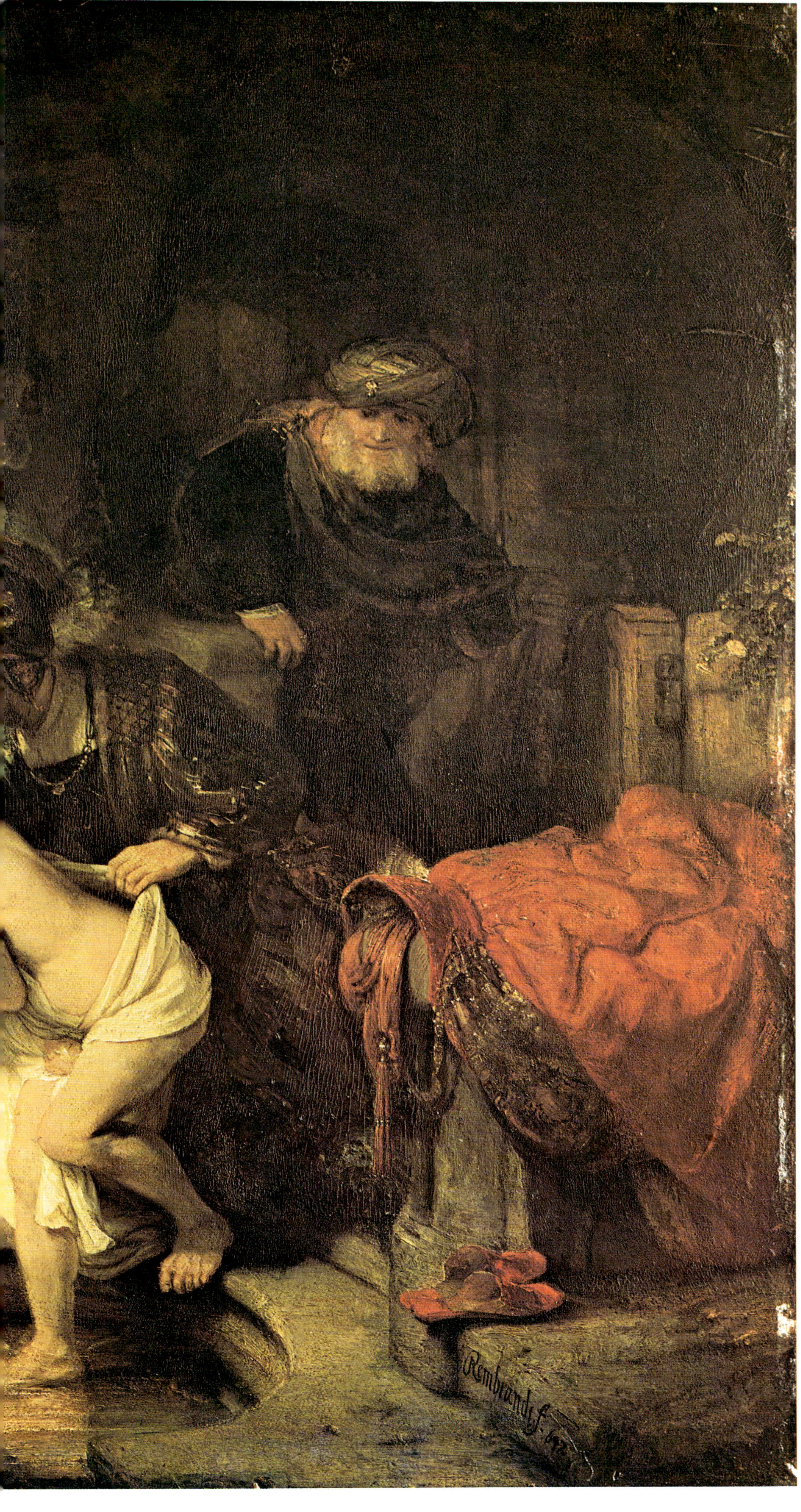

Plate 50
Susanna Surprised by the Elders
dated 1647
oil on panel
$30\frac{1}{8} \times 36\frac{1}{2}$ in (76.5 × 92.8 cm)
Gemäldegalerie, West Berlin

The earliest reference to this picture is in an Amsterdam sale in 1738. Later in the century in the collection of Sir Joshua Reynolds. Acquired by Wilhelm von Bode for the then Kaiser-Friedrich Museum, Berlin, in 1883. Now in the Dahlem Museum in West Berlin.

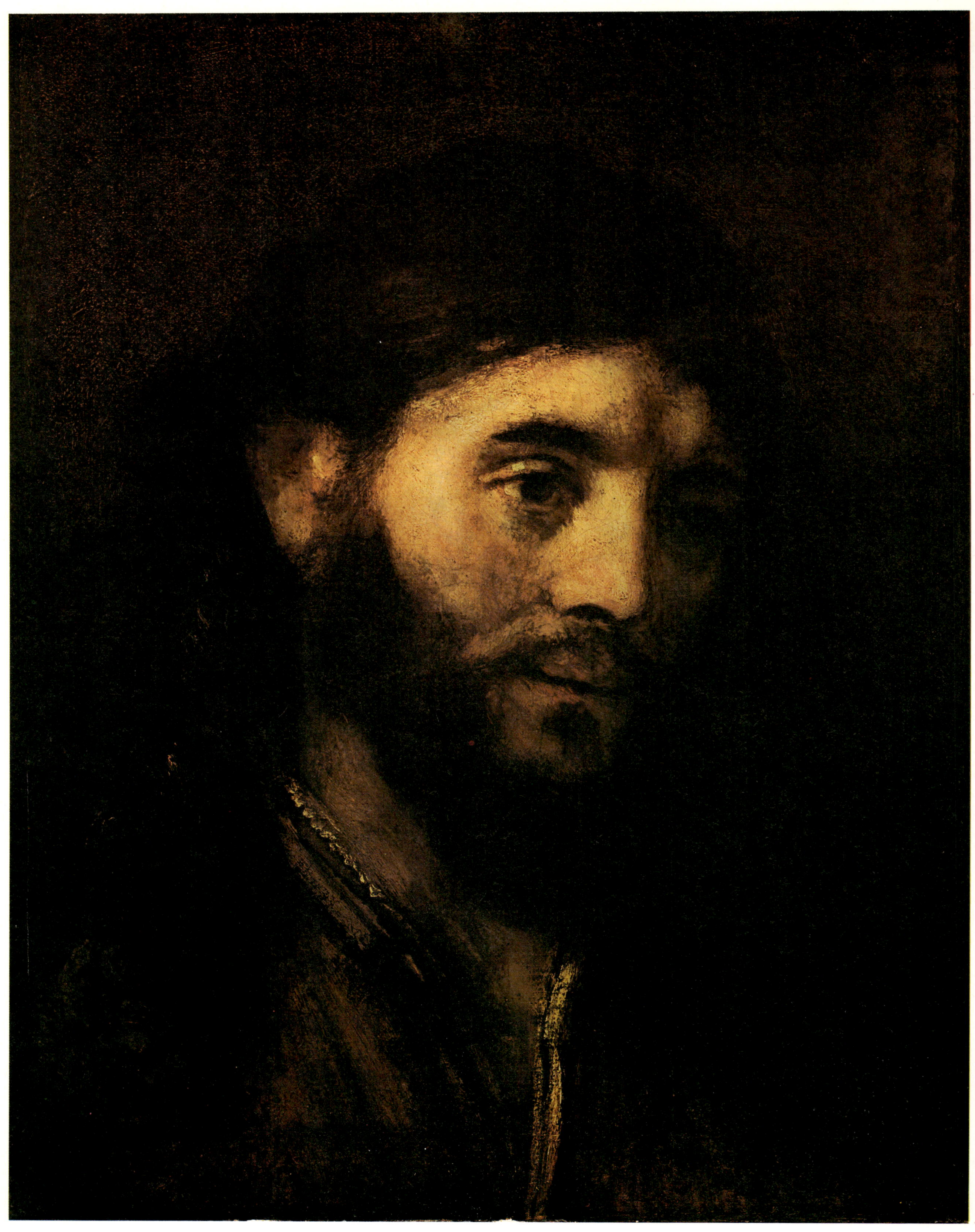

Plate 51
Head of Christ
about 1650
oil on canvas
$18\frac{3}{4} \times 14\frac{1}{2}$ in (47.5×37 cm)
Metropolitan Museum of Art, New York
Mr and Mrs I. D. Fletcher Collection, bequest of I. D. Fletcher, 1917

In this picture Rembrandt verges on the sentimental, which, according to modern taste, is no rare occurrence in 17th-century painting.

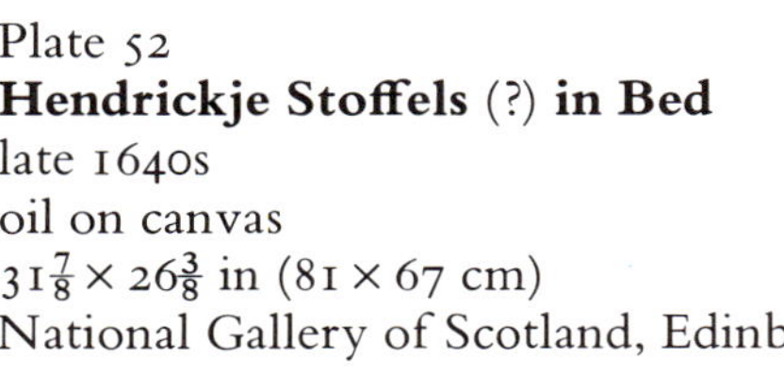

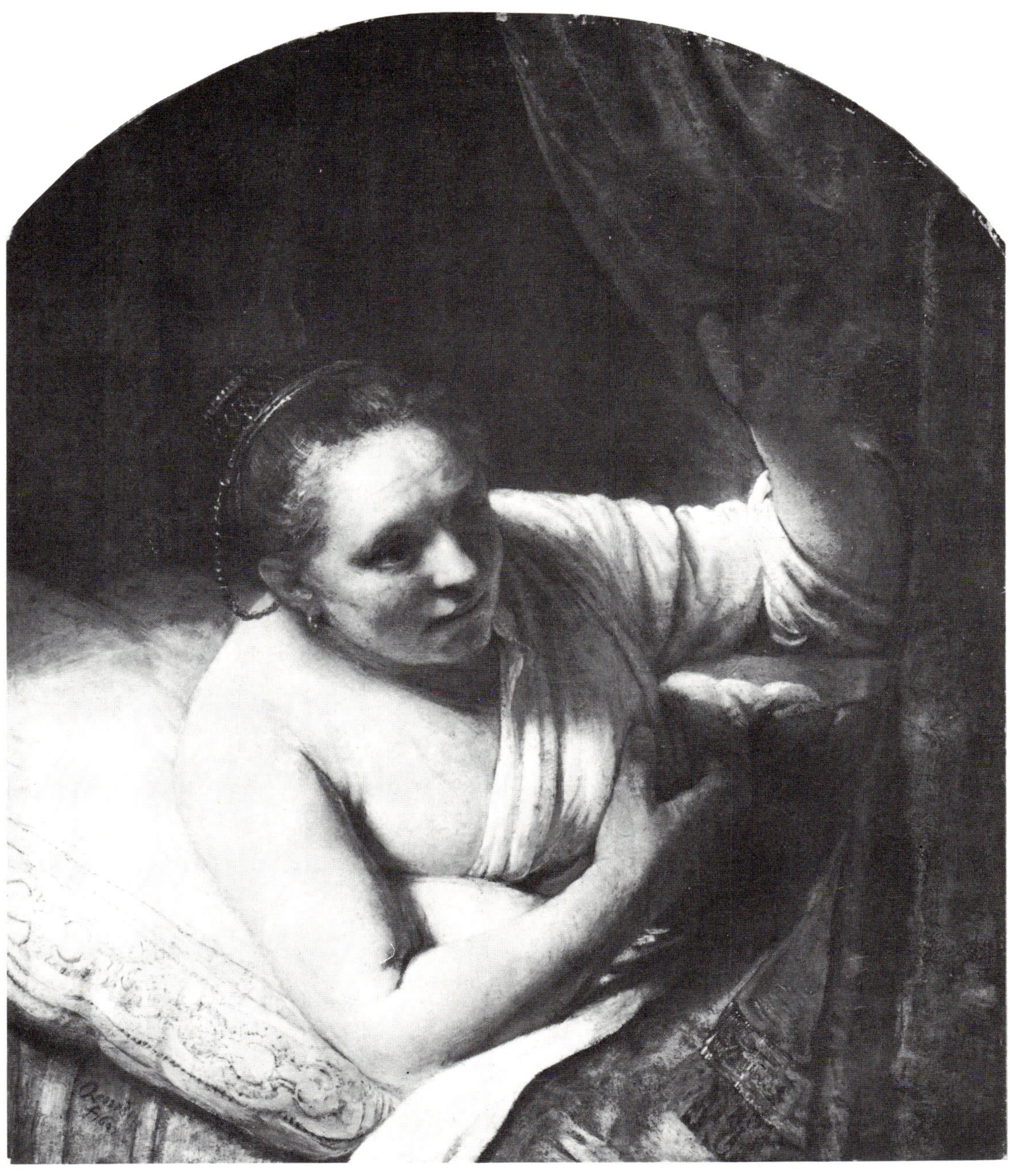

Plate 52
Hendrickje Stoffels (?) **in Bed**
late 1640s
oil on canvas
$31\frac{7}{8} \times 26\frac{3}{8}$ in (81×67 cm)
National Gallery of Scotland, Edinburgh

In the sale of the Prince de Carignan in Paris in 1742. In 1757 in the collection of François Tronchin at Geneva. Brought to England at the end of the 18th century. Sold at Christie's, London, in 1892 from the Wertheimer Collection. Given to the National Gallery in the same year by the Rt Hon. William McEwan.

The unlikely suggestion has been made that Rembrandt was Jewish; if so, he took the Christian religion seriously. But more likely he belonged to one of the obsure Protestant sects which sprang up in Amsterdam at the time, and which laid great emphasis on the reading and understanding of the Bible. If Rembrandt really did belong to the Mennonites it is almost as though these heads of Christ were painted for devotional purposes. They are usually of the same sitter, and there are versions in the Bredius Museum at The Hague, the Detroit Institute of Arts, Berlin, Philadelphia and in the Fogg Museum at Harvard.

Also in this vein but slightly more ambitious is the *King David with his Harp* formerly in the Kaplan Collection, New York. The sad-eyed king is made all the more touching with his elaborate gold harp. In this picture Rembrandt's gradual change in technique is beginning to be apparent. The celebrated late style is announced – the paint is much thicker in the highlights, in contrast to the very thin shadows. The sitter has a remote oriental quality which gives exactly the right feeling for this ancestor of Christ.

The *Hendrickje Stoffels (?) in Bed* (plate 52) in the National Gallery of Scotland at Edinburgh, which is of the late 1640s, has been a favourite for a long time on account of its intimate quality. Not one of the artist's best pictures, it seduces the spectator by the charm of the subject, the insight into the rarely recorded intimacies of a middle aged woman who, it appears, has just woken, or been woken. The paint has a certain heavy quality, a certain lack of transparency which records well the rather muddy flesh of the solidly built woman. The sitter has often been said to be Hendrickje, but this is by no means certain.

Like so many of Rembrandt's greatest works the *Man in a Golden Helmet* (plate 53) has been on too many calendars, tablemats and postage stamps to be generally taken as the gravely serious work that it is. It can either be interpreted as a tired but dignified old man dressed in a golden helmet, in order to give the artist an excuse to paint the object rather like a still-life; or more likely it is of a specific king who has not yet been identified, in the same way that the Glasgow *Man in Armour* (plate 67) can be shown to represent Alexander the Great with a reasonable degree of certainty. It has also been suggested that the sitter in the Berlin picture is Rembrandt's brother, and although the same old man appears in other pictures there is no real evidence either way. The man has a slight frown, and his tired and seemingly unwashed face is a sharp contrast to the glitter of the golden helmet. One is tempted to ask if this is not a kind of moral picture where the gold of the world is contrasted with the fragility of man. Croesus himself comes to mind, although he is more usually shown with the philosopher Solon who brings to his notice that happiness cannot be found in great wealth. Rembrandt has used every technical device to achieve the contrast between the untarnishable gold and the tragedy of the once strong and healthy man underneath it. There is never any mockery, but only an ineffable sadness which justifies the enormous fame of this picture. Its date is unknown, but it is generally thought to have been painted about 1650.

It would not be fair to ignore one of the most difficult problems to have faced Rembrandt scholars in the last few years, the famous *Mill* (plate 54) of about 1650, in the National Gallery, Washington.

Plate 53
Man in a Golden Helmet
early 1650s
oil on canvas
$26\frac{3}{8} \times 19\frac{3}{4}$ in (67×50 cm)
Gemäldegalerie, West Berlin

Acquired by Wilhelm von Bode on the London art market for the then Kaiser-Friedrich Museum in Berlin in 1897. Now in the Dahlem Museum in West Berlin.

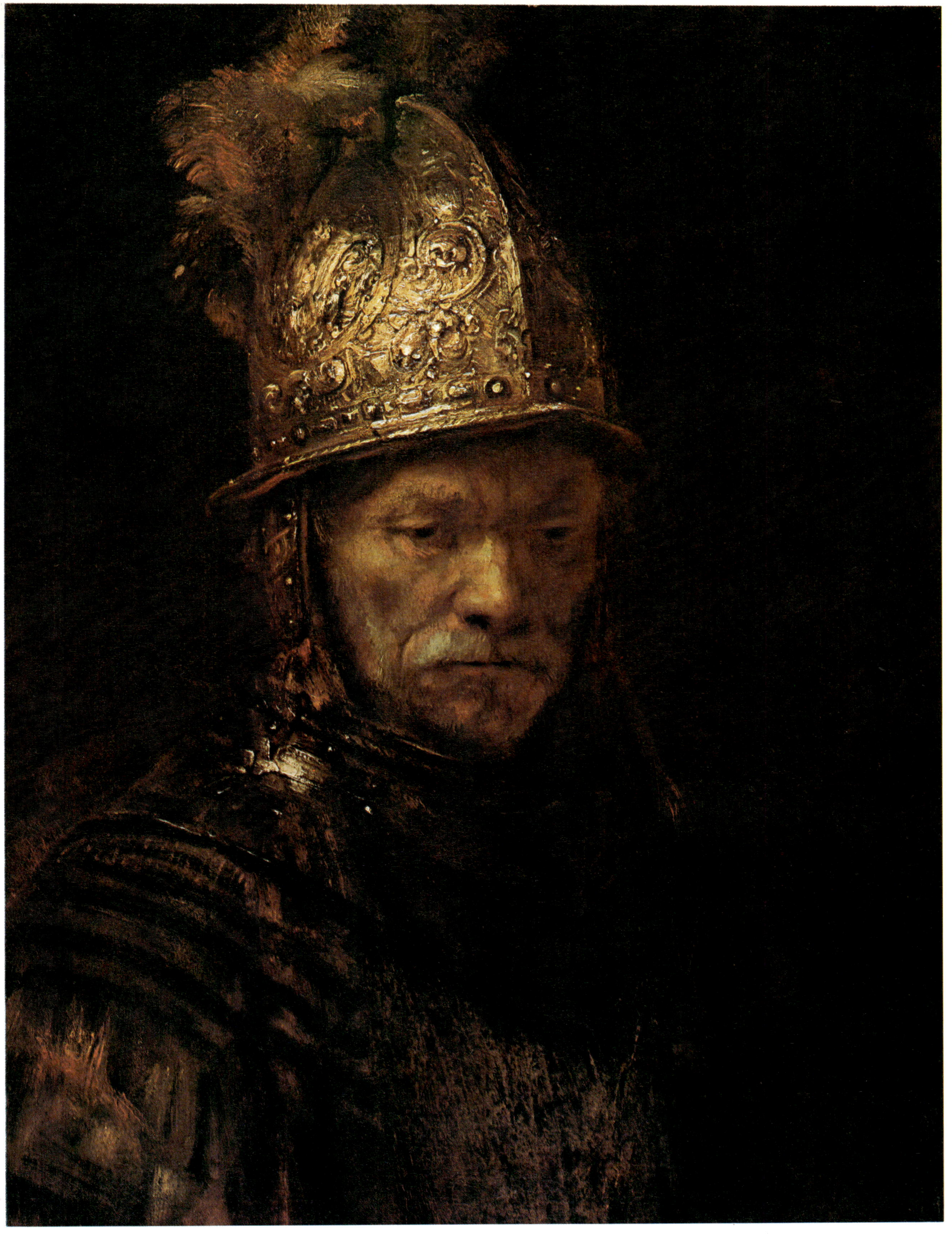

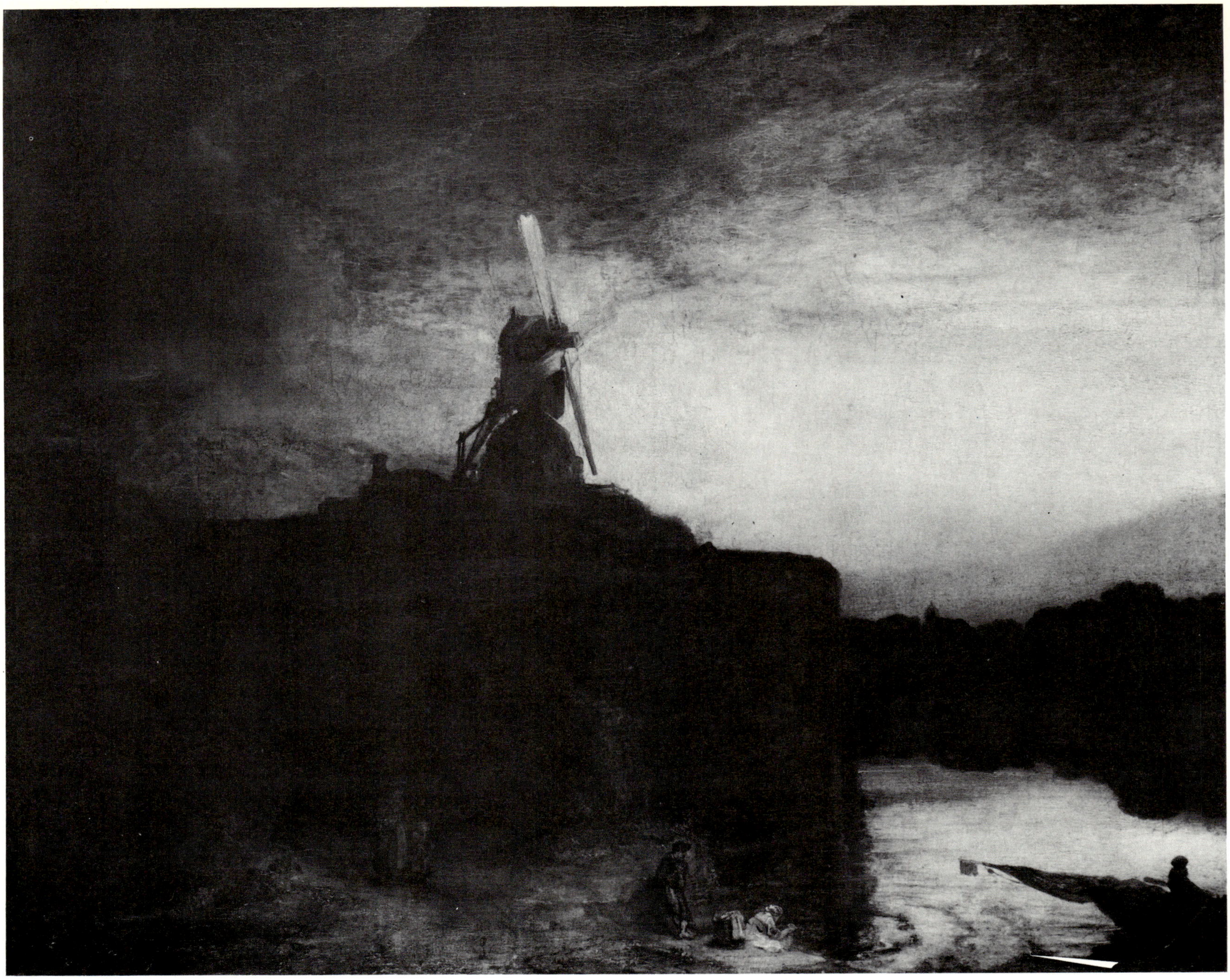

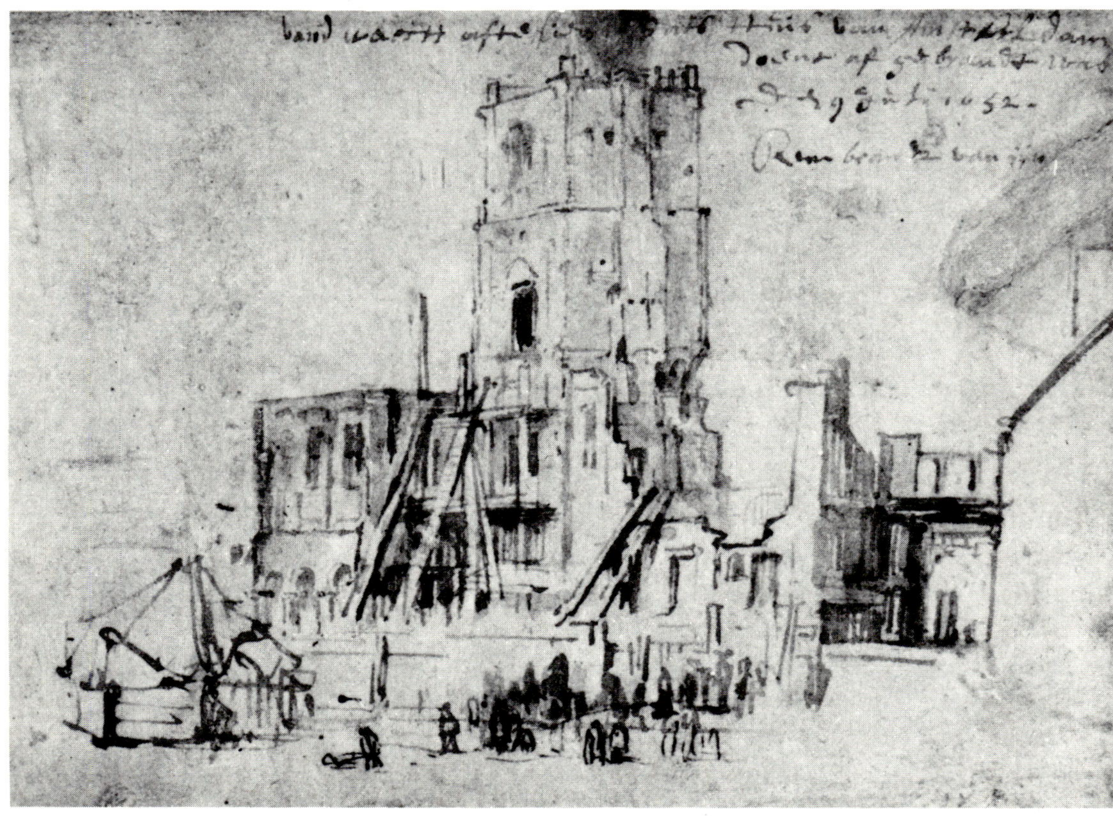

Plate 54
Rembrandt (?)
The Mill
about 1650
oil on canvas
$34\frac{1}{2} \times 41\frac{3}{8}$ in (87.5 × 105.5 cm)
National Gallery of Art, Washington
Widener Collection

Originally in the Orléans Collection and brought to England at the time of the French Revolution. Acquired by the Marquess of Lansdowne, who also owned the Kenwood *Self-Portrait* (plate 82). Sold with a great deal of publicity to P. A. B. Widener of Philadelphia in 1911 and subsequently given by Joseph Widener to the National Gallery, Washington. The picture has been so controversial in recent years that neither Bredius nor Gerson saw fit to discuss it in their catalogues.

Plate 55
Ruins of the Old Town Hall in Amsterdam after its Destruction by Fire
dated 1652
pen and wash
$5\frac{7}{8} \times 7\frac{7}{8}$ in (15 × 20.1 cm)
Rembrandthuis, Amsterdam

Recorded in several different sales in the 18th and 19th centuries. Finally in the J. P. Heseltine Collection before being acquired by the Rembrandthuis.

It would be better if the picture were not to exist; then there would not be the unfortunate necessity of suspecting that it is not by Rembrandt himself. In the late 18th and early 19th centuries this picture exerted a profound influence on the whole course of landscape painting in England, as it was exhibited several times, and many different artists came to know and to love it. The question uppermost in the present author's mind is that, if it is not by Rembrandt himself, who painted it? Such a question cannot at present be answered, as certainly no pupil known today produced a like object, and undoubtedly the painting itself is not an inferior work of art. Suffice it to say that modern scholarship has perhaps been hard on this masterpiece which inspired so much and that the invention is worthy of Rembrandt himself. The mill has a brooding feeling; there are none of the picturesque characteristics usually associated with windmills–rather the distant grandeur of the mill dominating a melancholy landscape. The conventional elements of a Dutch landscape have been rearranged by Rembrandt into something new in art, that of the deliberately emotive landscape, rather than one where topography or the play of light is uppermost in the artist's mind.

Rembrandt's interest in the topography of the surroundings of Amsterdam has already been remarked upon, and apart from the drawings of English subjects he occasionally drew architecture for its own sake. One example is the moving drawing of the *Ruins of the Old Town Hall of Amsterdam after its Destruction by Fire* (plate 55) which is dated 1652 and is in the collection at the Rembrandthuis, Amsterdam. It was to be just nine years later that Rembrandt was asked to decorate the new building which was to rise from the ashes of the old.

The considerable expansion of Rembrandt studies in the last two decades has never really grasped the nettle of the precise relationship with the pupils. Many of them merely imitated, but the most talented artist who worked in Rembrandt's manner in the early part of his all too short career was Carel Fabritius. The master of Vermeer, he was killed in the explosion of the powder magazine in Delft in 1654. In the small *Head of an Old Man* (plate 56) in the Walker Art Gallery, Liverpool, the artist's closeness to Rembrandt both in handling and in feeling is obvious. Later he developed a rather lighter style, and his few surviving portraits have a direct carefully observed approach which make it all the more lamentable that he died so young.

His brother Barent Fabritius also worked in Rembrandt's manner, and although an artist of some originality he never had Carel's acute powers of observation. A good example of his work

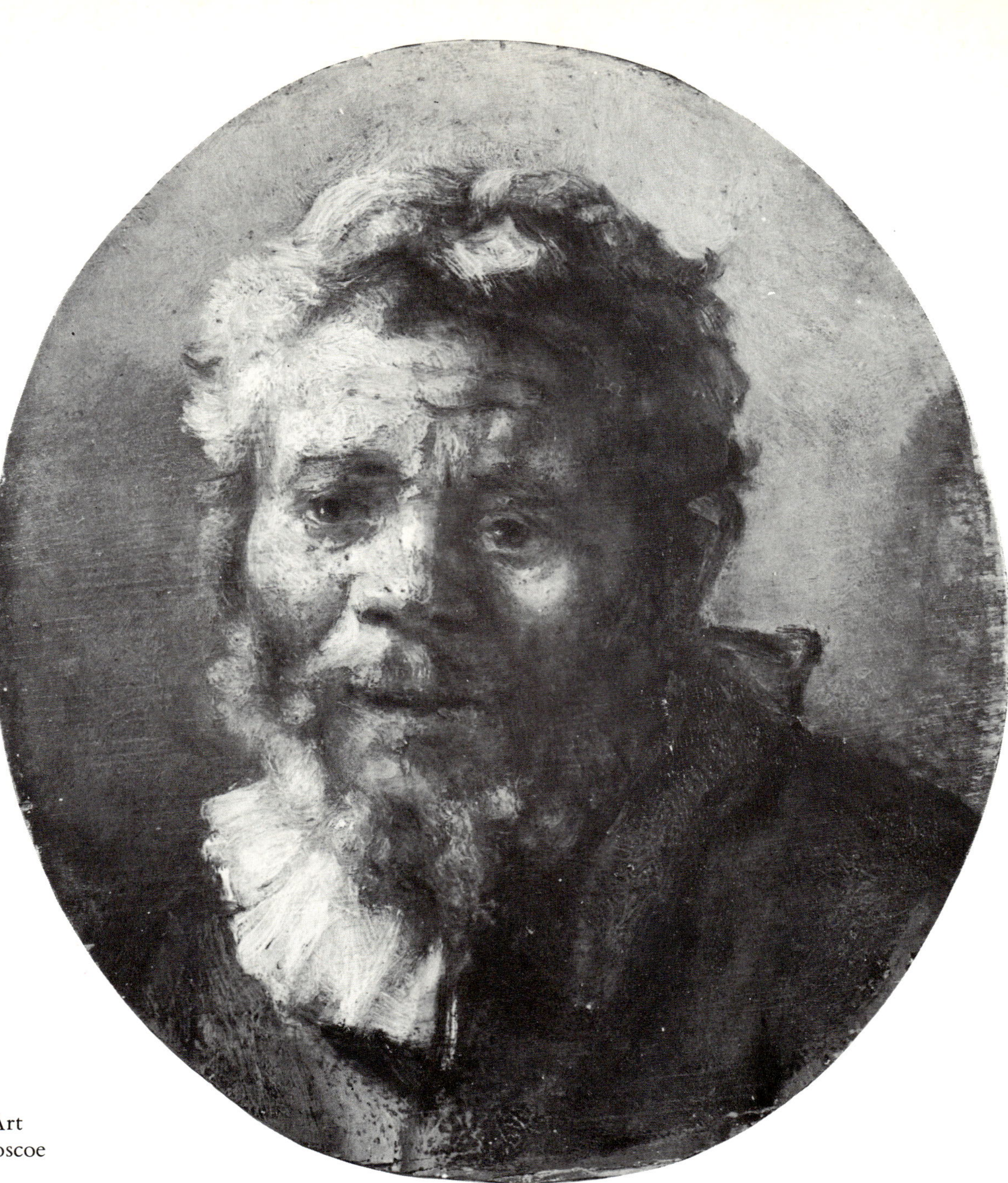

Plate 56
Carel Fabritius
Head of an Old Man
about 1650–52
oil on panel
$9 \times 7\frac{5}{8}$ in (22.8×19.3 cm)
Walker Art Gallery, Liverpool

Probably in the collection of William Roscoe of Liverpool in the early 19th century and bequeathed to the Walker Art Gallery by his descendant Mrs A. M. Roscoe in 1950.

is the *Dismissal of Hagar* in the Ferens Art Gallery at Kingston-upon-Hull, where much of the master's careful observation of the relationship between the figures remains, but little of his ability to hold the spectator's attention.

Even a brief study of Rembrandt's contribution to the art of etching would fill a considerable book, and his work in this medium can only be touched on here. Until the invention of photography artists were much more often interested in processes of reproduction than is generally realised today. Rembrandt was no exception: he made a whole series of advances in the way the medium of etching could be used to express a variety of moods.

Basically an etching is an engraving made on a copper plate, not by the action of a sharp tool, but by the action of acid which eats into the copper only where the protective coating of wax has

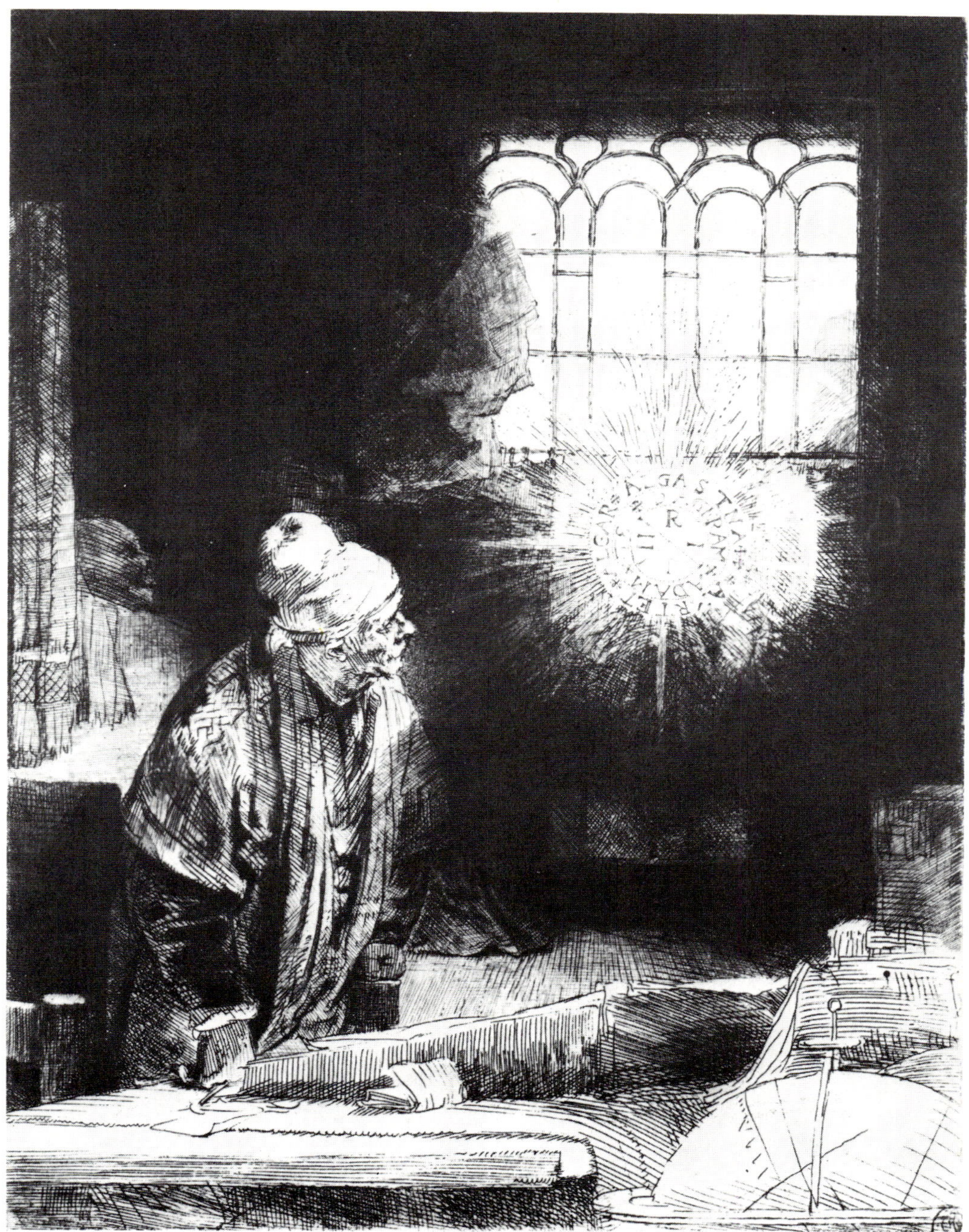

Plate 57
Dr Faustus in His Study
about 1652
etching
$8\frac{1}{4} \times 6\frac{1}{4}$ in (21×16 cm)
City Art Gallery, Leeds

Bequeathed to the City of Leeds in 1952 by Agnes and Norman Lupton who had made an extensive collection of Rembrandt's etchings.

been removed in the process of drawing on it. The resultant plate is very versatile, as the length of time in the acid can be varied, thus altering the intensity of the lines. Unfortunately a very limited number of good prints can be taken from each plate as the sensitive copper soon wears down with the action of the heavy press used in the printing.

The etchings of Rembrandt occupy a special position in the history of this medium, not only because they are technically brilliant, but because of his incessant experiments with the plate, which cause him to have several attempts on each plate, modifying the composition, and then printing it again. Each change made on the plate, after the first printing, is called a state. Before Rembrandt's time this had usually been limited to the adding of inscriptions or minor alterations, but in Rembrandt's case the

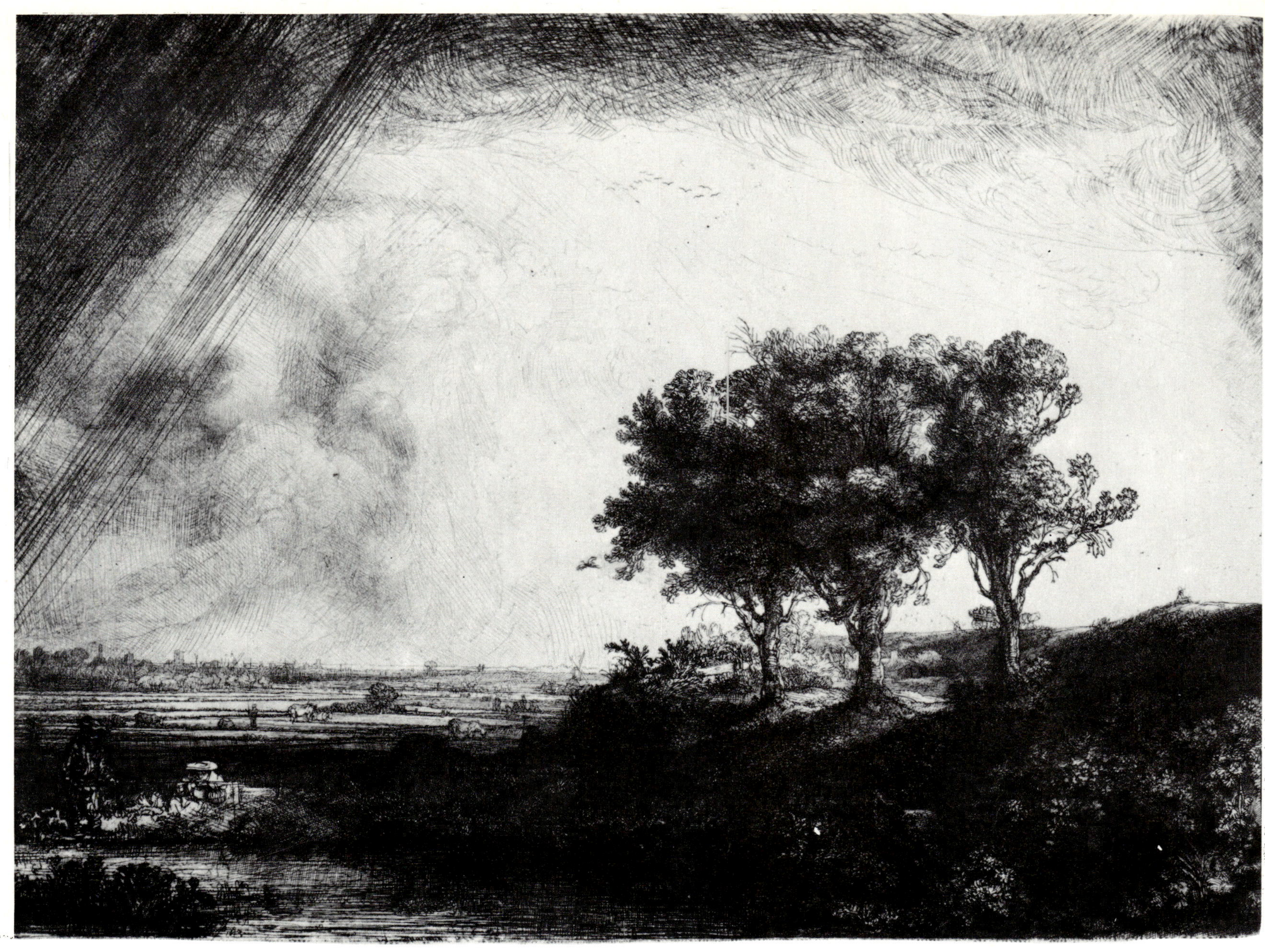

Plate 58
The Three Trees
dated 1643
etching
$8\frac{3}{8} \times 11$ in (21.3×27.9 cm)
British Museum, London

This etching has inspired many landscape artists. The composition is so simple and yet so subtly balanced that it appealed to many later artists, particularly those who worked up their compositions in the studio.

progress from the first to the last state of the plate can result in a complete metamorphosis. Many of Rembrandt's etchings are very well known, highly prized by print collectors and admired by the general public. They are, however, little exhibited, as they do not readily lend themselves to permanent display and are much more easily appreciated in the silence of a printroom, where their intimate quality is so much easier to see than on the walls of an exhibition gallery.

An excellent example of his etching style is the *Dr Faustus in His Study* (plate 57), the example chosen being that in the Leeds City Art Gallery. The special interest of this print is that not all the lines are etched on the plate: Rembrandt has added further strokes in pen, in order, it would appear, to see what some new changes would look like before taking the drastic step of altering the plate itself. The *Dr Faustus in his Study* gives an impression of the mystery of primeval magic. The magic disc appears in the air

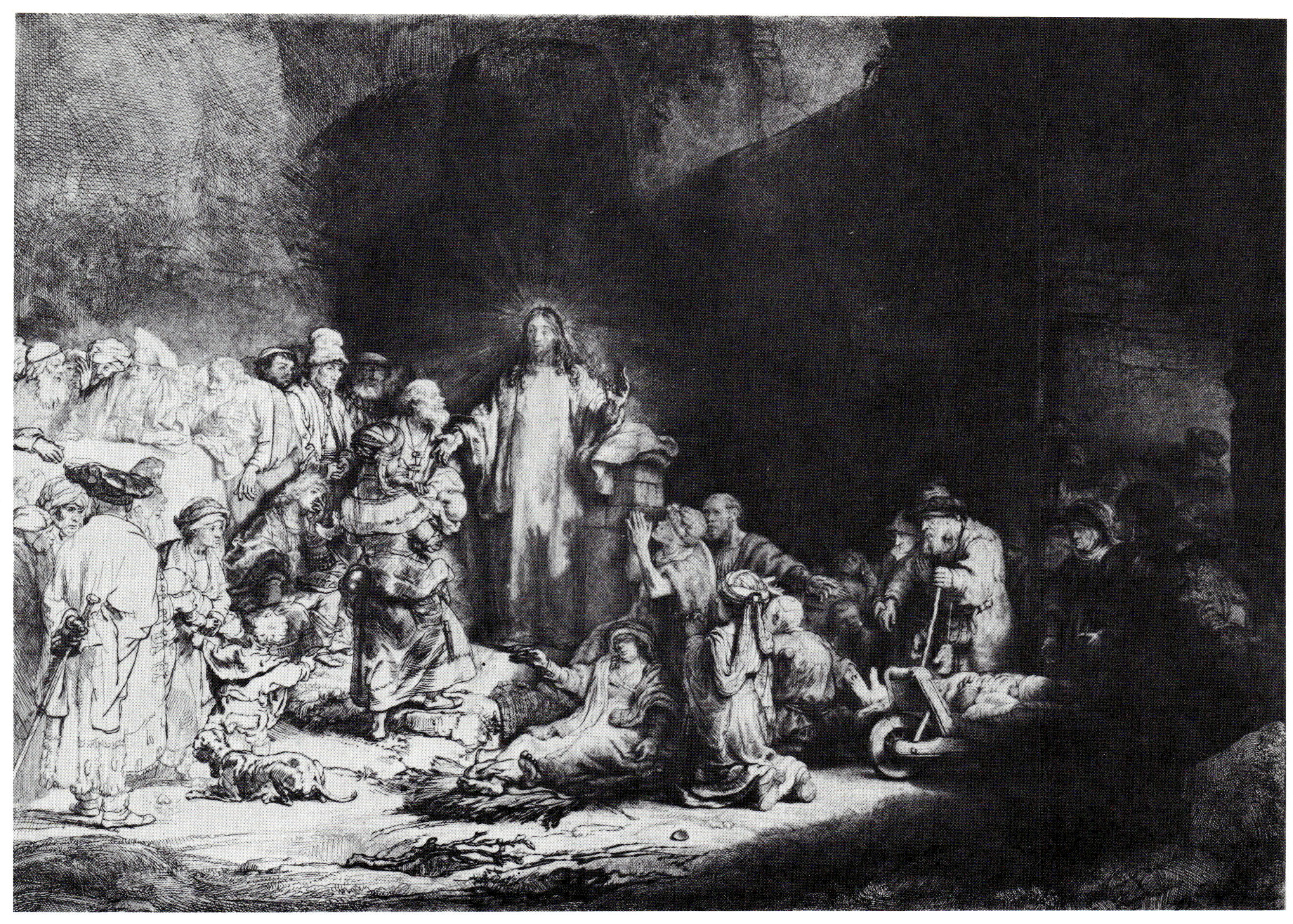

Plate 59
Christ Healing the Sick
The Hundred Guilder Print
about 1649
etching
11 × 15¼ in (27.8 × 38.8 cm)
British Museum, London

This is Rembrandt's best-known print.

undeterred by the light from the window. The skull at the extreme left echoes the face of the doomed Dr Faustus. This is one of Rembrandt's most intense and frightening etchings, made all the more mysterious by the complete failure of modern scholarship to discover the meaning of the letters in the magic disc.

Many of his etchings are of an unbelievable fineness, an infinite number of delicate lines adding up to a fragile image, whether it be the artist himself, a shell, or a spacious and wonderful landscape like *The Three Trees* (plate 58), the example in the British Museum, London, being reproduced here. It is easy to see that in such an etching the artist's drawing style has played a great part in its creation. There is a concentration on the immense breadth of the Dutch landscape contrasted with the three very solid trees which dominate the right-hand side.

One of the most significant of the artist's etchings is the *Christ Healing the Sick* (plate 59), usually known as the 'Hundred

Guilder Print'. A very complicated composition both in terms of the number of figures and in the lighting, it is generally dated in the years 1642–45, and in it the lessons learned in the creation of *The Night Watch* (plate 41) can be seen translated into the medium of etching. Christ dominates the composition, and in an uncanny way he radiates light over this sombre and touching scene where the sick lay all around him in various states of helplessness.

The 1650s, when the artist was aged 45–55, mark, in the opinion of the writer, the peak of Rembrandt's art. The first of the pictures from this period, the Berlin *Man in a Golden Helmet* (plate 53), has already been discussed. His last pictures after 1660 do not cease to be moving, but they lack the control which is seen in the 1650s.

The *Aristotle Contemplating the Bust of Homer* (plate 60) of 1653 in the Metropolitan Museum of Art, New York, apart from being one of Rembrandt's very best pictures, has a historical significance quite unsuspected by the average spectator. Unlike Rubens, Van Dyck or Gentileschi, to name only a few of the artists whose reputations became international in their own lifetimes, Rembrandt's international reputation was limited. Charles I of England's probable ownership of the Liverpool *Self-Portrait* (plate 14) has already been alluded to, but by far the most significant commission from outside his own country came from a certain Don Ruffio of Messina in Sicily who in 1654 received the *Aristotle*. It is known from the surviving documentation that Don Ruffio only asked for a half-length philosopher, and it must be presumed that Rembrandt elaborated on this initial request. Later Don Ruffio was to ask of Rembrandt two further pictures which are almost certainly the Glasgow *Man in Armour* and the *Homer* (plate 96) in the Mauritshuis in The Hague.

The Greek philosophers were held in very great esteem in 17th-century Holland, and it is therefore not surprising that the artist interpreted the subject in a solemn and almost religious manner. Aristotle is seen as a grand old man, the aristocrat of philosophers. There is in the figure not the slightest hint of scholarly asceticism, the only concession to this being the pile of books in the background. The bust of Homer, the greatest of poets, looks as if it were made of wax rather than marble, and Aristotle lays his hands on it, affectionately and with respect. There is an air of grandeur and gravity, without the depressing quality which this type of Rembrandt sometimes has. So often in the self-portraits the tragedy is almost too much to bear.

The series of outright masterpieces continues with the Louvre *Bathsheba with King David's Letter* (plate 61) which also suffers from

Plate 60
Aristotle Contemplating the Bust of Homer
dated 1653
oil on canvas
$56\frac{1}{4} \times 53\frac{1}{2}$ in (143.5 × 136.5 cm)
Metropolitan Museum of Art, New York
Purchased with special funds and gifts of friends of the Museum, 1961

In the collection of Don Ruffio in Messina by 1654 where it remained until about 1760. Sold by Lord Duveen in 1928 to Alfred Erickson, New York for the then astronomical sum of $750,000. Bought back by Duveen five years later for $500,000 who then resold it to Erickson in 1936 for $590,000. Acquired by the Metropolitan Museum in the Erickson sale at Parke-Bernet, New York, for $2,300,000, which, in 1961, was the highest price paid up to that date for a picture at auction.

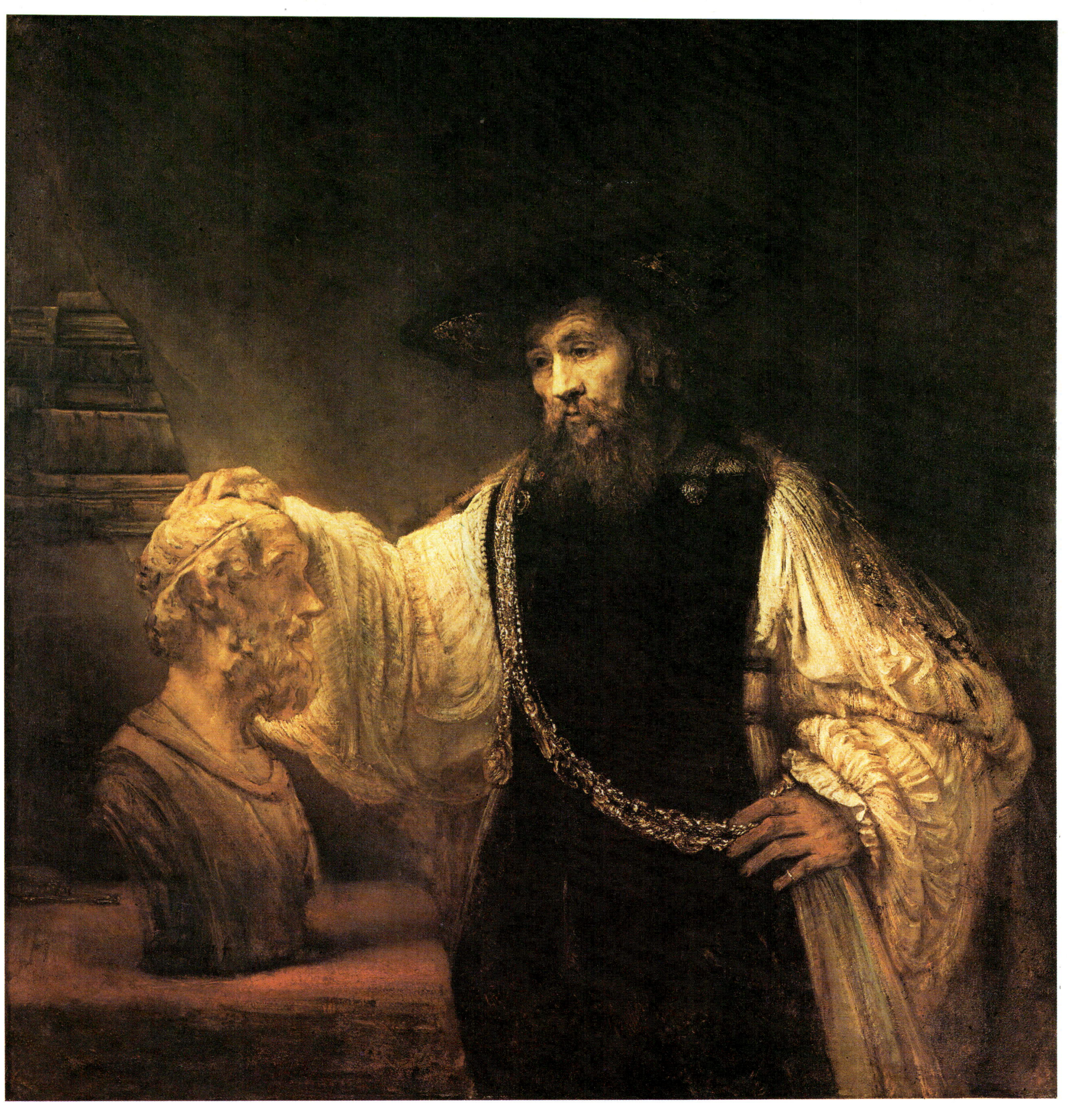

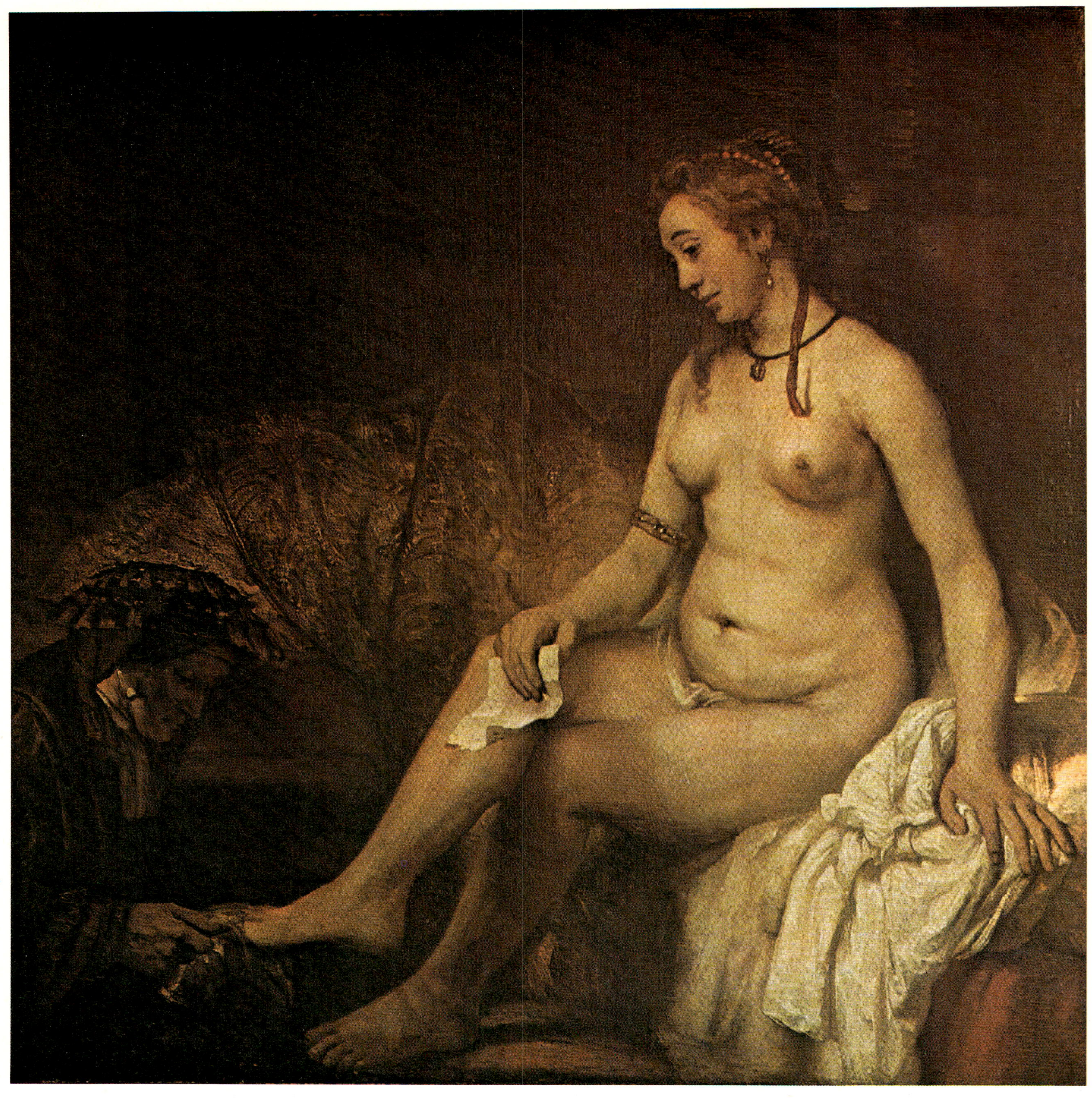

Plate 61
Bathsheba with King David's Letter
dated 1654
oil on canvas
$55\frac{7}{8} \times 55\frac{7}{8}$ in (142×142 cm)
Musée du Louvre, Paris

Surprisingly enough the earliest mention of this picture comes from the sale of William Young Ottley in London in 1811. Sold again in London in 1837 when it was purchased by the dealer Peacock for 105 guineas. Subsequently in Paris and bequeathed to the Louvre by Dr La Caze in 1869.

overfamiliarity. In the English-speaking world the painting of the nude has always been treated with a certain amount of caution, and few writers until the present time have considered it a worthy object of study. In this, his most famous nude, Rembrandt is very much part of the Western tradition, deriving ultimately from Venice. However, there is a precedent much closer to home. Cornelis Cornelisz. van Haarlem's *Bathsheba* (plate 62) of 1594 in the Rijksmuseum, Amsterdam, is an early attempt at the sensuous nude. The style is highly artificial, but the artist succeeds in creating a mood of relaxed sensuality. Rembrandt took up the idea, not very far removed from the Cornelis Cornelisz. Yet the artist has been able to glory in the painting of an amply proportioned female nude without any sexual or moral undertones. Bathsheba holds King David's letter while her elderly serving maid dries one of her feet. The whole attitude of Bathsheba is completely natural: there is none of the embarrassment so brilliantly painted in the Berlin *Susanna* (plate 50), neither is there the feeling that the model is bored or in a draught. Today Bathsheba would be considered fat, but it is an immensely lyrical picture, in which the gentle curve of Bathsheba's head is matched by that of the serving woman. The whole has a very subdued colour scheme, perhaps partly caused by the layer of heavy varnish.

Related in both mood and style is the much smaller *Woman Bathing* (plate 63) in the National Gallery, London. This title is not quite accurate as she is standing up to her calves in the water and holding up her shift in order to stop it getting wet. The picture has an innocent quality: it is an intimate scene painted very freely on a small scale. The technique is quite surprising as the seeming precision dissolves on approaching the picture closely, and it is seen to be made up of rough slabs of thickly applied paint, in particular her hand and the white shift which is painted with great sweeps of the loaded brush. When such a technique is used by Rembrandt on a larger scale, as in the *Man in an Armchair* in the same gallery, it gives an immense feeling of power, but in the context of this little picture it is all the more daring as such a technique was rarely used for a cabinet-type picture.

The Leningrad *Danaë* (plate 64), although one of Rembrandt's largest and most significant canvases, has posed many problems. Probably begun about 1636 it is likely to have been completed almost twenty years later. Unless a new document turns up we shall never know whether he just kept it in the studio as a large picture which he continued to work on or whether some client returned it and asked him to rework it in his later manner. The debt to the Italian Renaissance here too is obvious. Less elegant

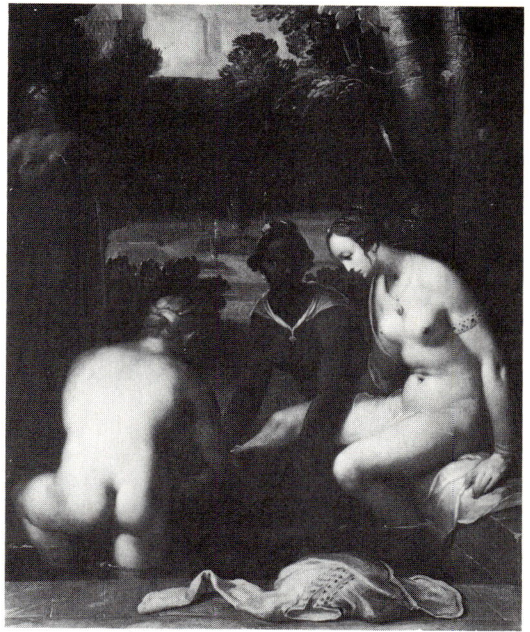

Plate 62
Cornelis Cornelisz. van Haarlem
Bathsheba
dated 1594
oil on canvas
$30\frac{1}{2} \times 25\frac{1}{4}$ in (77.5 × 64 cm)
Rijksmuseum, Amsterdam

Acquired by the Rijksmuseum from a collection in Paris in 1955. The previous history of the picture is at present unknown.

Plate 63
A Woman Bathing
dated 1655
oil on panel
$24\frac{3}{8} \times 18\frac{1}{2}$ in (62 × 47 cm)
National Gallery, London

Sold frequently in the 18th century always for small sums. Acquired by Sir Joshua Reynolds in 1759 for £16 5s. 6d. It is not known when the picture left Reynolds' collection but it was acquired by the Rev William Holwell Carr for 165 guineas in 1829. Bequeathed by him to the gallery two years later.

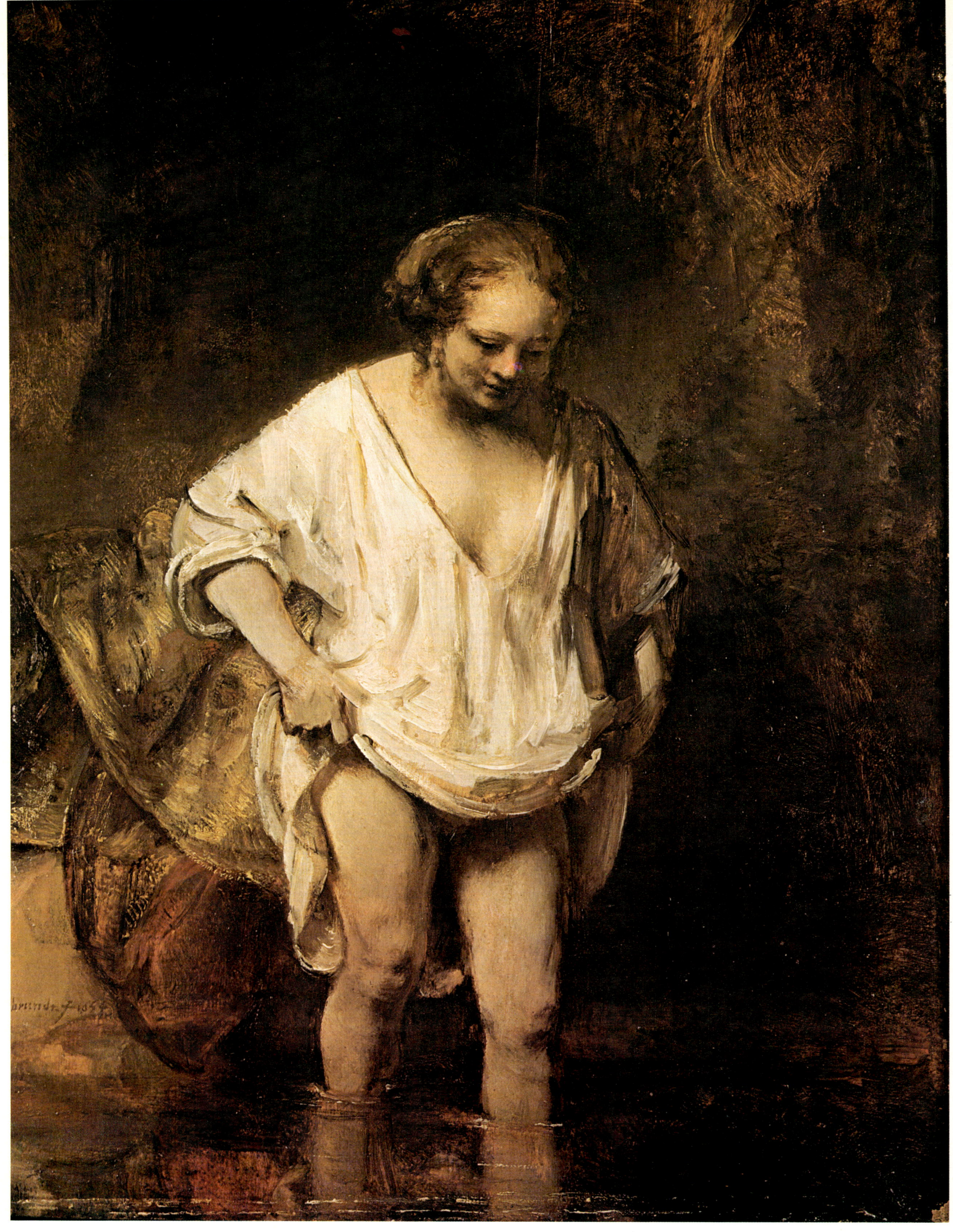

Plate 63 *see page 79*

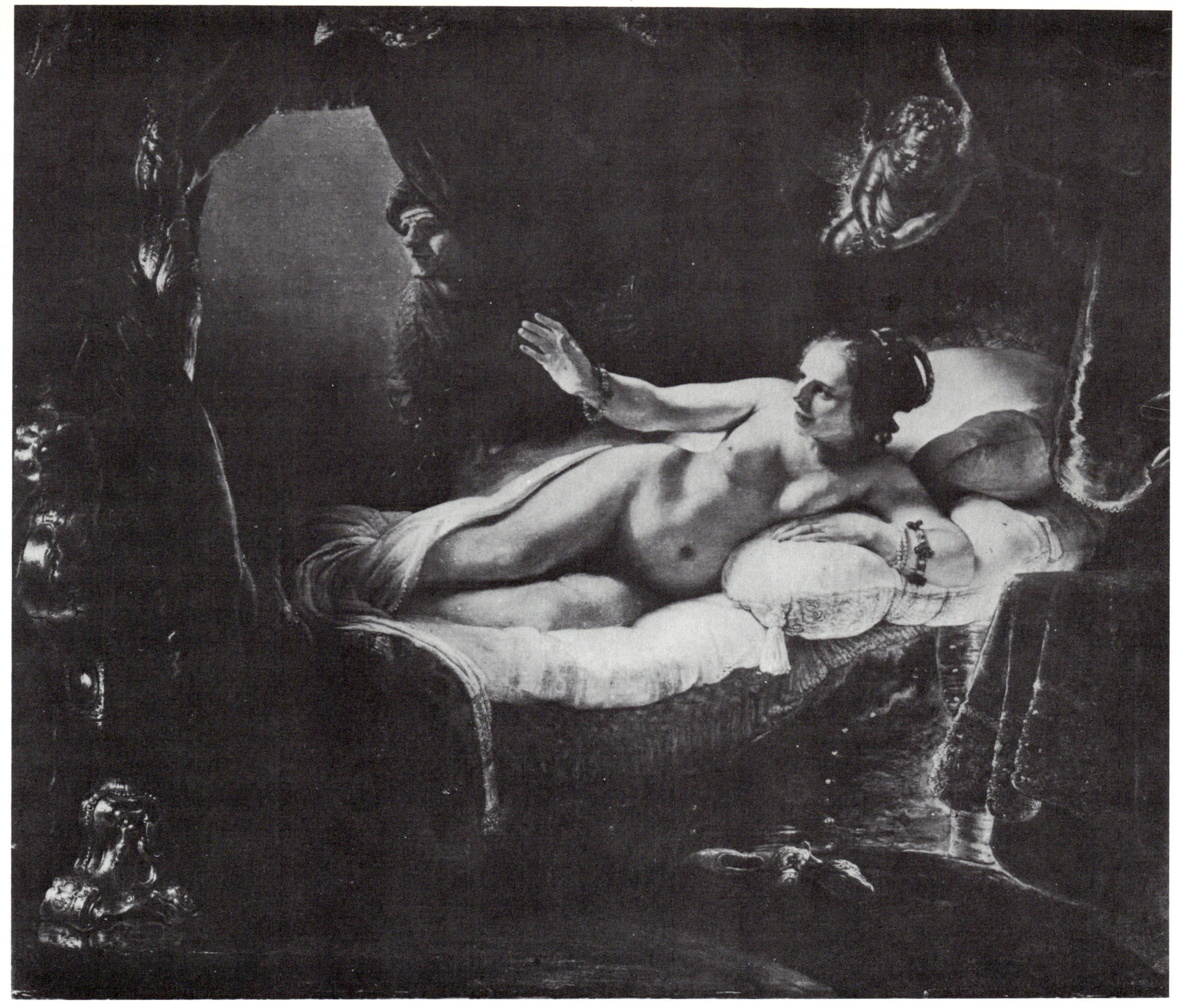

Plate 64
Danaë
begun 1636 but finished much later
oil on canvas
$72\frac{3}{4} \times 80$ in (185×203 cm)
Hermitage, Leningrad

Bought by Catherine the Great of Russia in 1772 from the Crozat Collection in Paris. Since then in the Hermitage, Leningrad.

than the similar works of Titian, *Danaë* still gives an impression of voluptuous luxury surrounded as she is by ample pillows and extravagant curtains.

It is a common fault to try to relate specific events or circumstances of an artist's life to his art and to see in his pictures the outcome of this or that personal tragedy. Vermeer, that most silent of painters had a dozen (noisy?) children in his house and died in penury, while his art has a comfortable serenity. In Rembrandt's case the problem is more complicated. When he used members of his family or immediate circle in his pictures clearly that is an accurate record of a particular person at that particular moment.

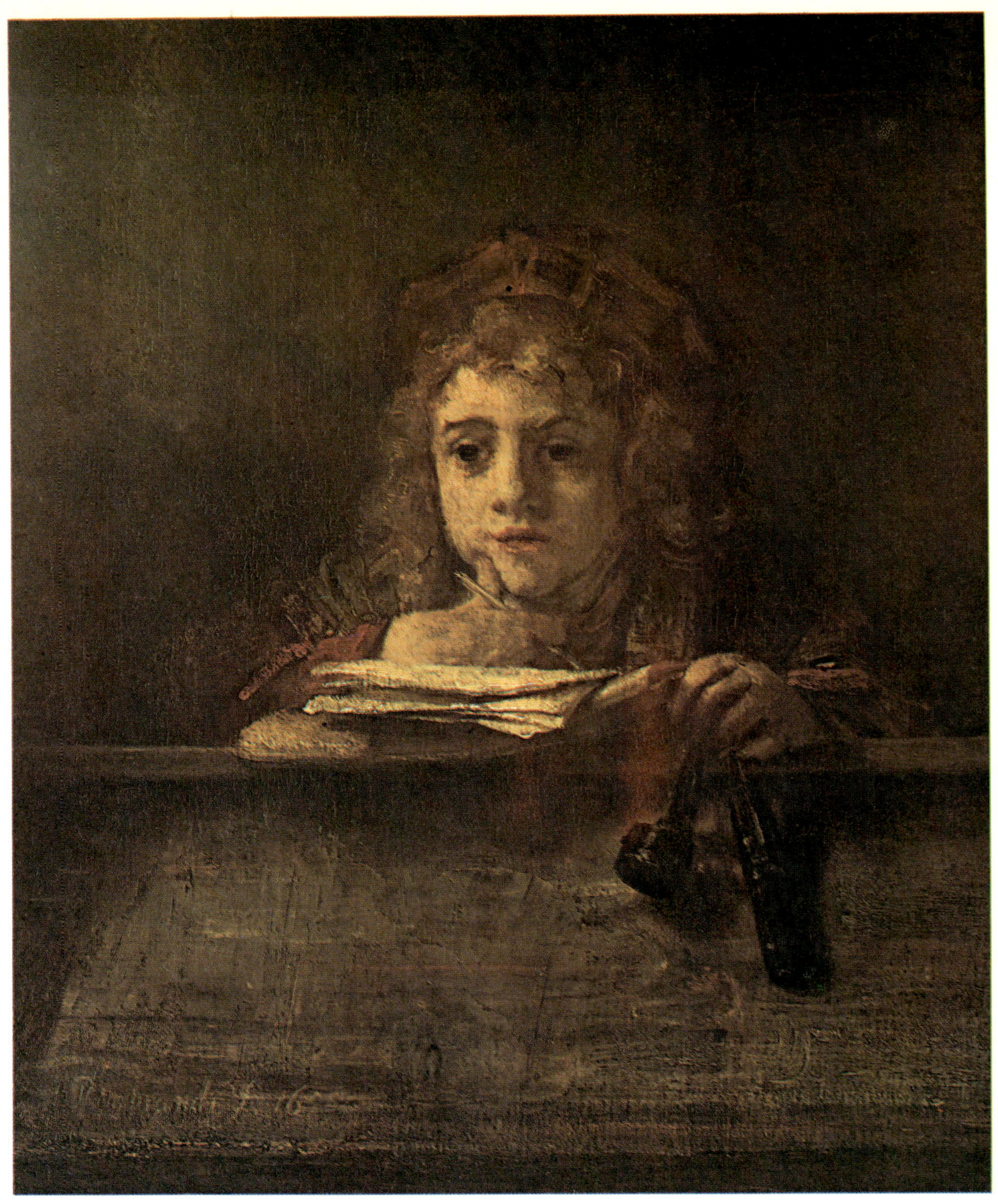

Plate 65
Titus Puzzling over His Lessons
dated 1655
oil on canvas
$30\frac{1}{4} \times 24\frac{3}{4}$ in (77 × 63 cm)
Boymans-van Beuningen Museum, Rotterdam

In the collection of the Earl of Crawford and Balcarres. Acquired by the Boymans Museum in 1940 with the aid of the Friends of the Museum.

The death of Saskia in 1642, although a personal tragedy for the artist, is not reflected in his painting. Rembrandt was perfectly capable of introducing melancholia into his pictures before he experienced such events in his life. The early *Jeremiah Contemplating the Destruction of Jerusalem* (plate 9) is an exercise in the depiction of this emotion.

Saskia had left Rembrandt with a small income from her estate with the proviso that it ceased if he were to remarry. He did not immediately take a mistress in order to have the best of both worlds; but it seems that a serving maid in his household by name of Hendrickje Stoffels gradually found a place in the artist's affections, and in 1654, some nine years or so after she had entered the household, she bore him a daughter Cornelia. Hendrickje must have acted as mother to Titus, who had been born just before

Saskia's death, and Rembrandt began to paint one of the most touching series of pictures in the whole of the Western tradition of painting: that is, the careful observation every year or two of the growing up of his son and then of his gradual, tragic dissolution and death just before Rembrandt himself. They range from the ever-popular *Titus Puzzling over His Lessons* (plate 65), which is dated 1655, in the Boymans-van Beuningen Museum, Rotterdam, to the last record of the dying young man whose ravaged features speak so eloquently from the darkened canvas in the Dulwich College Picture Gallery (plate 91). The Rotterdam painting is the sort of picture that can only be inspired by the deepest sense of affection. The viewpoint, which seems strange at first, is in fact taken from the conventional type of Italian portrait where the sitter is placed behind a parapet: a perfect example of this is the *Unidentified Boy* by Giovanni Bellini in the Barber Institute at Birmingham. Rembrandt has transposed the idea completely by altering the viewpoint. The spectator, instead of being on a level with the sitter, a prisoner behind the parapet, is placed slightly lower. No Italian had dared, or even perhaps been interested, in such a caprice. The edge of the desk has taken the place of the parapet. It is amusing to speculate on the idea that poor Titus was having a hard time remembering the lessons upon which his learned father insisted. There is no doubt that Rembrandt was a man of the most enormous intellectual experience. His seven surviving letters show that he was little interested in the art of writing, but all his pictures, whatever their subject, show a complete mastery of the subject-matter, which indicates a wide and enquiring intellect.

Rembrandt has caught perfectly the moment when the problem has got the better of the child. Titus' expression is a mixture of puzzlement and childish sorrow designed to appeal to the all-too-susceptible parent who will soon come to the rescue with the answer.

It is rare to be able to have an exact record of Rembrandt's personal life. Such an insight is found in the inventory of his effects made at the time of his bankruptcy in 1656, but far more eloquent is the visual record of *A Corner of Rembrandt's Studio* (plate 66) in the drawing in the Ashmolean Museum, Oxford. The studio appears cluttered with easels, canvases and furniture, while the model, naked to the waist, is seated in the chair at the right. As is so often the case in his drawings, an immense amount of detail is suggested with the minimum of means, while the feeling of light which filters rather than streams through the relatively small and high window is masterly.

Plate 66
A Corner of Rembrandt's Studio
1650s
pen and brush
$8 \times 7\frac{1}{2}$ in (20.5 × 19 cm)
Ashmolean Museum, Oxford

This drawing shows the room known as the Grootschilderskammer ('large picture room') which was in the house sold by Rembrandt in 1656. Formerly in the Chambers Hall Collection before entering the Ashmolean Museum.

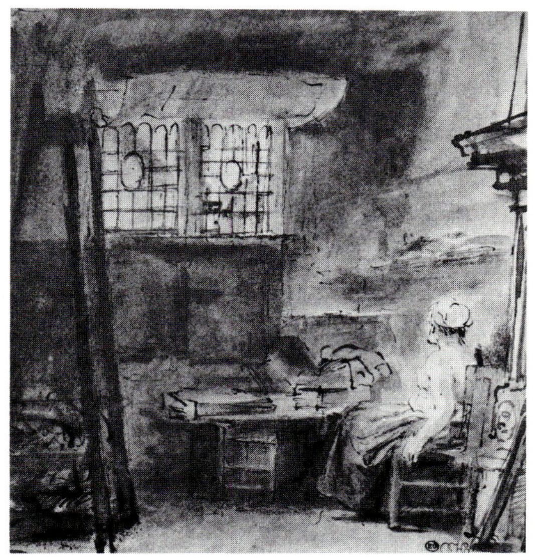

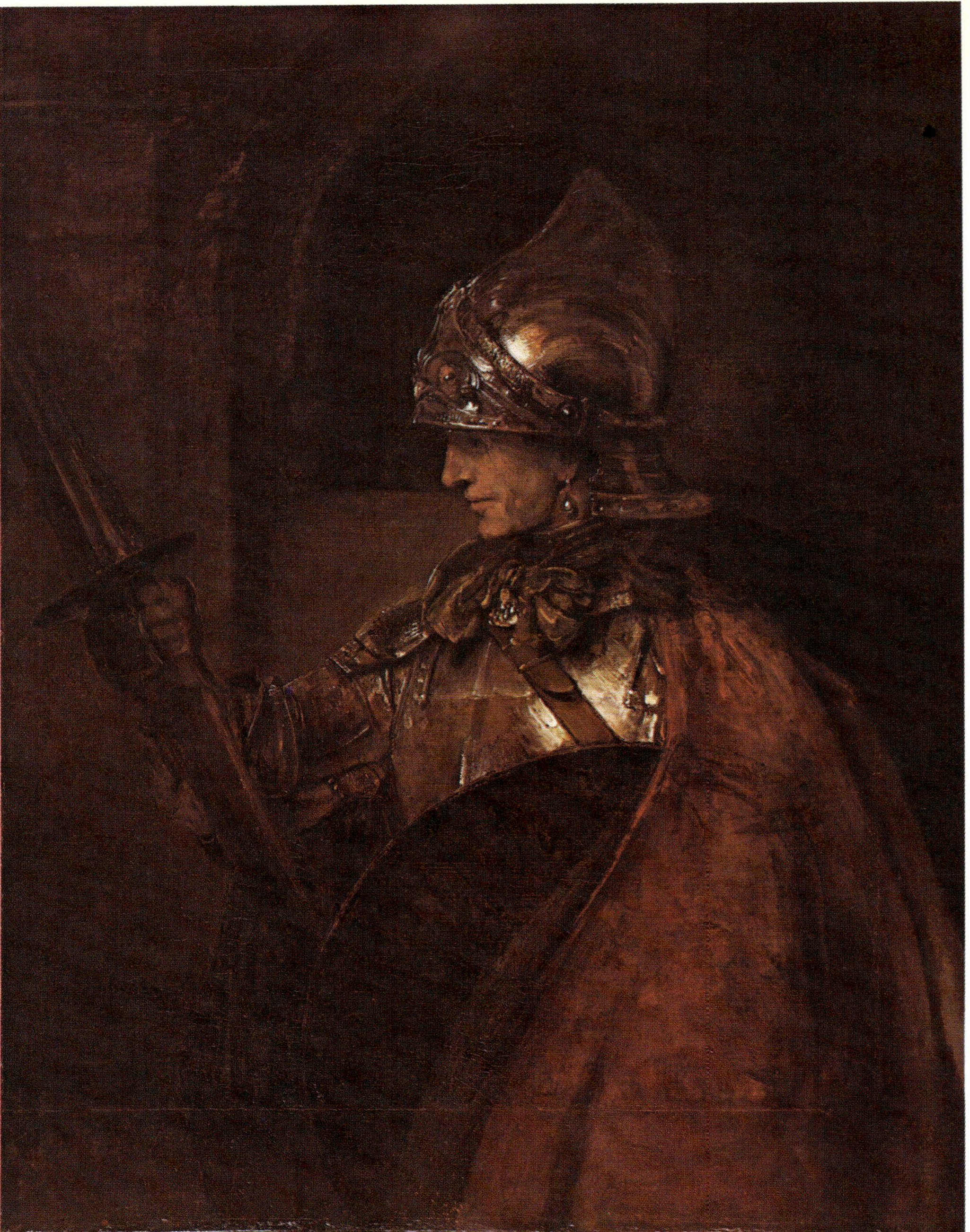

Plate 67
A Man in Armour
Alexander the Great (?)
dated 1655
oil on canvas
$45\frac{3}{8} \times 34\frac{1}{2}$ in (115.5 × 87.5 cm)
Art Gallery, Glasgow

The history of this picture is complicated, controversial and confused. The documentary evidence for Don Ruffio's ownership of it is weak as the early descriptions are not a convincing identification. Nevertheless if Don Ruffio did not own this very picture it was one rather similar in style. The picture was probably in the Count de Fraula sale in Brussels in 1738, and it was certainly in the collection of Sir Joshua Reynolds by 1764. He sold it to the Earl of Warwick in 1790 at whose sale in 1837 it was bought by Samuel Woodburn. In the collection of John Graham Gilbert by 1860 whose widow bequeathed it to the Glasgow Art Gallery in 1877.

From the same year is the *Man in Armour* (plate 67) in the Corporation Art Gallery, Glasgow. Although one of the artist's best pictures of this type the numerous problems which surround it have helped to confuse rather than emphasise its extraordinary quality. It is almost certain that this is the *Alexander the Great* asked of Rembrandt by Don Ruffio (see page 76 for the beginning of the story), because of the strips of canvas which have been added on all sides of the picture, thus throwing it completely off balance. It just so happens that on receiving the *Alexander* Don Ruffio was not satisfied with it as it was not of the same dimensions as his *Aristotle*. He therefore insisted that the picture should be enlarged to match. The demanding patron had already asked Guercino for a further philosopher, of which only a drawing survives, and he forced the distinguished Italian painter to produce his philosopher

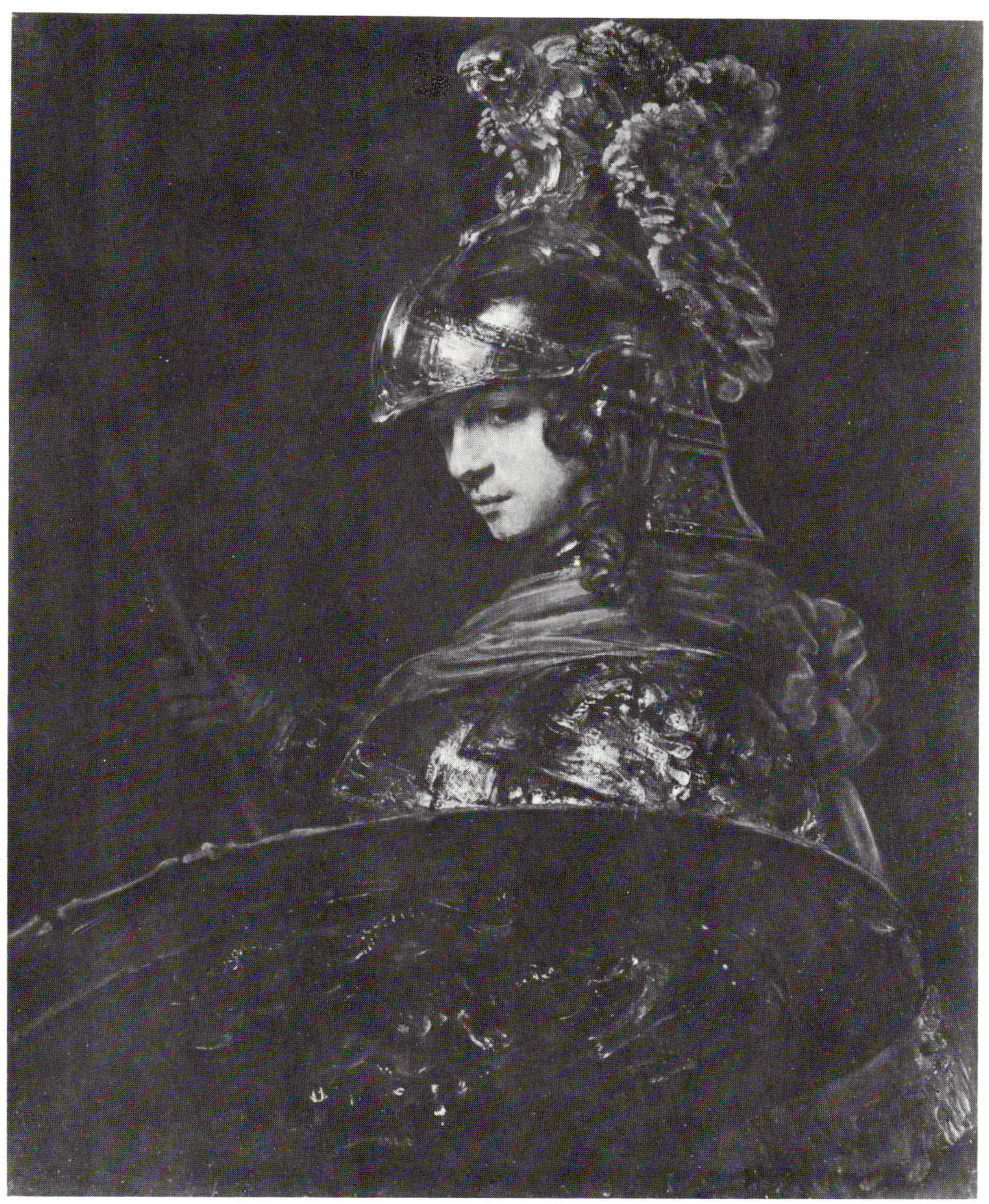

Plate 68
Youth in a Helmet
early 1660s
oil on canvas
$46\frac{1}{2} \times 35\frac{3}{4}$ in (118 × 91 cm)
Gulbenkian Foundation, Lisbon

One of Rembrandt's gentlest pictures, it was formerly in the Hermitage. Its present fame is entirely justified.

in his earlier, darker, manner in order that it should match his growing collection of Rembrandts. Unfortunately the strips of canvas on the Glasgow picture appear to be of later date than the painting, but the coincidence is too great for the possibility that it is Don Ruffio's *Alexander* to be ignored.

The other representation of the subject is in the Calouste Gulbenkian foundation in Lisbon (plate 68), which shows a much younger and less worried man. It has the character of a 'fancy piece', not exactly light hearted, but with a certain fragile charm which is rare in Rembrandt. The picture is usually dated rather later and may be as late as the early 1660s. The general colour scheme of the Glasgow picture is cool, as the helmet is of silver. All the richness of texture has been subordinated to the expression of the man, whose face is mostly in shadow. Generally

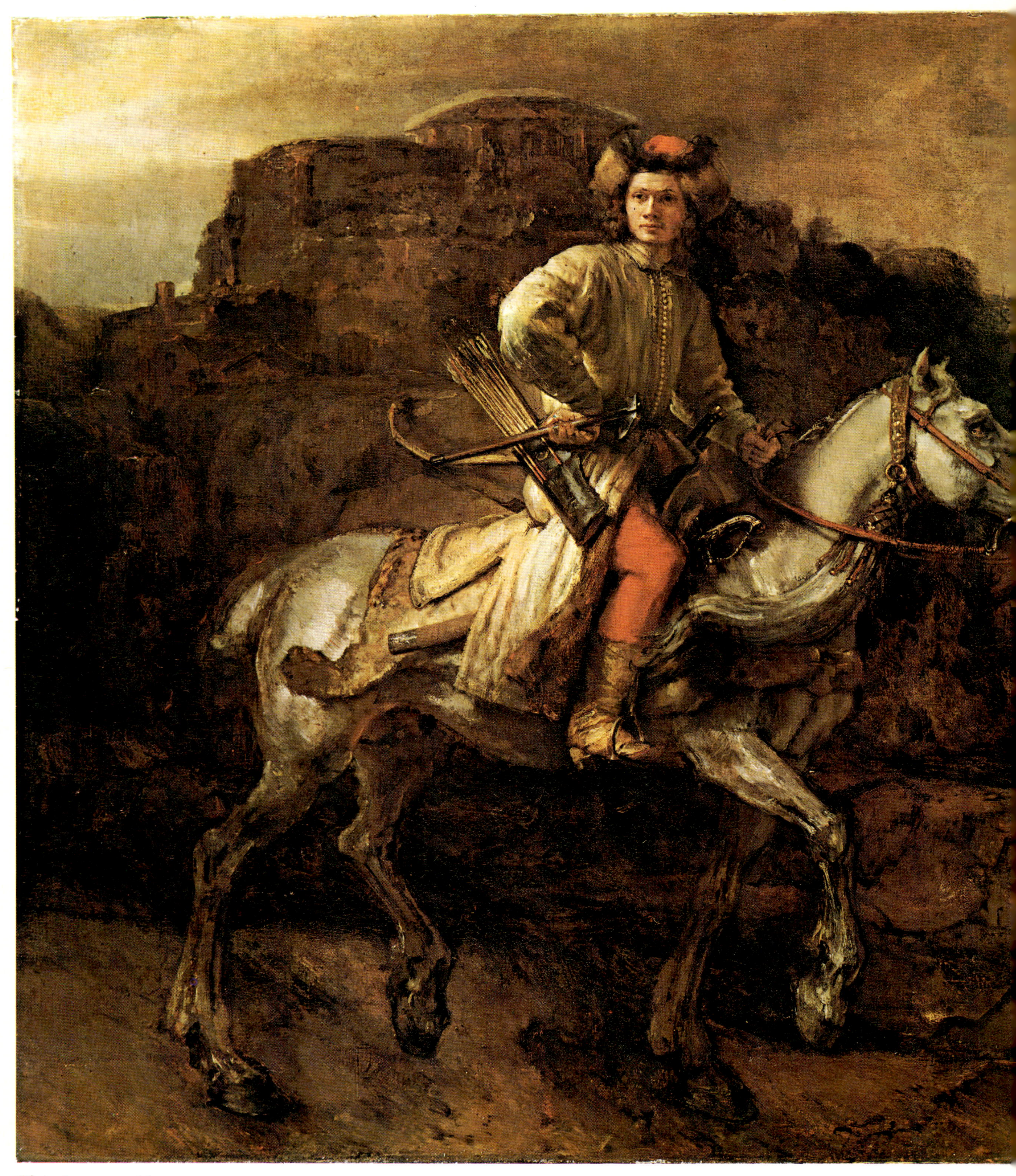

Plate 69 *see page 88*

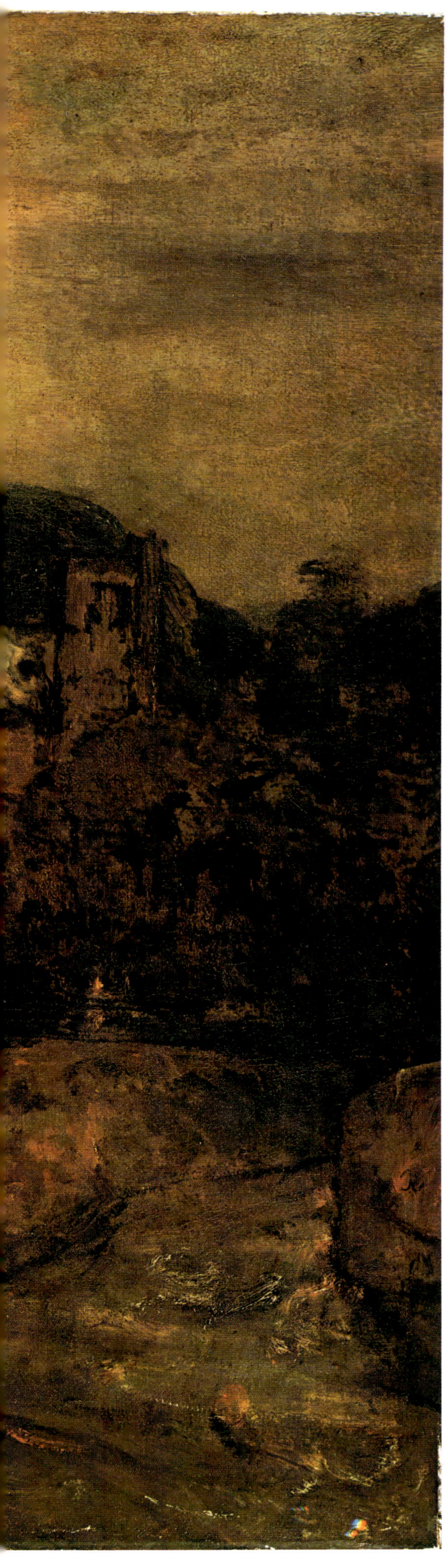

in a dark picture such as this the lightest areas are those where the artist wished to place the most emphasis, and quite naturally the darker areas, lost in shadow, were less important. Here Rembrandt has defied this convention and painted all the glitter of the armour and the helmet without detracting from the face. Indeed the attention is drawn to the sad face of the young man, which is partly obscured by the helmet. Alexander the Great is not usually seen in art as a tragic figure but rather as a conqueror. Here, however, the man, although hardly more than a youth, seems weighed down by his own greatness.

Nobody is quite sure when Rembrandt painted *The Polish Rider* (plate 69) in the Frick Collection, New York, but it must date from the 1650s. In reproduction the picture always gives an impression of infinite grandeur – the scale of the immense *Man on Horseback* in the National Gallery, London, is imagined. In front of the painting one is immediately struck by its relatively small scale which adds to its mystery and excitement. The interpretations of the exact subject of this picture have been very varied, some of them plausible, but none of them entirely convincing. The title *The Polish Rider* is derived from the fact that the man on the horse is in Polish uniform, but his exact intention in this Don Quixote-like scene is not clear. One of the most tempting interpretations is that it is the Prodigal Son, having dissipated his patrimony, and on the point of returning to his father to ask forgiveness. Hence the shadowed city in the background where he has lived a corrupt life.

The question which the picture poses the spectator is why this rather handsome young man, on an underfed-looking horse, should be riding through this gloomy landscape. There is a terrible feeling of melancholy which is not defined by any specific element. The rider is lost in the landscape: he is perhaps leaving the spectral city in the background. The real magic lies in the fact that after long contemplation the spectator comes to the conclusion that he does not know at all what is going on, and the mind wanders endlessly on, touched by the mystery of this meaningless scene. The technique is bold but controlled – a characteristic of most of his pictures in the 1650s, the middle years of which saw the artist's bankruptcy. Yet, as has already been noted, it is neither possible nor relevant to pinpoint such a personal problem in his paintings.

In keeping with the artist's burst of creativity in the 1650s the drawings take on a new intensity of feeling. One could wish for a painting incorporating the excitement of the drawing of *The Prophet Jonah before the Walls of Nineveh* (plate 70), in the Albertina, Vienna, of about 1655. The prophet is seen lamenting the

Plate 69
The Polish Rider
about 1655
oil on canvas
$45\frac{1}{4} \times 53\frac{1}{4}$ in ($115 \times 135{\cdot}5$ cm)
Frick Collection, New York

For long in Polish collections, hence the title. In the collection of King Stanislas Augustus II of Poland in the 18th century and bought by Henry Clay Frick from Poland in 1910.

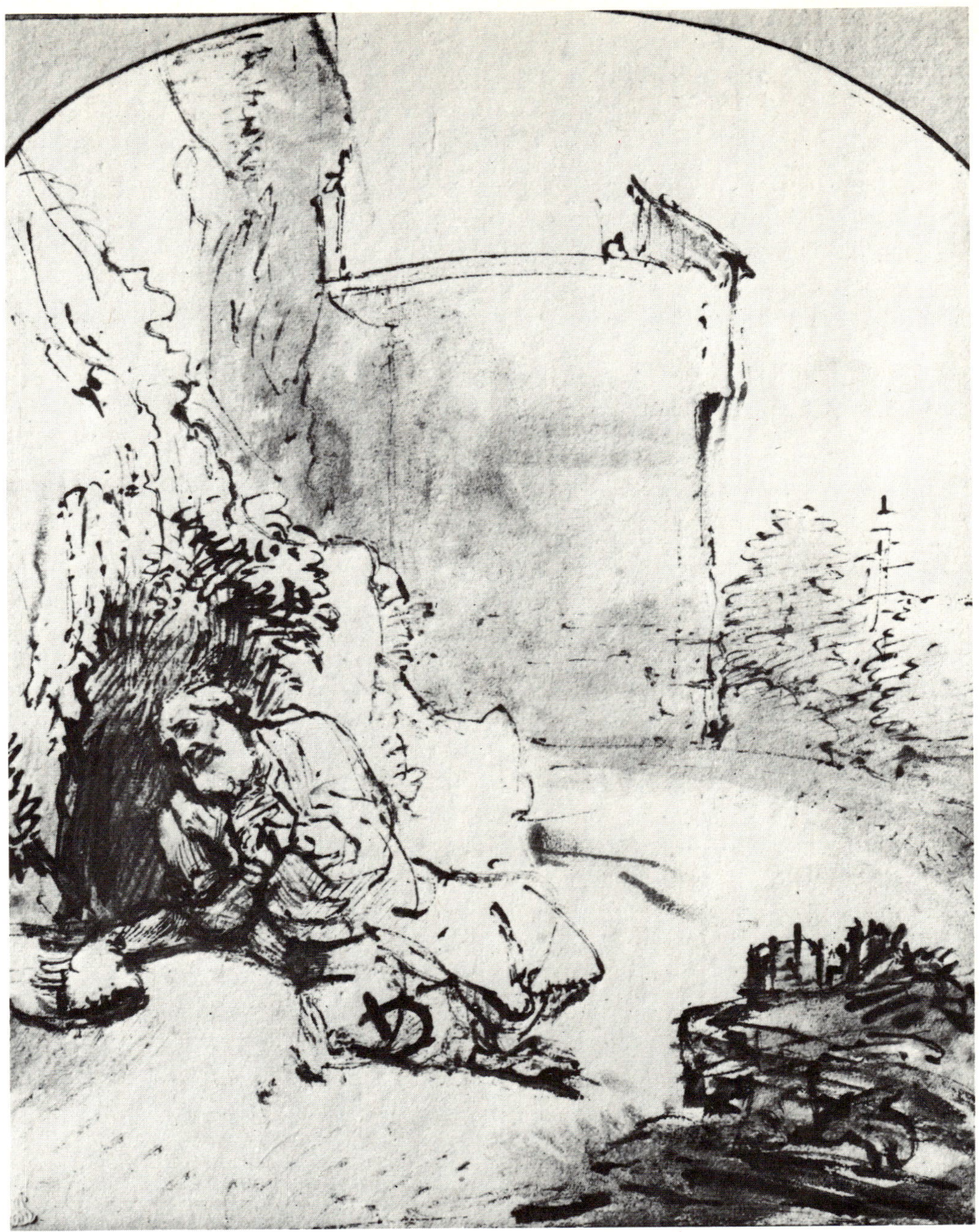

Plate 70
The Prophet Jonah before the Walls of Nineveh
about 1655
pen and wash
$8\frac{1}{2} \times 6\frac{3}{4}$ in (21.7×17.3 cm)
Albertina, Vienna

The earlier history of the drawing is unknown before it entered the Albertina.

Plate 71
The Anatomy Lesson of Dr Joan Deyman (fragment)
dated 1656
oil on canvas
$39\frac{3}{8} \times 52\frac{3}{4}$ in (100×134 cm)
Rijksmuseum, Amsterdam

Originally placed in the Anatomical Hall, Amsterdam. Sold in Amsterdam in 1841 when it passed to a London dealer who sold it to the Rev. Pryce Owen of Cheltenham. In 1882 acquired by the City of Amsterdam who lent it to the Rijksmuseum three years later on a permanent basis.

wickedness of that most corrupt of cities, but what a change from the Amsterdam *Jeremiah Lamenting the Destruction of Jerusalem* (plate 9) of more than twenty years before. The prophet is in an attitude of lamentation and prayer, while the city is suggested by a vast expanse of blank wall, which takes the form of a great curved bastion. Translated into paint this would have been one of the artist's best works.

The artist's ability to paint the horrific, either explicitly or implicitly, occurs at regular intervals throughout his career, from the Frankfurt *Blinding of Samson* (plate 20), to the Stockholm *Conspiracy of Julius Civilis* (plate 84). *The Anatomy Lesson of Dr Joan Deyman* (plate 71) of 1656, of which only a fragment survives in the Rijksmuseum, Amsterdam, is very much more explicit than the gentlemanly experiments of Dr Tulp. Here the doctor has dismembered the corpse, removed entrails and, having

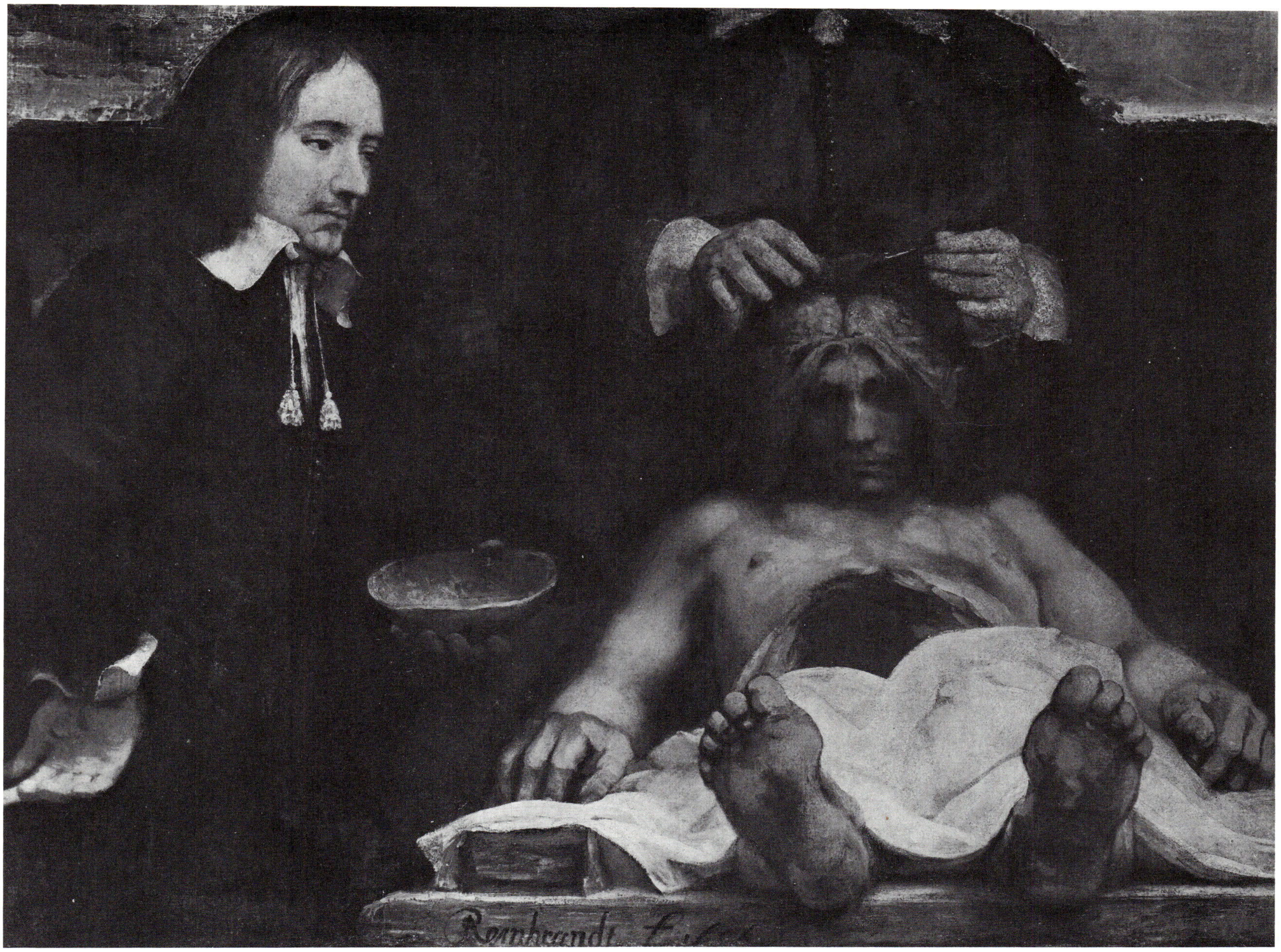

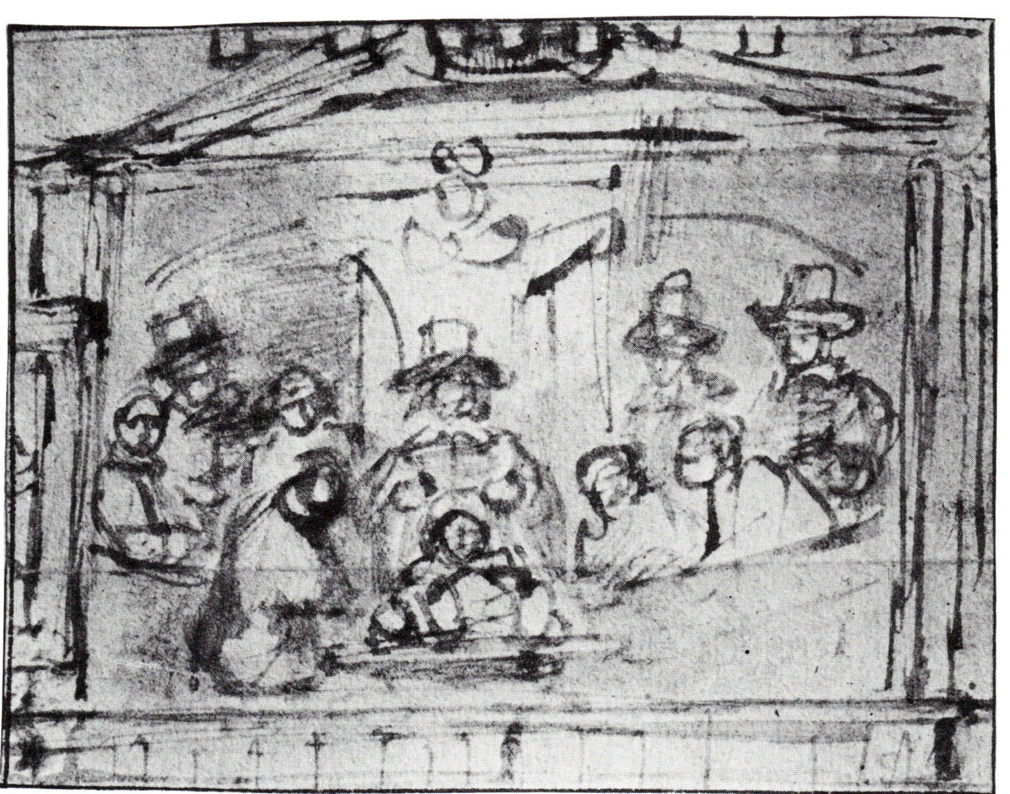

Plate 72
The Anatomy Lesson of Dr Joan Deyman
about 1656
pen
$4\frac{3}{8} \times 5\frac{1}{4}$ in (11 × 13.3 cm)
Rijksprentenkabinet, Amsterdam

Formerly in the collection of Jan Six. Sold in Amsterdam in 1928.

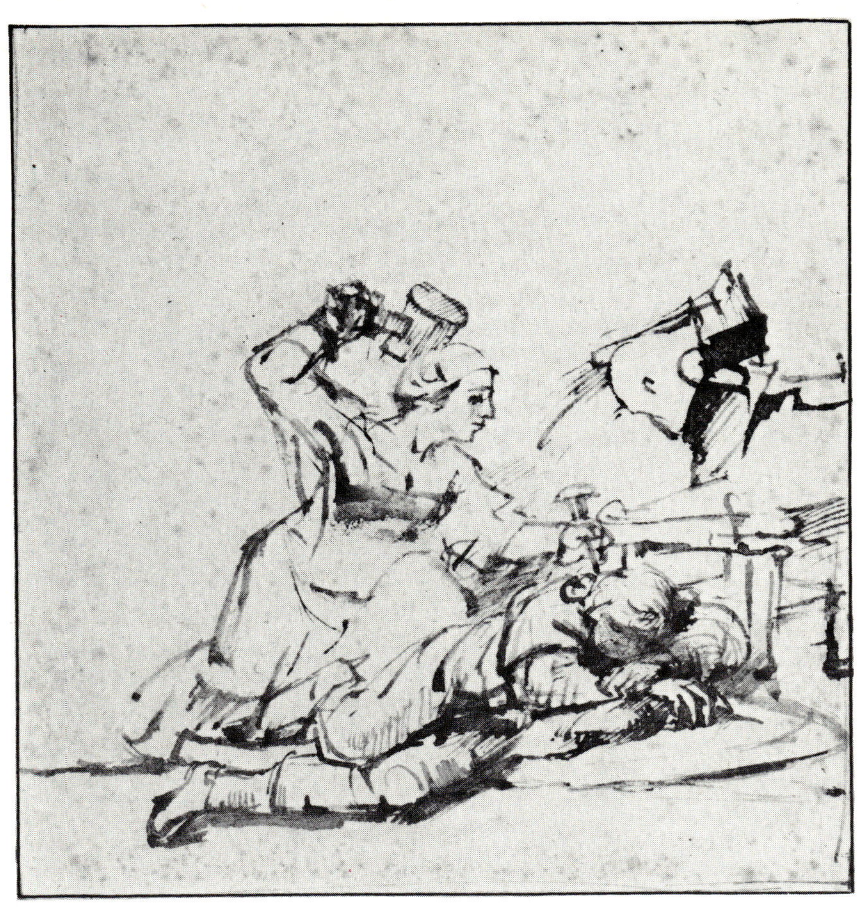

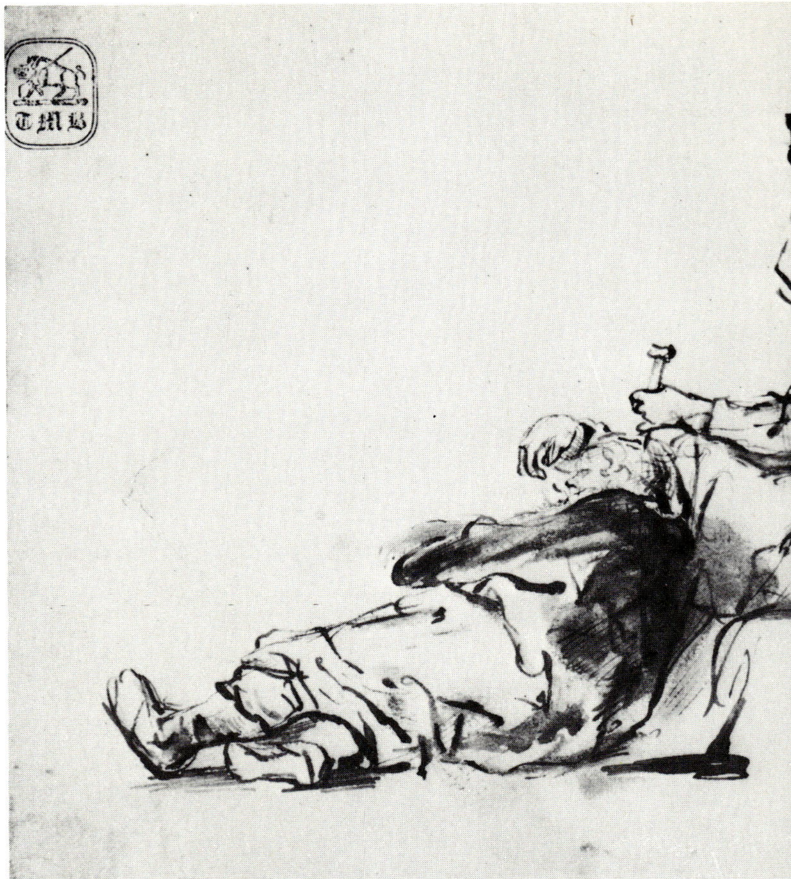

sawn off the top of the skull, is in the process of examining the brain. The corpse is seen from what appears to be a very unusual angle, feet first, but it must be derived in some way from Mantegna's famous depiction of *The Dead Christ* in the Brera Gallery, Milan. In spite of the clinical nature of the mortuary scene there is a surprising feeling of serenity about the picture. There is no drama. The dead human is painted with a sense of detachment found in the *Slaughtered Ox* in the Louvre, Paris. The drawing for the whole composition survives in the Rijksprentenkabinet, Amsterdam (plate 72), which shows it to have been very large indeed, with numerous figures carefully arranged round the central figure of the doctor and the corpse.

In order to illustrate Rembrandt's infinite variety of imagination, a series of drawings of the same subject with different interpretations are shown here (plates 73–75). Rembrandt chose the moment of extreme violence, that of Jael knocking a nail into the head of the sleeping Sisera. The drawing in Amsterdam (plate 73) shows Jael with an enormous hammer with which she is about to crush the skull of Sisera, who sleeps, lost in shadow, at the front of the composition. She has put the nail in place and is about to administer the *coup de grâce*. The same situation is shown in the drawing, which is possibly a studio production, in the Public

Plate 73
Jael and Sisera
about 1659–60
pen
$7\frac{1}{2} \times 6\frac{3}{4}$ in (19×17.2 cm)
Rijksprentenkabinet, Amsterdam

Bequeathed to the Print Room in Amsterdam by Cornelis Hofstede de Groot.

Plate 74
Rembrandt (attributed)
Jael and Sisera
1650s
pen and wash
$6\frac{1}{2} \times 9\frac{5}{8}$ in (16.5×24.5 cm)
Public Library, Museum and Art Gallery, Folkestone

Nothing is known of the earlier history of the drawing and its first recorded owner, Thomas Mann Bridge, whose mark is on the drawing, also remains elusive. The drawing passed by descent to Mrs Masters of Folkestone who presented it to the local Public Library in 1924, where it was first noticed by A. M. Hind in the late 1920s, although it remained completely unknown until exhibited at the Royal Academy in 1962.

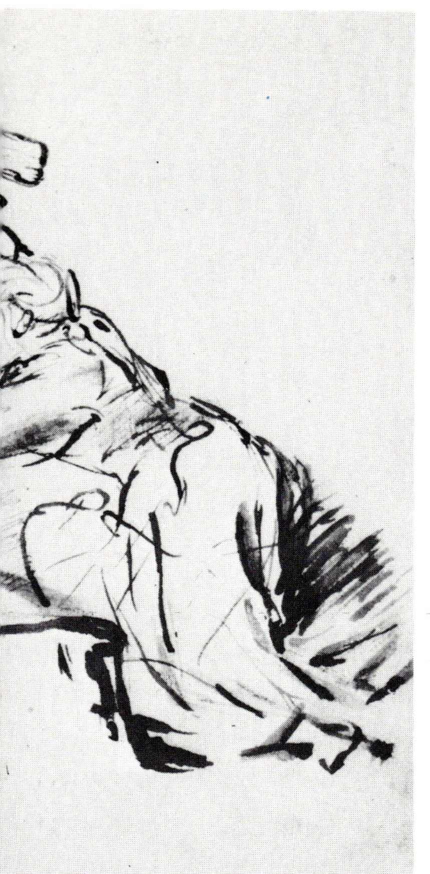

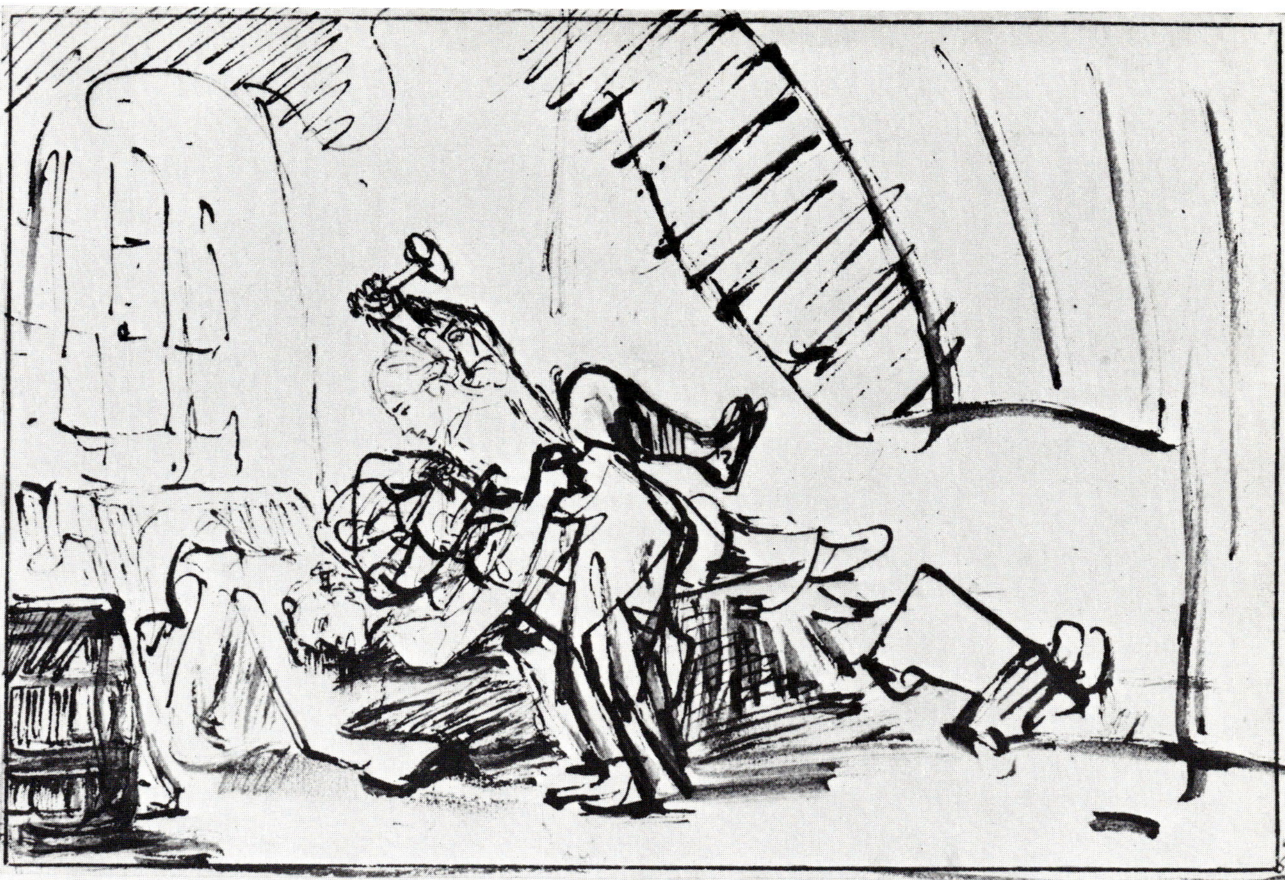

Plate 75
Jael and Sisera
1650s
pen
$8\frac{1}{8} \times 7\frac{1}{2}$ in (20.5 × 19 cm)
Ashmolean Museum, Oxford

In the collection of the Viscount Fitzharris. Sold Christie's on 21st April 1950. Acquired by Sir Karl Parker for the Ashmolean Museum.

Library at Folkestone (plate 74), but the figures are seen at a different angle. If the Folkestone drawing should turn out not to be by Rembrandt himself, the pupil is to be congratulated in copying the mood and expression of Jael, as it is very close to that in the Amsterdam drawing. A good copy of the Folkestone drawing is in the Louvre (Inv. No. 22,986) which further illustrates the problems which beset the Rembrandt connoisseur. The most moving drawing in the series is that in the Ashmolean Museum, Oxford (plate 75). Jael has already delivered a terrible blow, the nail is deep inside Sisera's head, his face is twisted with agony, while the unrelenting Jael raises her arm in order to bring the hammer crashing down yet again on Sisera's shattered skull. Rembrandt never, it seems, turned this idea into a painting, but kept mulling it over in his head, and it found its way out in this series of drawings. They all must date from the 1650s.

Rembrandt's last phase as an artist, about which it is too easy to be sentimental, is heralded by the *Jacob Blessing the Sons of Joseph* (plate 76) at Kassel. It is dated 1656, but it has been suggested that the artist worked on it again, rather later; this explains its uneven quality. From an emotional point of view this is one of the artist's most complex pictures, as it is not quite clear on whose side the artist is, for he changed the intention of the Bible story. Jacob,

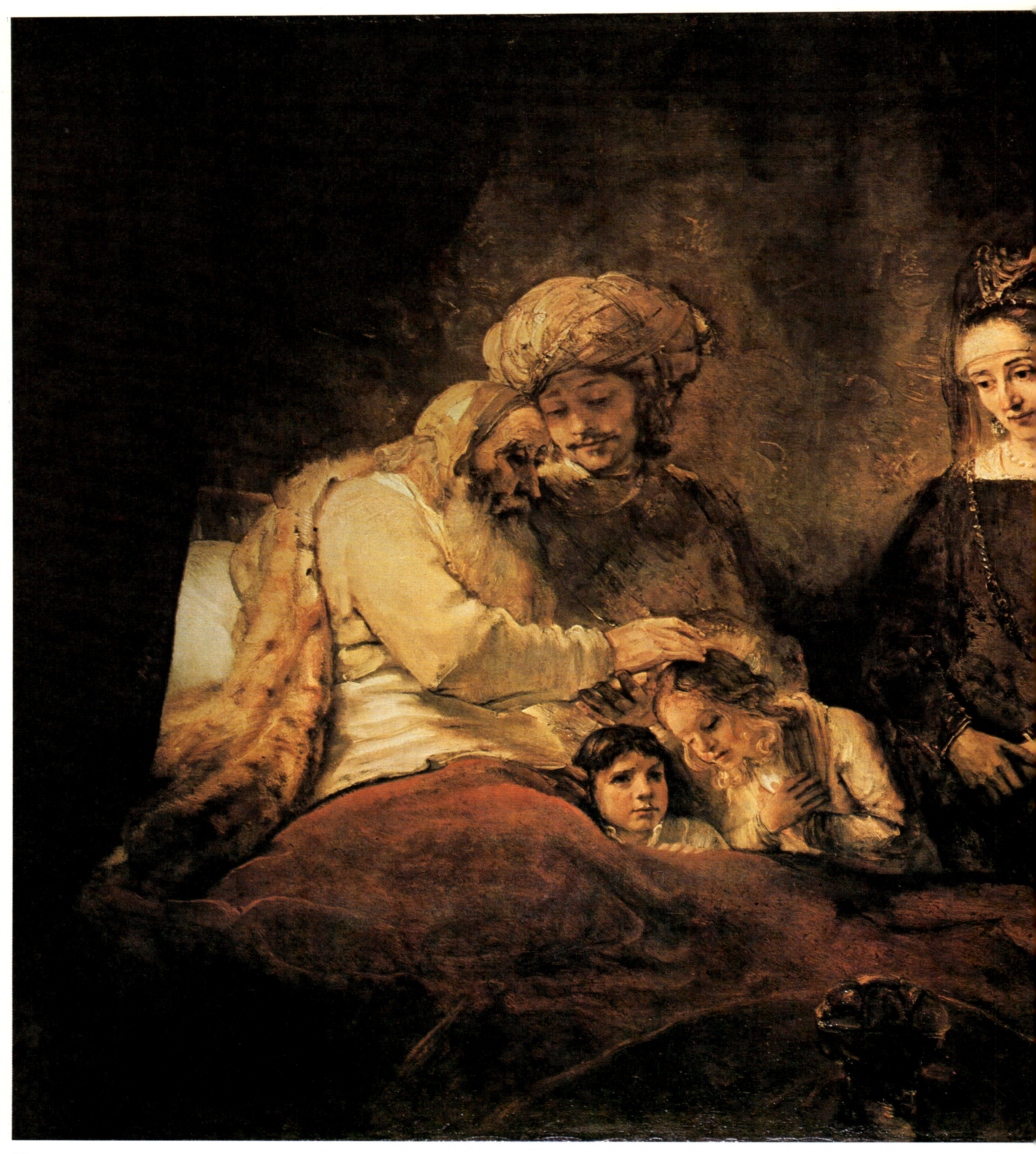

Plate 76 *see page 94*

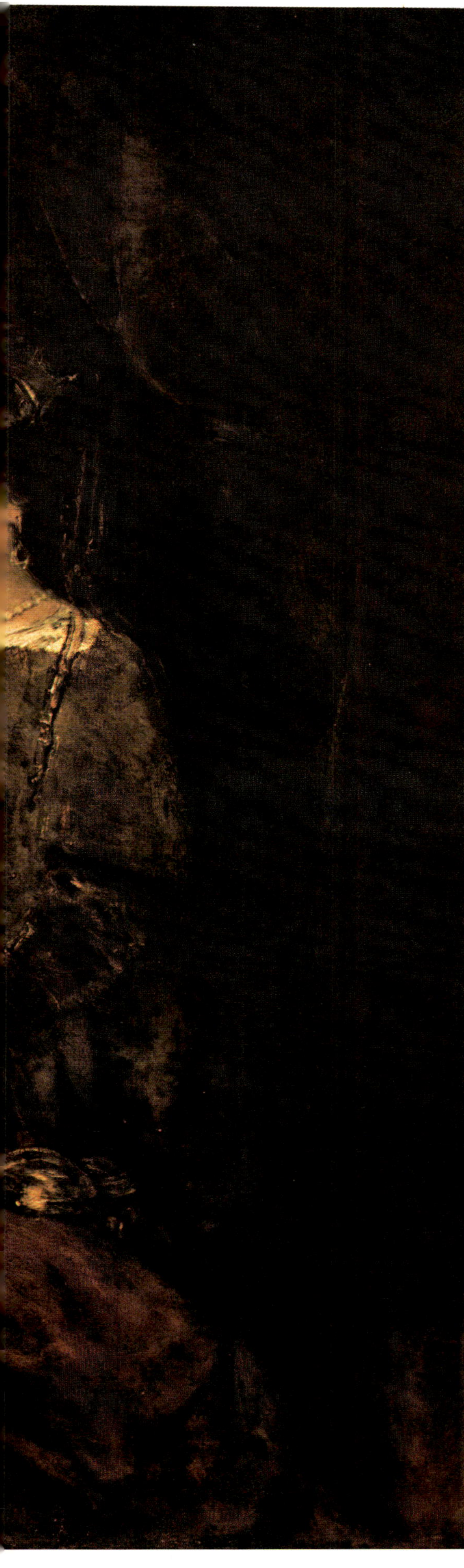

bedridden and in his dotage, required of his son Joseph to bring his two sons, Manasseh and Ephraim, in order that they may be blessed by their grandfather. Jacob deliberately blesses Ephraim, who is the younger son, much to the surprise and annoyance of Joseph, who naturally assumed that Manasseh should be blessed. Jacob remarked, 'Ephraim *shall* be greater than Manasseh.' Rembrandt has changed the situation in a mysterious way. Jacob appears to be blessing the wrong child by accident–the older child hardly seems to be realising what is going on, while Ephraim has the angelic look of the favourite. Now the Bible specifically states that Joseph was annoyed at the mistake, but in the picture he seems to have a resigned, even satisfied look which implies that he knew about the plot, and indeed may have had a part in it. Asenath, Joseph's wife, appears much more detached, and there is almost a sense of resignation of the parents bending to the will of the old man.

This picture is one of Rembrandt's most important observations on the human condition. Joseph's head is placed so close to that of his father, and both are so close to the children, that the picture forms a kind of three ages of man. This theme was very popular in Renaissance Italy. The idea was to depict the growth and decline of the human being in a visual sense. Shakespeare used the image for his 'All the world's a stage . . .' and it seems likely that the dramatic juxtaposition in this picture has the very same intention. Thus at one stroke Rembrandt has created both a generalisation about humanity, told a Bible story in an enigmatic way and, in terms of paint quality, painted one of his most touching masterpieces.

The *Portrait of Titus* (plate 77) in the Wallace Collection, London, is generally dated some three years or so later than the Rotterdam picture, and thus about 1658. Here Rembrandt has returned to the convention of the full frontal portrait in order to record the by now adolescent features of his son. The only strong colour in the picture is the red velvet cap, the rest is a quiet arrangement of browns, with a touch of gold on the hair and the chain round his neck. The artist has painted his son with the same sense of penetration usually reserved for his own features. He has not forgotten the convention of half the face in shadow, which he had used so many years before in The Hague *Self-Portrait* (plate 7). Titus emerges as a slightly moody young man, although it is tempting to suggest that Rembrandt had unconsciously imposed his own melancholy on the sitter.

He also painted *Hendrickje Stoffels as the Goddess Flora* (plate 78) in the Metropolitan Museum, New York, at approximately this

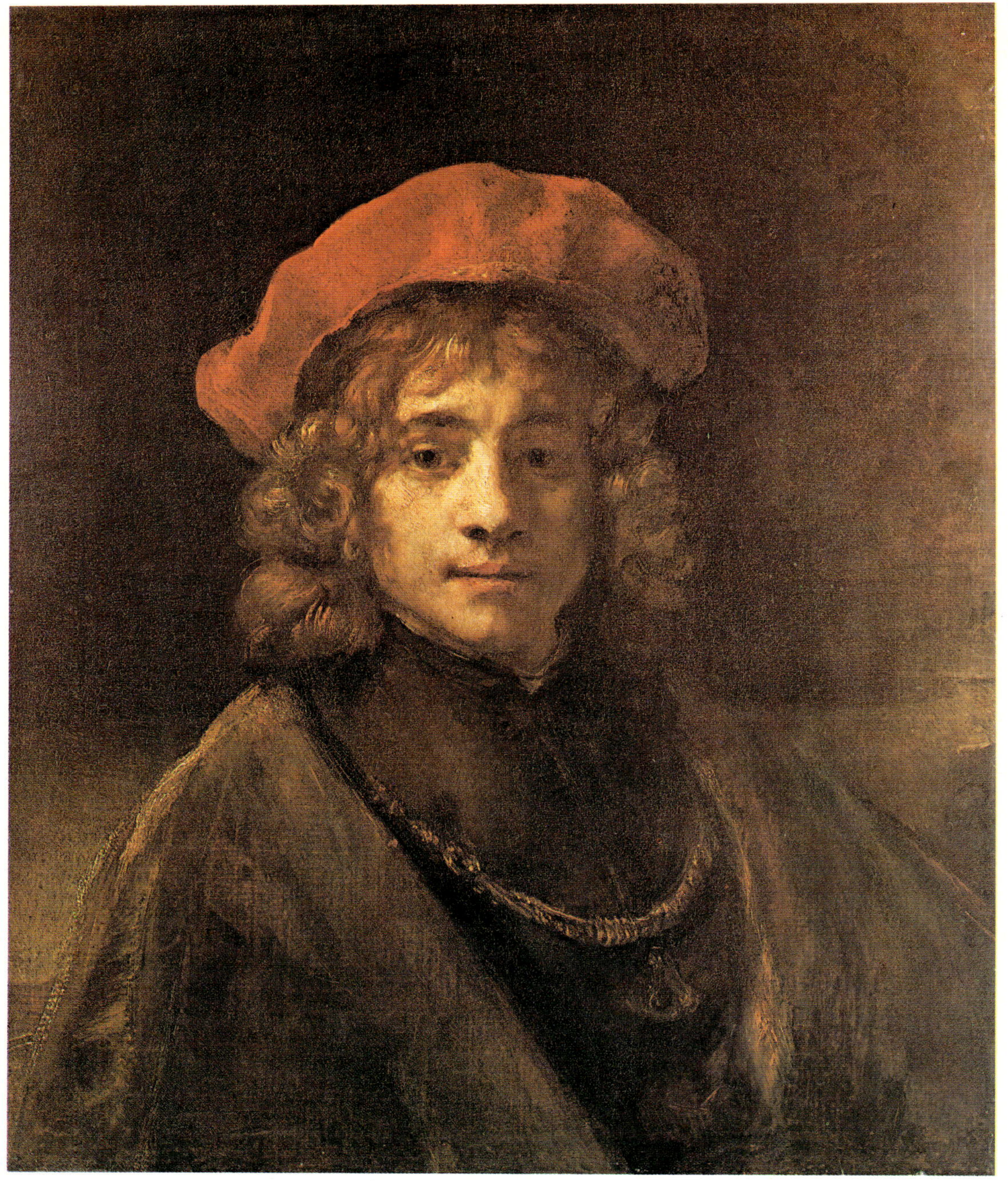

Plate 76
Jacob Blessing the Sons of Joseph
dated 1656, possibly retouched later
oil on canvas
$46\frac{1}{4} \times 83$ in (117.5×210.5 cm)
Staatliche Gemäldegalerie, Kassel

At Kassel since the middle of the 18th century, although the earlier history of this important picture is unknown. Taken to Paris in 1806 by the Napoleonic troops and returned to Kassel in 1815.

Plate 77
Portrait of Titus
about 1656
oil on canvas
$26\frac{3}{8} \times 21\frac{5}{8}$ in (67×55 cm)
Wallace Collection, London

The history of this masterpiece is unknown until it appeared in the sale of King William II of Holland in 1850 when it was acquired by Brondgeest for 4,000 florins. Soon after it was evidently in the collection of Lord Hertford, since he lent it to the Art Treasures exhibition in Manchester in 1857. Bequeathed to the nation along with the rest of his collection in 1897.

Plate 78
Hendrickje Stoffels as the Goddess Flora
about 1657
oil on canvas
$39\frac{3}{8} \times 36\frac{1}{4}$ in (100×92 cm)
Metropolitan Museum of Art, New York
Gift of A. M. Huntington in memory of his father C. P. Huntington, 1926

Formerly in the collection of the Earls Spencer at Althorp, Northamptonshire.

time. Her expression is almost identical to that of the figure in the Louvre *Bathsheba* (plate 61), so it is not unlikely that Hendrickje was the sitter for that picture too. In the New York painting a very different mood is apparent. Hendrickje appears fragile and aloof. There is almost the feeling that this type of 'fancy piece' was a (legitimate) excuse for the artist to experiment with and to express his delight in his technique. This is very obvious in the elaborate headgear and simple dress she is wearing; both made very heavy demands on the painter from the point of technique.

In the same room as *The Polish Rider* (plate 69) in the Frick Collection, New York, is the *Self-Portrait at the Age of 52* (plate 79). This is certainly the most monumental of all the self-portraits in its

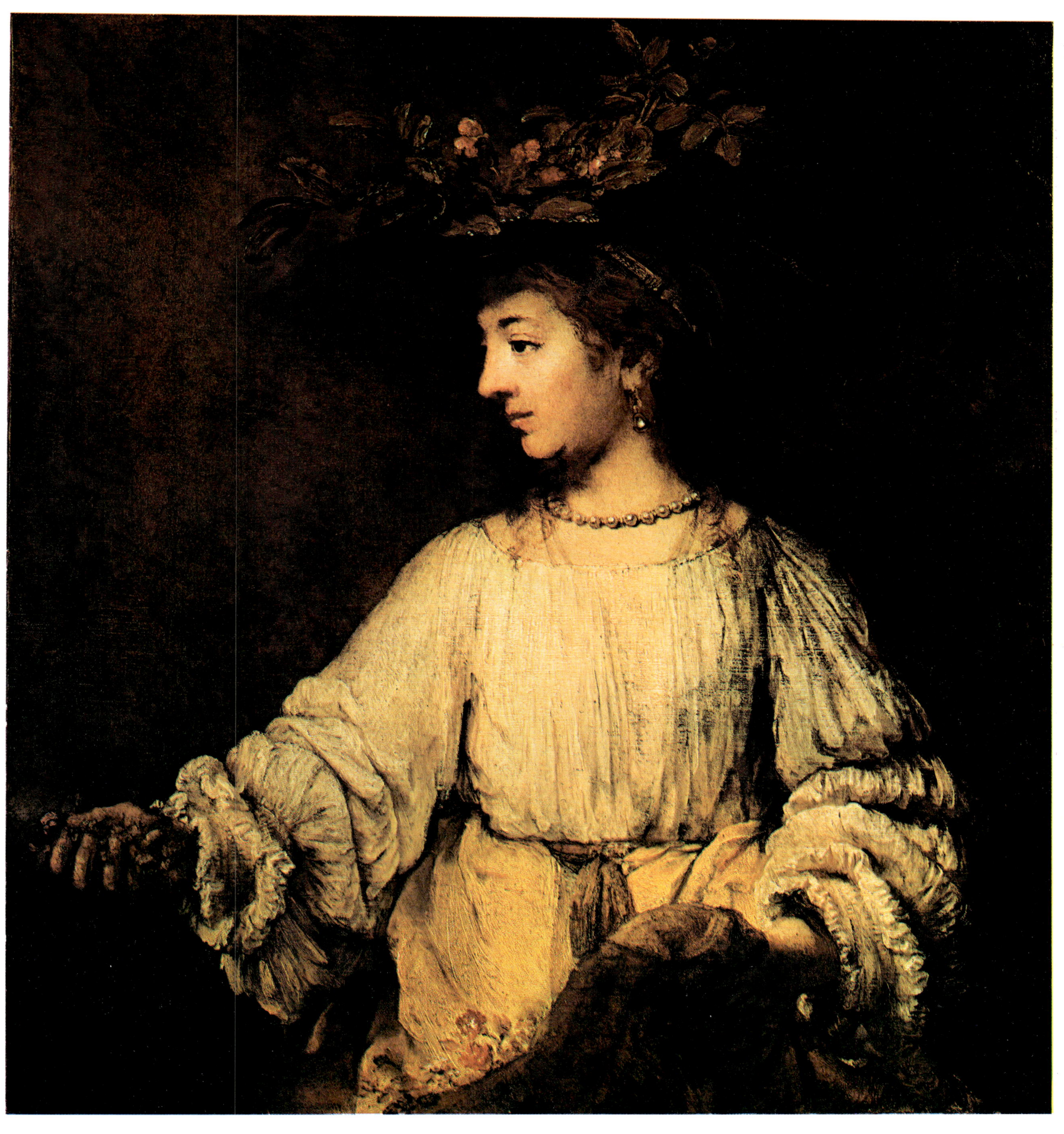

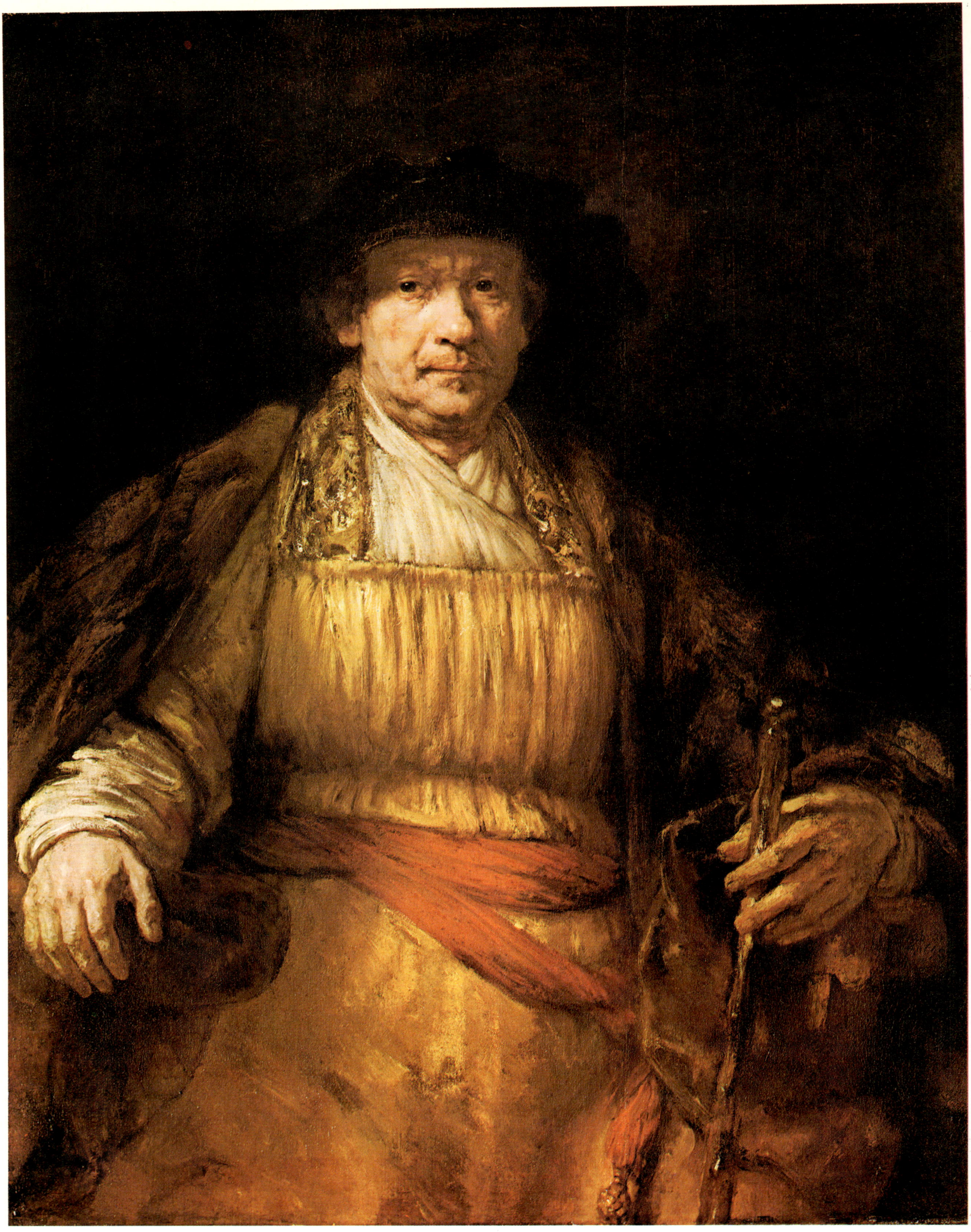

Plate 79
Self-Portrait at the Age of 52
dated 1658
oil on canvas
$52\frac{3}{4} \times 41$ in (133.5×104 cm)
Frick Collection, New York

In the 19th century in the collection of the Earls of Ilchester in England. Acquired by Henry Clay Frick from Knoedler in 1906.

simplicity of composition and directness of observation. The picture creates a tremendous impression of physical weight which forms a sharp contrast to the diffident quality of *The Polish Rider*. A careful analysis of this picture reveals a number of inconsistencies which were deliberately introduced. The composition is a simple pyramid with the head of the artist at the apex. Below the waist the anatomy is generalised in an astonishing way to the point of being out of focus. Indeed Rembrandt was one of the first artists to realise that the human eye does not record every object it sees with equal intensity. The eye can only focus on the object which is more or less in front of it. When related to painting this statement appears less naïve. Most artists, in particular the Dutch, sought to paint every object with an equal degree of focus. The completest statement in this direction is of course the art of Vermeer who corrected the imperfections and distortions the eye creates at the edge of the vision. Rembrandt took the opposite step and deliberately blurred the edges of his pictures, particularly in his last years. This then gives an impression of reality in the comparatively small space on the canvas. The eye comes to rest on the central, focal point in the picture, and therefore the rest of the painting appears perfectly natural since it corresponds to our own vision. Quite the opposite is true of the average Dutch still-life, where the eye has to rove over the whole painting in order to focus on each lovingly painted object.

The Frick *Self-Portrait* is one of the best examples of this problem of focus–Rembrandt's last works were in fact to become almost completely blurred in outline and only from a considerable distance do the forms begin to make sense. This is perhaps why his very last pictures have achieved such fame only in the 20th century, the century when Impressionism was appreciated. The colour scheme of the portrait is predominately gold and red, which was to be used with such dazzle a few years later in that unforgettable picture *The Jewish Bride* (plate 97) in the Rijksmuseum, Amsterdam.

Following the artist's bancruptcy in 1656 it seems that his pictures are less often dated, and so there is some uncertainty as to the exact order in which they were painted. There are two particularly memorable self-portraits from approximately 1660. The first is a tiny panel in the Musée Granet at Aix-en-Provence (plate 80). Until recently this picture was regarded as a sketch for an unexecuted or lost large picture, but modern views have insisted that it is not by Rembrandt at all–so much so that it is often deleted from serious works on the painter. Those who have visited the Aix museum will have been struck by the dominating

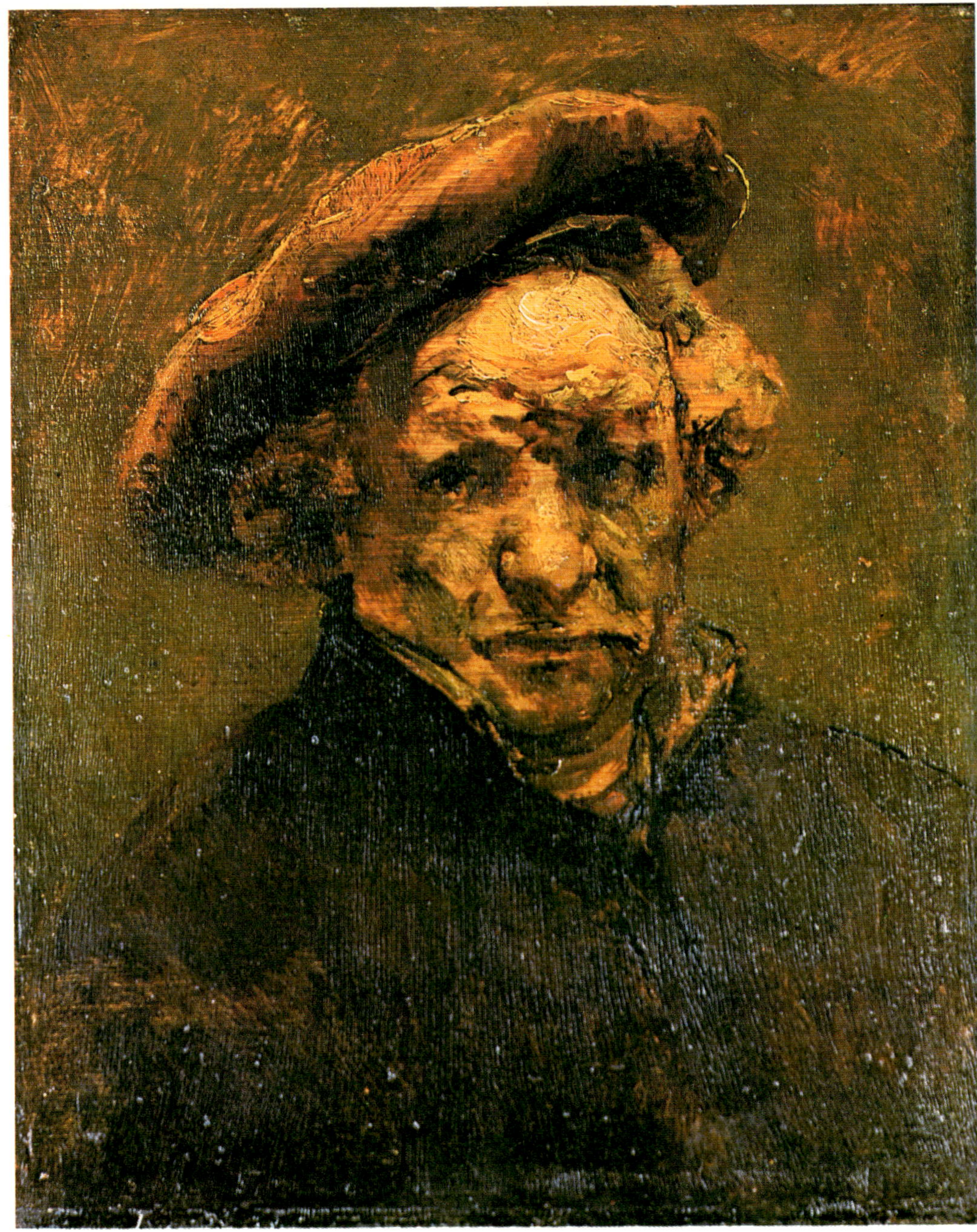

Plate 80
Self-Portrait
about 1660
oil on panel
$11\frac{3}{4} \times 9$ in (30×23cm)
Musée Granet, Aix-en-Provence

The early history of the controversial picture is unknown; it belonged to J. B. Bourguignon de Fabrigoules and was given to the museum by his son in 1860. Always accepted as a masterpiece by Rembrandt until the recent doubts by Gerson.

quality of this diminutive work. The features are clearly those of the artist himself in a very much more lively mood than is usual in these years. The paint is applied briskly with the impression that it was done at one sitting. He has given himself a sense of determination which is almost aggressive. This is such a contrast to the sad, almost gloomy, self-portrait in Washington (plate 81) of 1659, where the artist has shown himself as an old man who has failed in the world. It is true that even some of the most dignified of human spirits have been surrounded by a sense of failure, which may be caused by a dissatisfaction with what they have achieved, and the realisation that as their lives draw to a close there is no further possibility of improvement or change of direction.

Plate 81
Self-Portrait at the Age of 53
dated 1659
oil on canvas
33¼ × 26 in (84.5 × 66 cm)
National Gallery of Art, Washington
A. W. Mellon Collection

First recorded in the collection of the Dukes of Montague, by inheritance to the Dukes of Buccleuch. Acquired by Andrew Mellon for the National Gallery, Washington, before 1939.

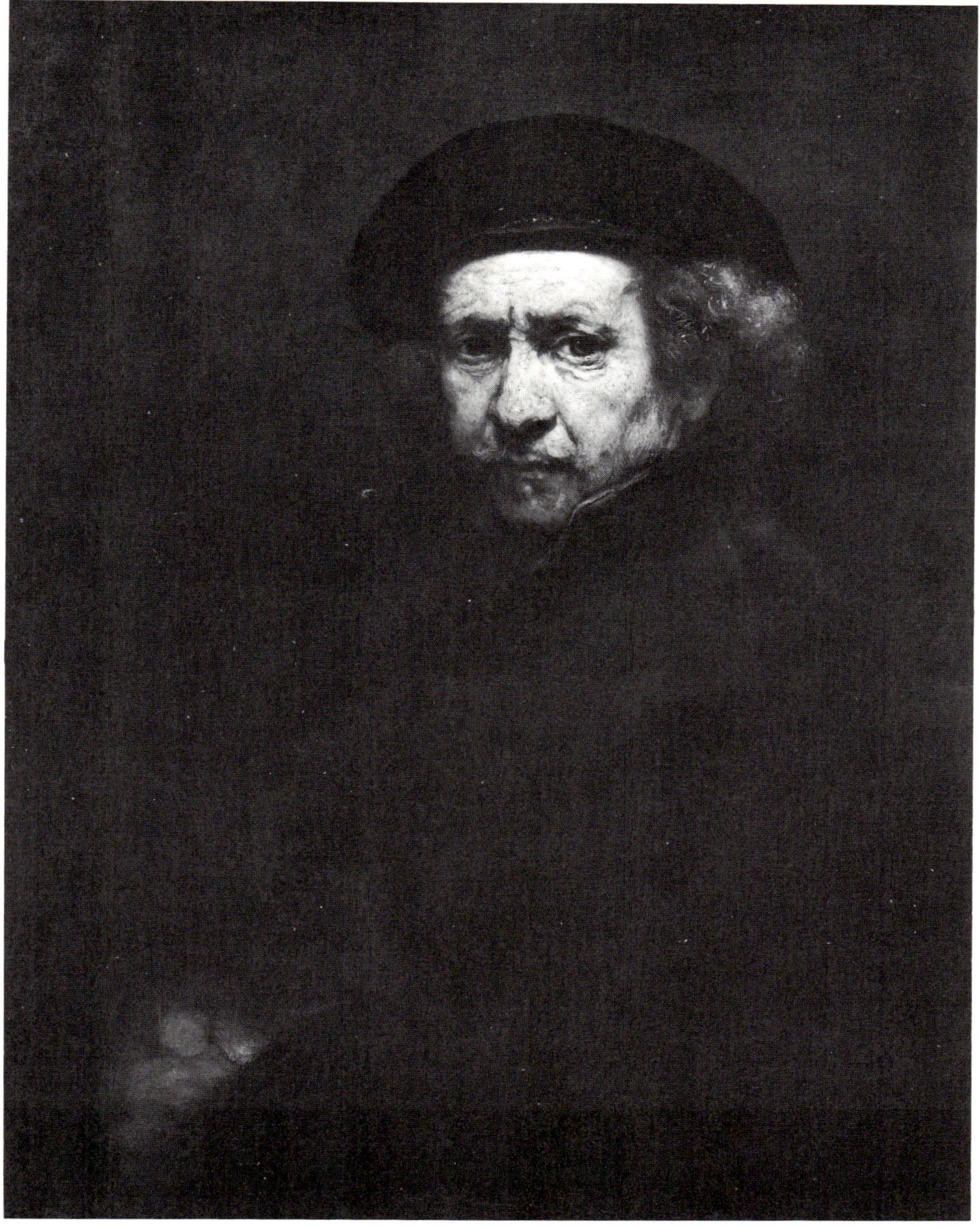

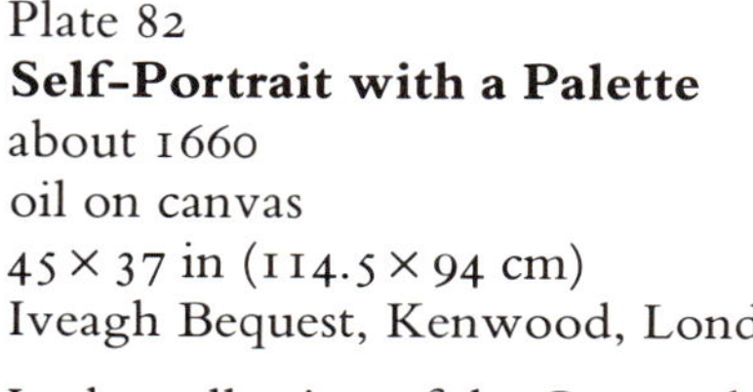

Plate 82
Self-Portrait with a Palette
about 1660
oil on canvas
45 × 37 in (114.5 × 94 cm)
Iveagh Bequest, Kenwood, London

In the collection of the Comte de Vence in Paris in 1750. In the Danoot Collection in Brussels in 1781 until sold in 1828. Brought to England by Buchanan and Niewenhuys and sold to the Marquess of Lansdowne in 1836. Acquired by the Earl of Iveagh from him through Agnew in 1888 and bequeathed by Lord Iveagh to the then London County Council in 1927.

Plate 83
Titus Dressed as a Monk
about 1660
oil on canvas
31¼ × 26½ in (79.5 × 67.5 cm)
Rijksmuseum, Amsterdam

Formerly in the Stroganoff Collection, St Petersburg, and then in the Museum of Fine Arts in Moscow. Left Russia in 1933 in which year it was acquired by the Rembrandt Society and placed in the Rijksmuseum.

A complete contrast to the Aix picture is the grave self-portrait (plate 82) in the Iveagh Bequest at Kenwood, London. This is one of the few pictures where Rembrandt has revealed himself as an artist pure and simple, as he is more usually in some sort of fancy dress. The geometric quality of the composition has frequently been commented on, in particular the strange circle in the backround. The artist has now become so totally self-absorbed that all the external elements have disappeared. There is no longer any reliance on theatrical 'props': only the analysis of character is left. The premature ageing process has speeded up, the sitter seems almost in dissolution. In fact he still has nine more years to live, though one would not think it. He has returned to the cool colour

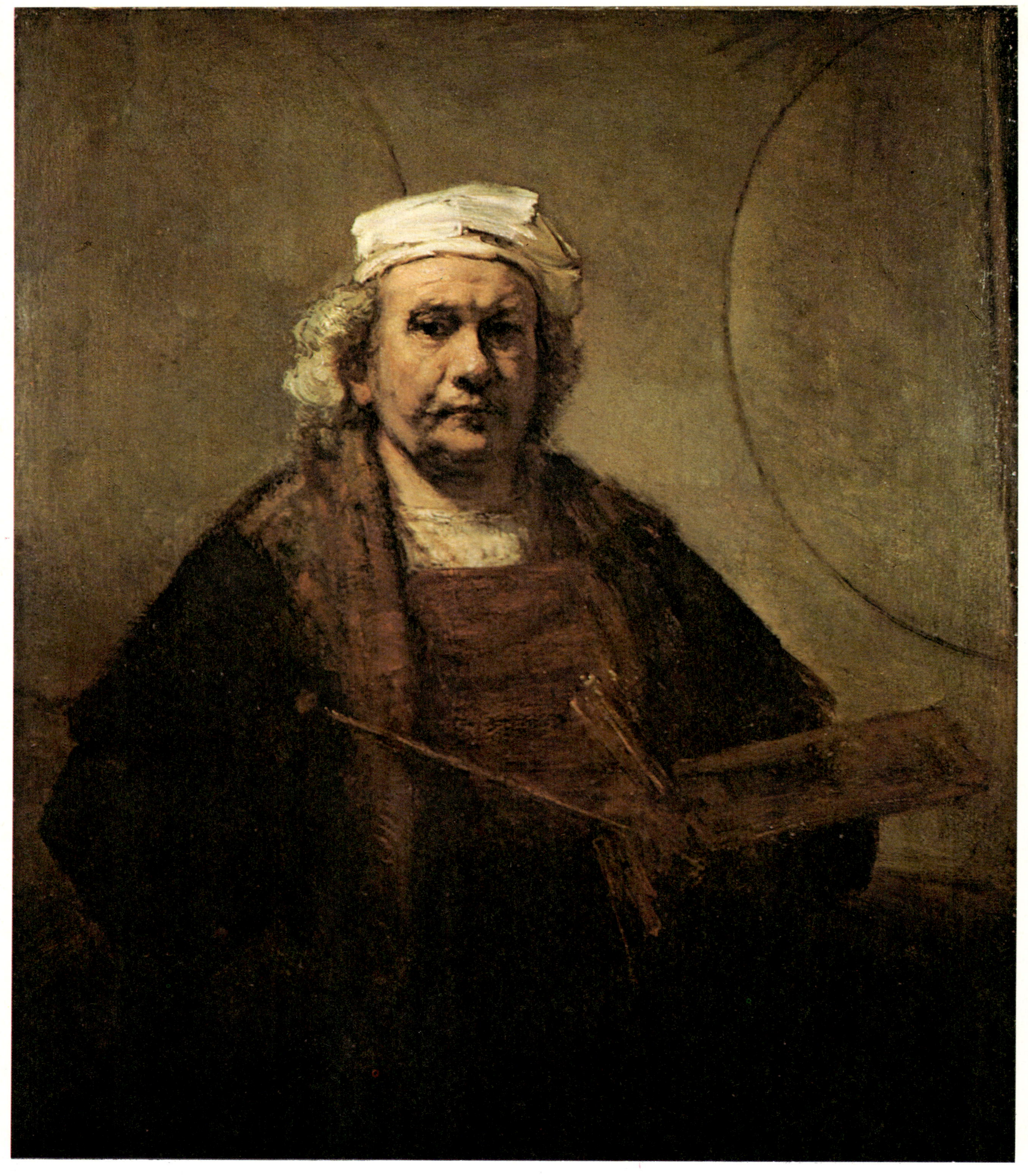

Plate 82 *see page 99*

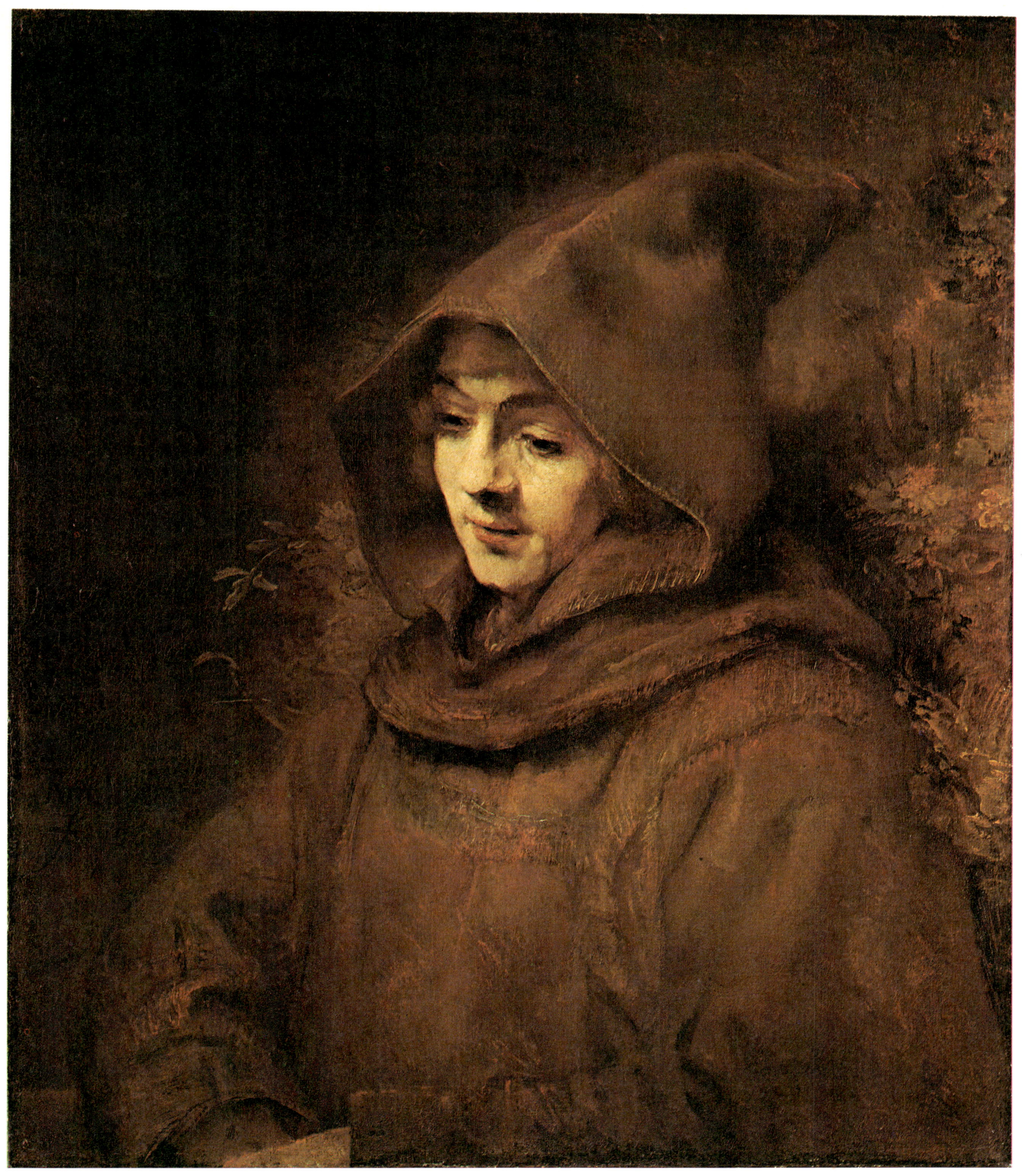

Plate 83 *see page 99*

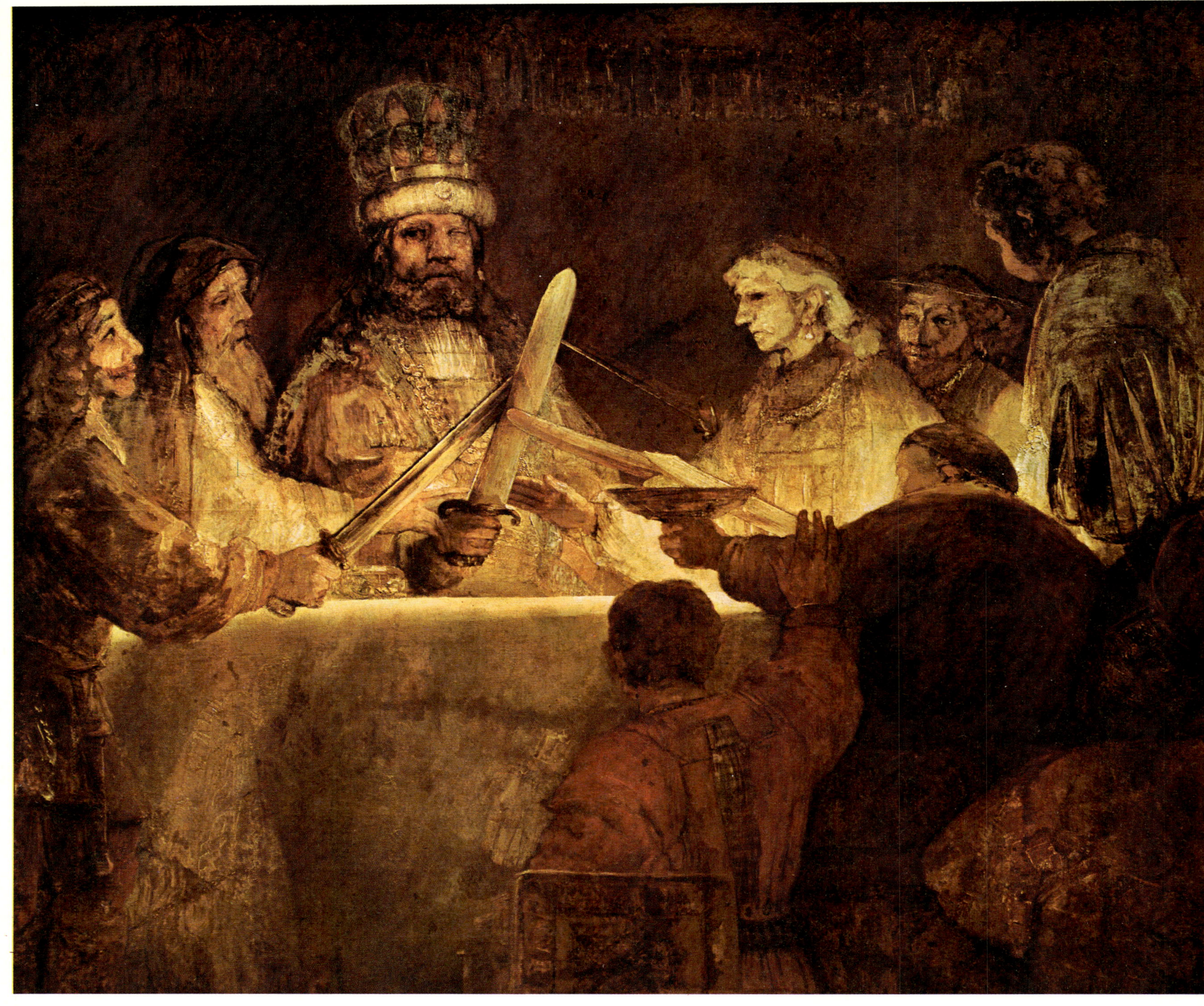

Plate 84
The Conspiracy of Claudius Civilis
(fragment)
dated 1661
oil on canvas
$77\frac{1}{8} \times 121\frac{5}{8}$ in (196×309 cm)
Nationalmuseum, Stockholm

Following its removal from the Town Hall, Amsterdam, about 1661, the subsequent history of the painting is unknown, until it appeared in Sweden in the 18th century. In the Academy in Stockholm in the 19th century and transferred to the Nationalmuseum there in 1864.

scheme of his earlier years, the grey/greens and broken whites. By now we know the features well, but what is less familiar is the man behind the mask. Sad, dignified and bursting with that imagination which was still to produce a whole range of pictures wonderful in their inventiveness, touching in their human content but, in the writer's opinion, lacking in that taut control which makes the *Aristotle* (plate 60) and *The Polish Rider* (plate 69) supreme.

The sweetly charming *Titus Dressed as a Monk* (plate 83) in the Rijksmuseum, Amsterdam, is generally dated about 1660, more or less the same time as the Kenwood self-portrait (plate 82). It is

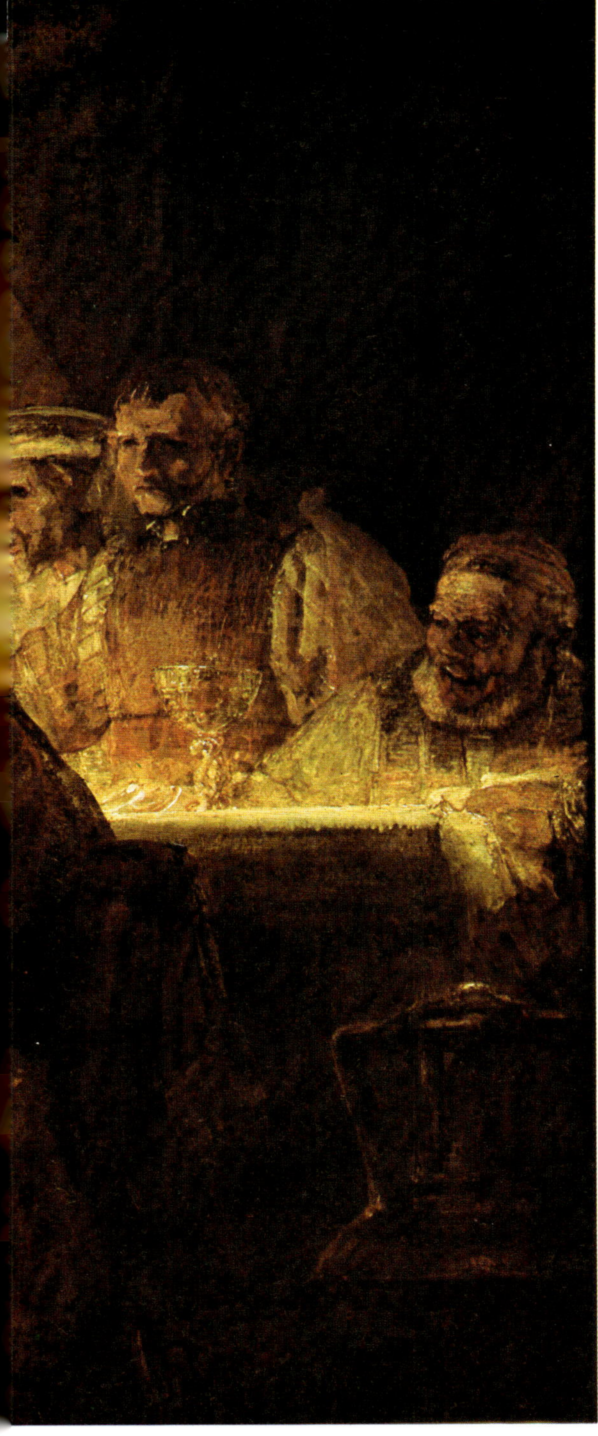

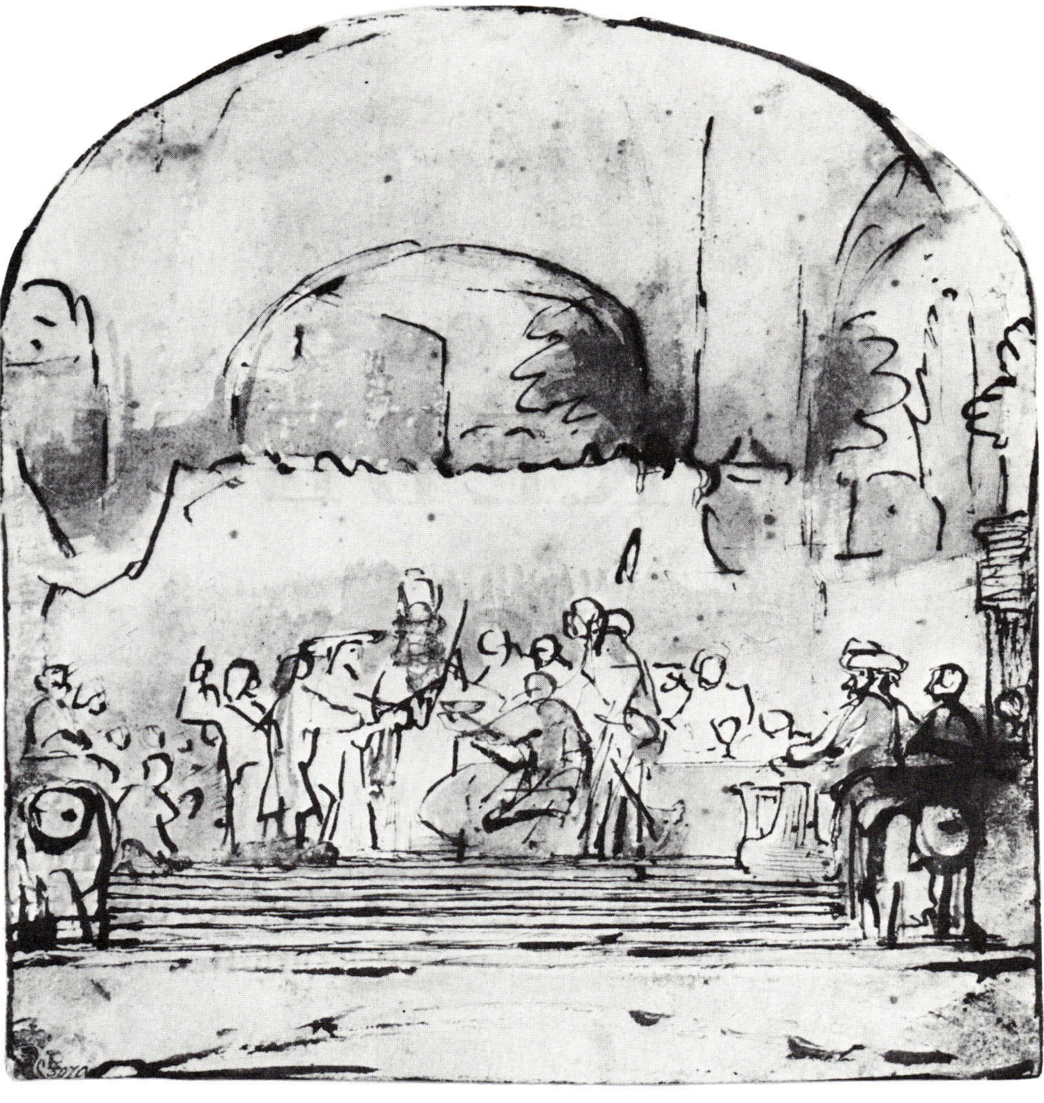

Plate 85
The Conspiracy of Claudius Civilis
about 1660
pen and wash
$7\frac{3}{4} \times 7\frac{1}{8}$ in (19.6 × 18 cm)
Staatliche Graphische Sammlung, Munich

Before being acquired by the Munich Print Room the drawing was in the collection of the Counts Palatine.

likely that it serves no other purpose than the artist's own private pleasure in painting his beloved son in yet another garb. Titus must have been almost twenty years of age, and like his father the ageing process began early. His expression is almost coy and singularly inappropriate for his monkish habit.

Rembrandt met his Waterloo when he painted *The Conspiracy of Claudius Civilis* (plate 84), of which a mangled fragment survives in the Nationalmuseum, Stockholm, for the new Town Hall at Amsterdam (the building survives as the Royal Palace there). Its greatness as a work of art, even in its present state, is unquestionable, but in the eyes of his contemporaries it was this

Plate 86
St Matthew and the Angel
dated 1661
oil on canvas
$37\frac{3}{4} \times 31\frac{7}{8}$ in (96 × 81 cm)
Musée du Louvre, Paris

Seized at the time of the French Revolution from the collection of the Count d'Argivillier and placed in the Louvre where it has remained ever since.

picture which made Rembrandt a monumental failure. Modern art criticism is no less tolerant of failure than it was in Rembrandt's day. Sir Frank Brangwyn's decorations for Swansea Town Hall, or the series of panels in the Leeds City Art Gallery are failures in the eyes of present day society in just the same way that the *Claudius Civilis* was a disaster in its own time. It contributed greatly to the myth that Rembrandt was a misunderstood genius.

Amsterdam, in trying to rival the great cities of the Italian Renaissance, had erected a vast but sober Town Hall, following the destruction by fire of its predecessor, and had intended that the Great Central Hall should be decorated with suitable historical subjects as befitted a newly rich city trying to establish a not altogether illustrious cultural heritage. The main commission went to Govaert Flinck, who had been one of Rembrandt's better pupils in 1659, but he died a year later, and Rembrandt was commissioned to paint a truly vast arched composition which was to occupy one end of the main hall. The drawing in Munich (plate 85) gives a vague idea of the layout of the composition. The subject was *Claudius Civilis Appealing to the Batavians to Go to War* which was generally seen to be a thinly disguised allegory on the Netherlanders' own revolt, under William of Orange, against their Spanish governors.

The exact circumstances concerning the ultimate rejection of the picture are unknown. The picture was certainly installed in the room, but it seems that the artist had it taken down again in order to retouch it–it is likely that everybody had grumbled that it appeared 'unfinished'. The painting was never replaced. The artist had failed.

The remaining fragment in Stockholm is difficult to admire on casual inspection. It is dominated by one of Rembrandt's most terrifying images–the one-eyed Claudius Civilis brandishing his sword, which is so lit that it appears almost white hot. Rembrandt's ability to paint the benevolence of old age, which is so touching in so many of his pictures throughout his career, is here transformed into an image of disgusting cruelty. If the story were unknown to the spectator it would seem as if some diabolical rite is about to be performed. Through aeons of time the wickedness of the world oozes out of Claudius Civilis' face. His rich clothes are blurred at the edges through centuries of corruption. Shakespeare used this type of image when recording the cruelties of King Lear, also taking place in a distant and indefinable past. Small wonder that the *Civilis* has never been loved by the public, but conveniently forgotten, a fragment in distant Stockholm, where it serves as a reminder that the very great in art is not always a cosy image of

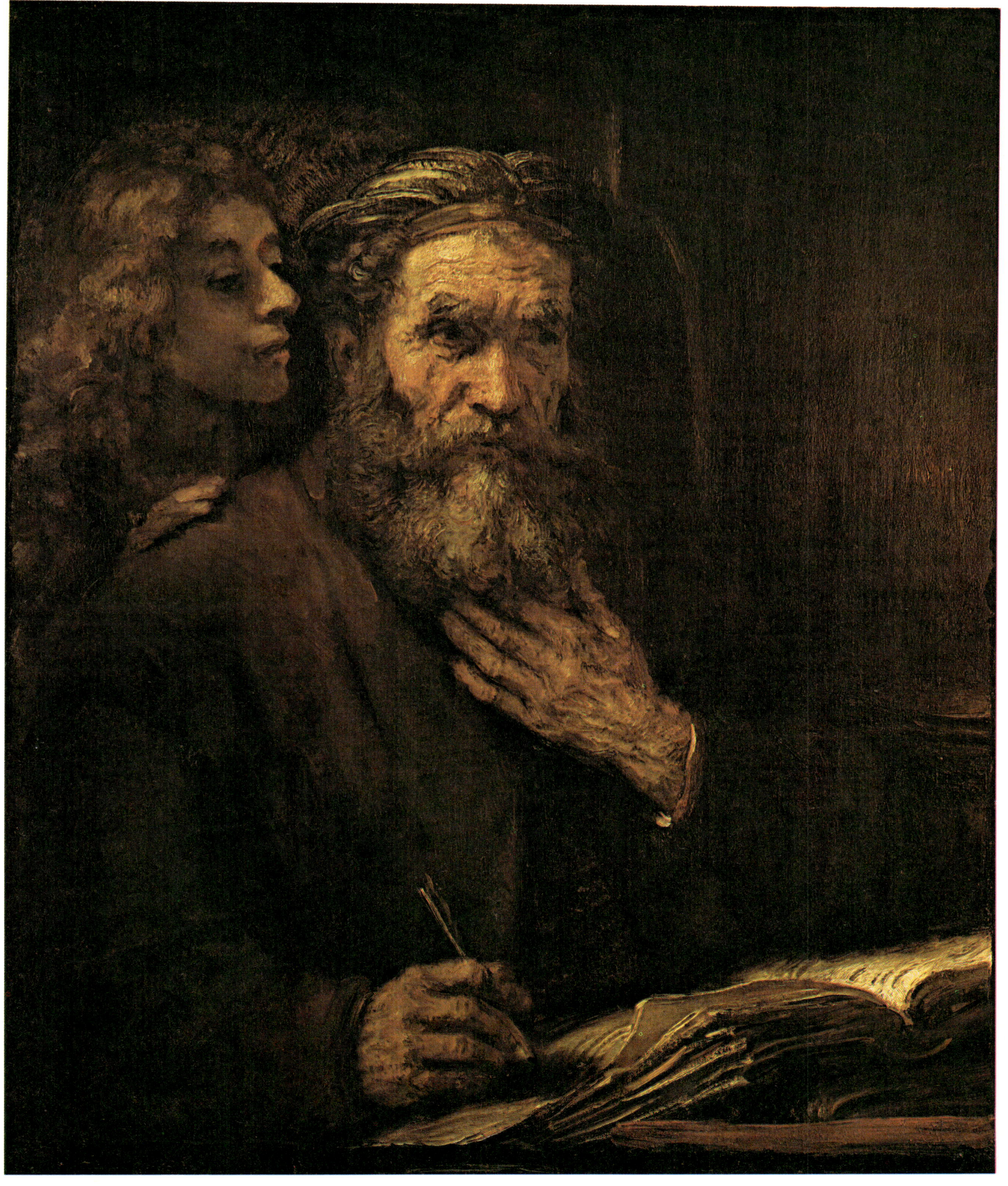

Plate 87
Man with a Falcon
about 1661
oil on canvas
$38\frac{3}{4} \times 31\frac{1}{8}$ in (98.5 × 79 cm)
Konstmuseum, Gothenburg

In the Lesser Collection, London, then in the Brodin Collection, Stockholm, before entering the Gothenburg Museum.

Plate 88
Portrait of Jacob Trip
about 1661
oil on canvas
$51\frac{3}{8} \times 38\frac{1}{4}$ in (130.5 × 97 cm)
National Gallery, London

Plate 89
Portrait of Margaretha Trip, Wife of Jacob Trip
about 1661
oil on canvas
$51\frac{3}{8} \times 38\frac{3}{8}$ in (130.5 × 97.5 cm)
National Gallery, London

These two pictures have always been together, but their early history is obscure. The first certain record is as late as 1837 when they were lent by Sir William Fowle Middleton Fowle to the British Institution. Purchased from his great-niece Lady de Saumarez by the National Gallery in 1899.

the dignity of the spirit in man.

The Louvre *St Matthew and the Angel* (plate 86) is one of the rare pictures from this period, indeed from any point in his career, where the artist exhibits a sense of humour. The aged Apostle is in the process of being guided by the angel while he writes the Gospel. How different the angel appears from Rembrandt's solid but airborne creatures! He is youthful and has what seem to be the half-remembered features of the now grown-up Titus – the face is certainly close to the rather earlier *Titus Reading* in the Kunsthistorisches Museum, Vienna. Matthew is solemn but kindly and, unusually, can almost be seen to have a twinkle in his eye while the angel whispers corrections to the manuscript in his ear.

The surface of the pictures in these years become gradually more encrusted with paint. There is almost the effect of the petrifying well. The same thing is found in the late works of Titian, who broke up the surface of his canvas with ever-increasing varieties of textures, until, in the very last pictures, they almost become texture for its own sake. This is beginning to happen in Rembrandt's little-known *Man with a Falcon* (plate 87) in the museum at Gothenburg in Sweden. The variety of texture is considerable in the painting of this rather grand but unemotional old man. Such a picture must come into the category of painting for painting's sake. Here Rembrandt's art has lost all the didactic quality of which it was so full. There is no longer any story to be told; there is no specific message to convey, although as always Rembrandt makes the spectator look again and realise that he has made a unique statement about the particular problem in front of him.

The pair of portraits *Jacob Trip* (plate 88) and his wife *Margaretha de Geer* (plate 89) are fortunately preserved together in the National Gallery, London. They take up the tradition with which the artist had begun his career, that of the successful husband-wife portrait. This shows that at this stage he was not devoid of commissions. There is another portrait of Margaretha de Geer (plate 90), which is dated 1661 in the same gallery, and the pair has usually been dated to approximately the same year or very close to it.

The *Jacob Trip* is the less striking of the two, although he occupies a very much larger proportion of the picture plane. He is in very sombre shades of brown, almost no other colour being used to any extent. The *Margaretha* is an exercise in the painting of black and white. Her ruff is a *tour de force*, both in the observation of its elaborate folds, and in the tonal relationship of that most difficult of colours, white. Much of the rest of the picture is an

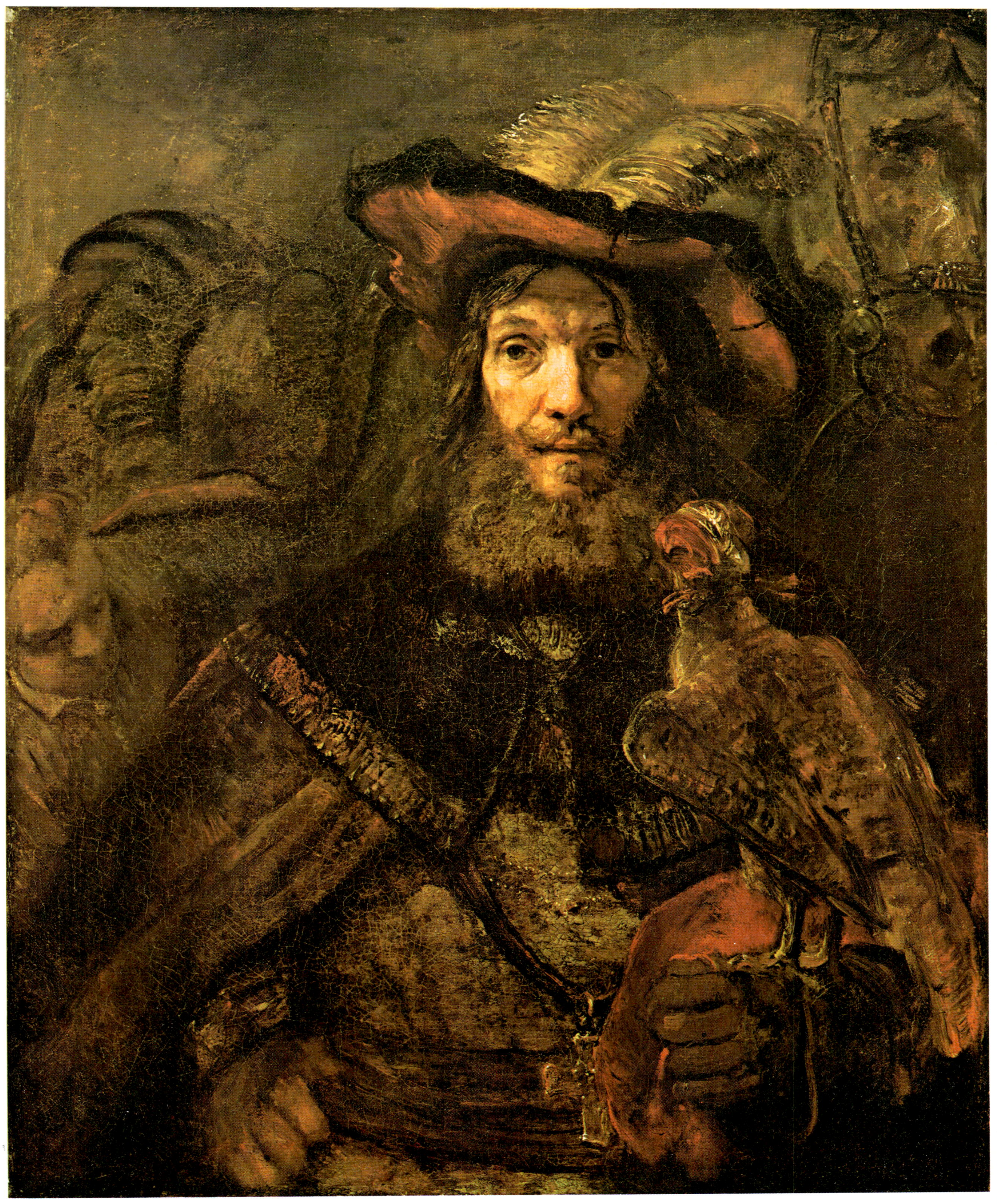

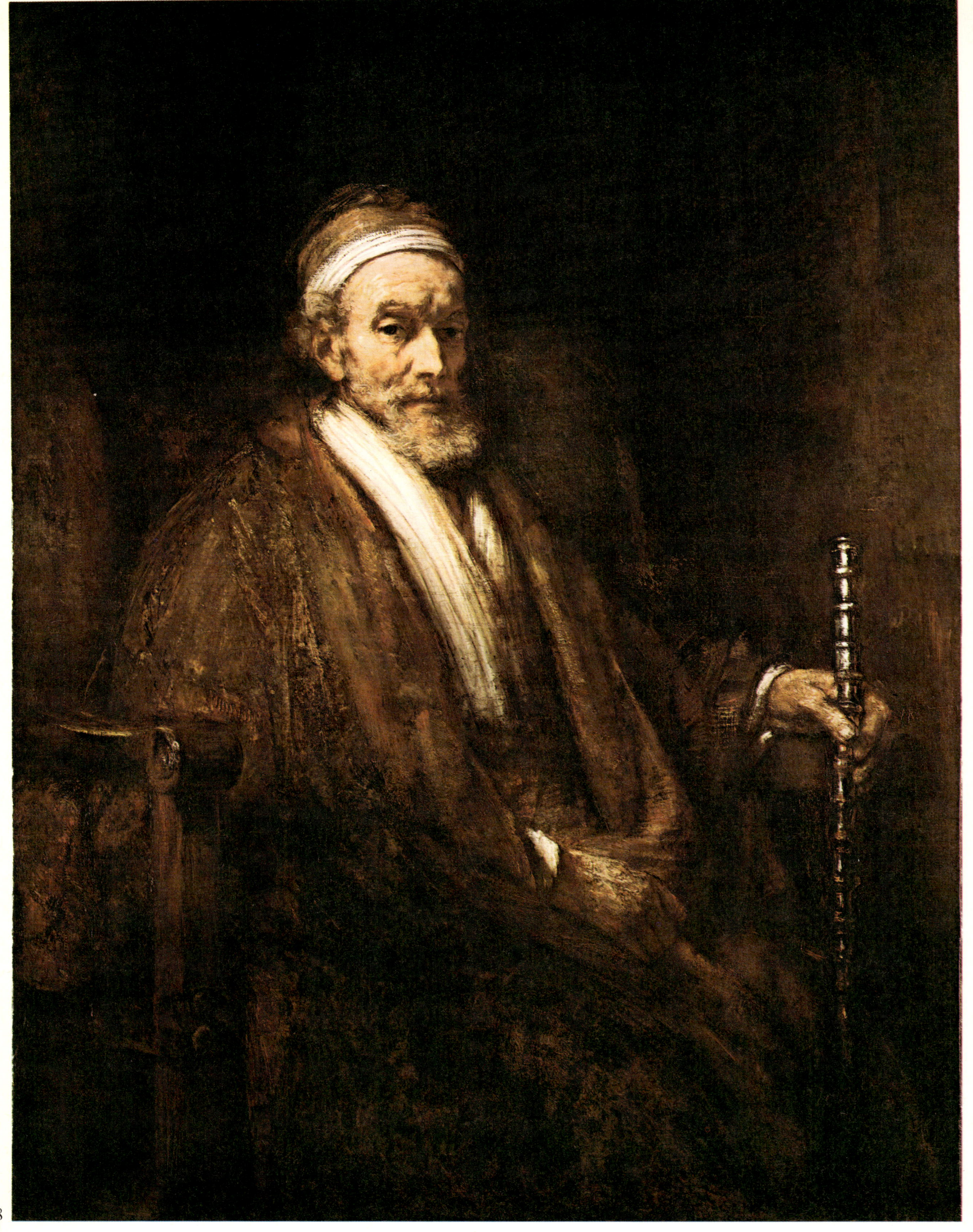

Plate 88 *see page 106*

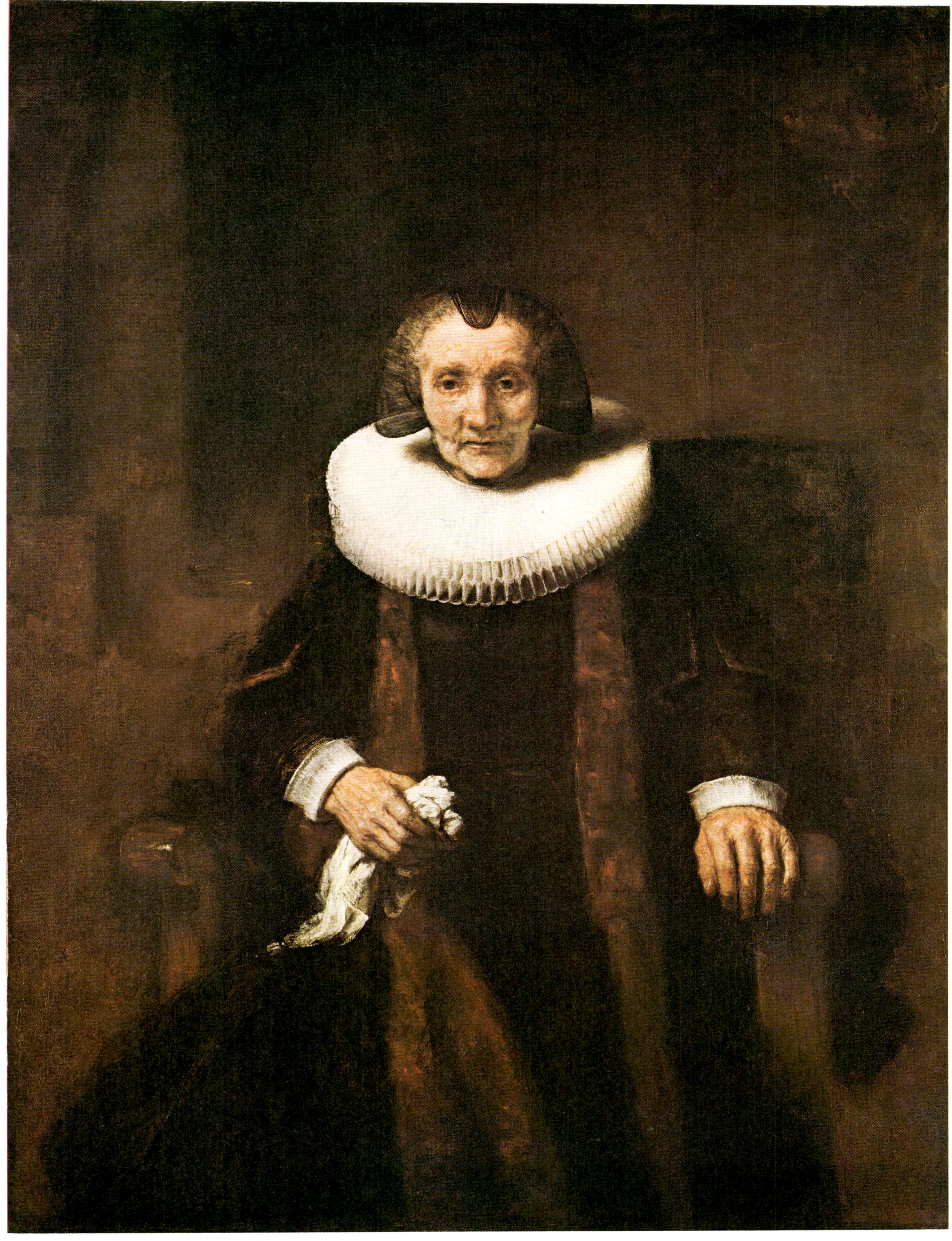

Plate 89 *see page 106*

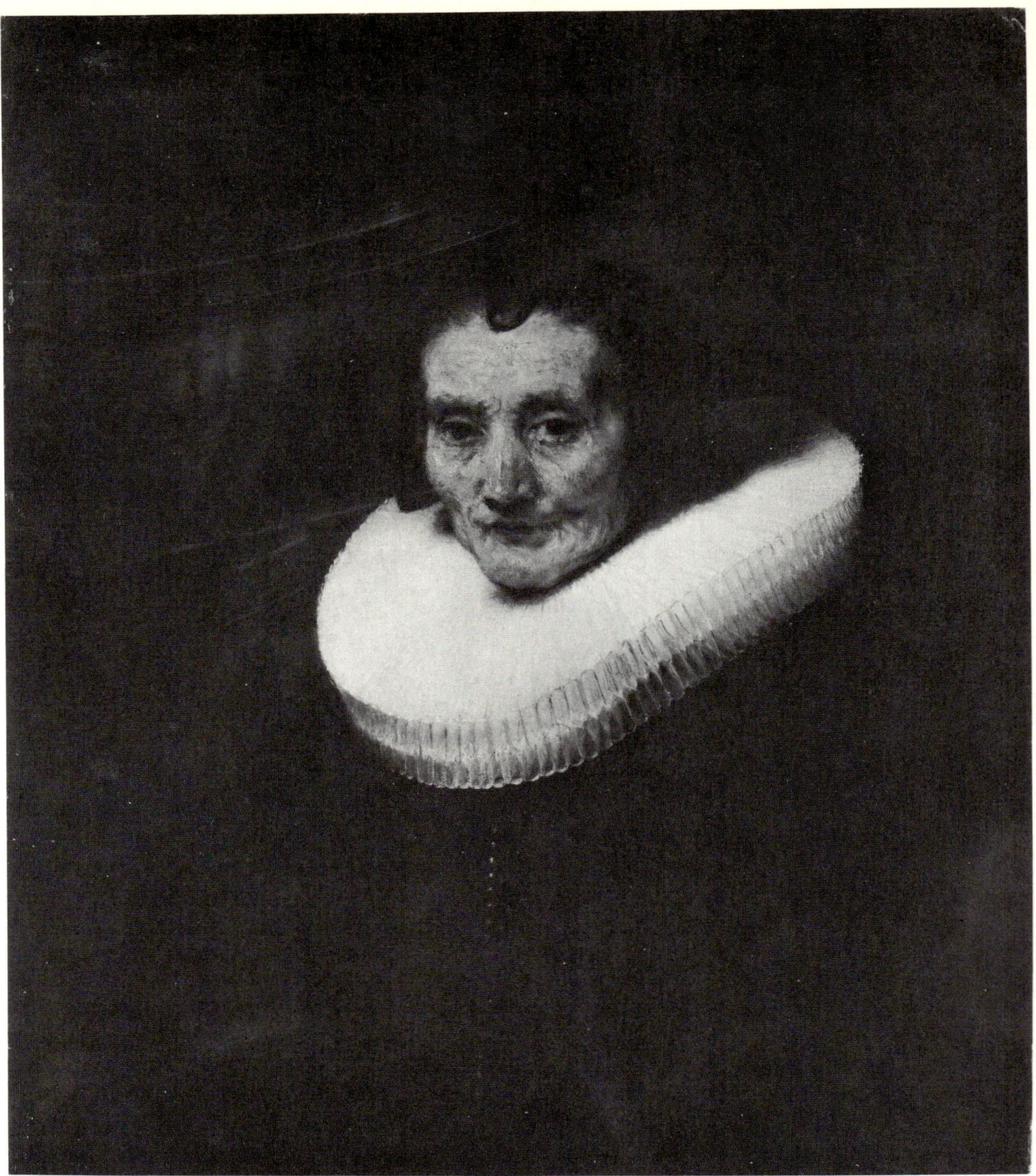

Plate 90
Portrait of Margaretha Trip
dated 1661
oil on canvas
29 × 25¼ in (75.5 × 64 cm)
National Gallery, London

Like so many of the pictures by Rembrandt now in England, the history of this one goes back no further than the early 19th century when, in 1818, it was exhibited at the British Institution. The picture then passed to a collection in The Hague and came back to England in 1846 when it was acquired by S. Jones Loyd who bequeathed it to his daughter Lady Wantage. The latter gave it to the Earl of Crawford and Balcarres from whom it was purchased by the National Art Collections Fund and presented to the National Gallery in 1941.

exceptionally deep black, the only relief being the face and hands of the sitter. Her hands deserve special mention, as they dominate the composition in a peculiar way. They seem to come forward at the spectator in direct contrast to those of her husband, which are lost in shadow.

Considering the relative extravagance of Rembrandt's colour scheme and of his experiments in composition, there is the feeling that when he had to paint this staid and respectable couple the artist toned down his current style and reverted, to all intents and purposes, to his earlier manner. The Trips are elderly, humourless and almost vexed in their expressions. Rarely has bourgeois old age been depicted with such objectivity–there is neither that near-mockery sometimes found in Frans Hals, nor indeed is there any sympathy with the couple who have been well endowed with goods in this world and who now face the uncertainty of the next.

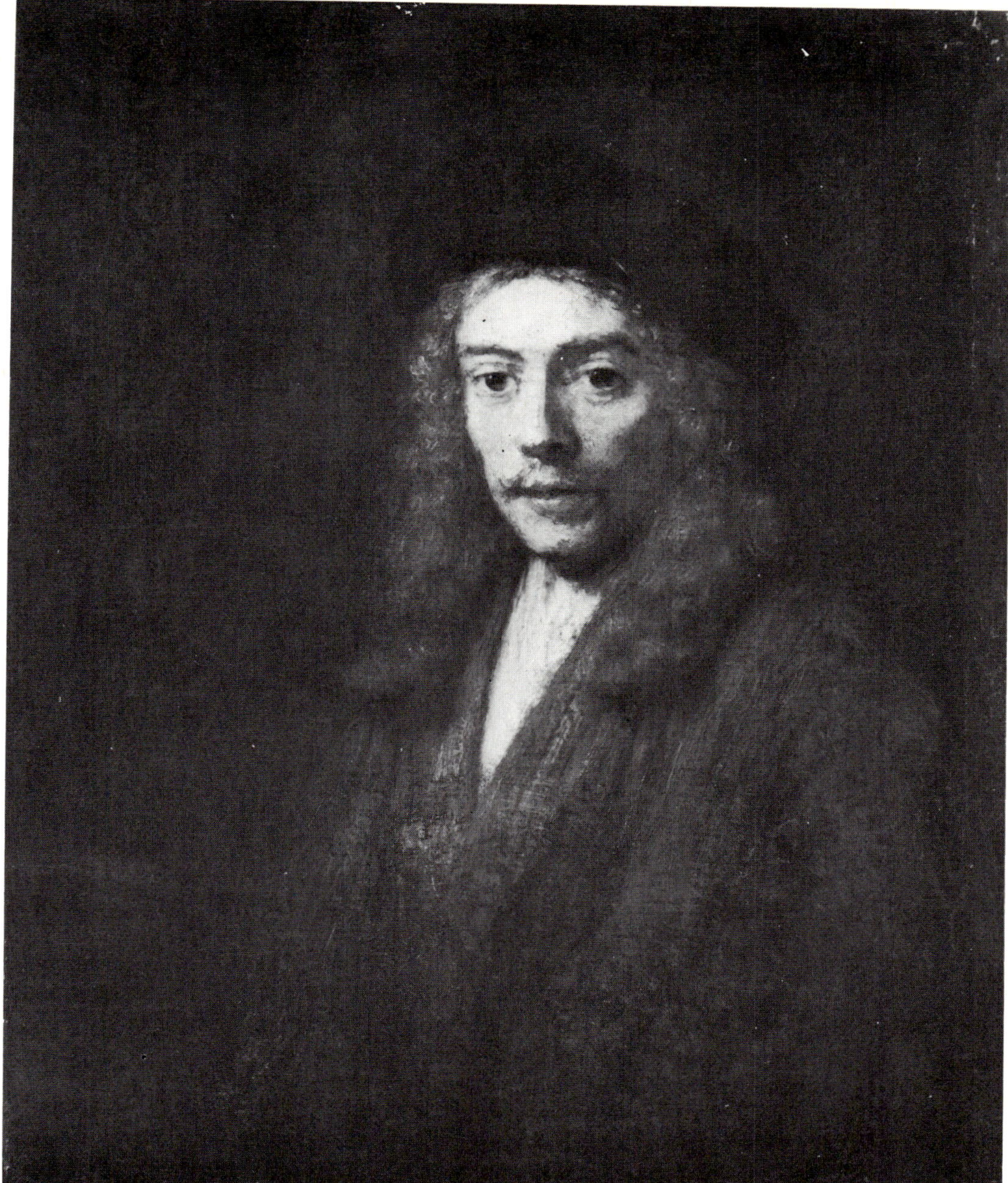

Plate 91
Portrait of Titus
early 1660s
oil on canvas
$28\frac{3}{4} \times 23\frac{5}{8}$ in (73×60 cm)
Dulwich College Picture Gallery, London

In his *Beauties of the Dulwich Gallery* (London, 1824) Hazlitt, without realising that the painting represented Titus, described it as follows: 'Nothing can be richer than the colouring, more forcible and masterly than the handling, and more consistent and individualized than the character of the face. It is one of those portraits of which it is common to say–"That must be a likeness".' Belonged to Noel Desenfans who bequeathed it to his friend Sir Peter Francis Bourgeois who bequeathed it to Alleyn's College of God's Gift, Dulwich, where it has remained since 1811.

The last surviving portrait of Titus (plate 91) is the little-known work in the Dulwich College Picture Gallery, which is of the early 1660s. The face seems that of a weak old man ravaged with disease. Of course we look at it with hindsight–we know that Titus will predecease his father, and therefore it is all the more tempting to read tragedy into this canvas. Most of the shadows have darkened considerably and only the face retains some of its original freshness, but what a face! Titus' big watery eyes look appealingly, almost imploringly, out of the canvas, and his thick lips are partly open, which gives an even greater impression of life. In this picture Rembrandt may have failed to captivate the spectator on account of the fact that it is almost too mysterious, but he saw his son with a devastating accuracy and not through a film of sentiment.

Both the previously discussed *Anatomy Lessons* fall into the

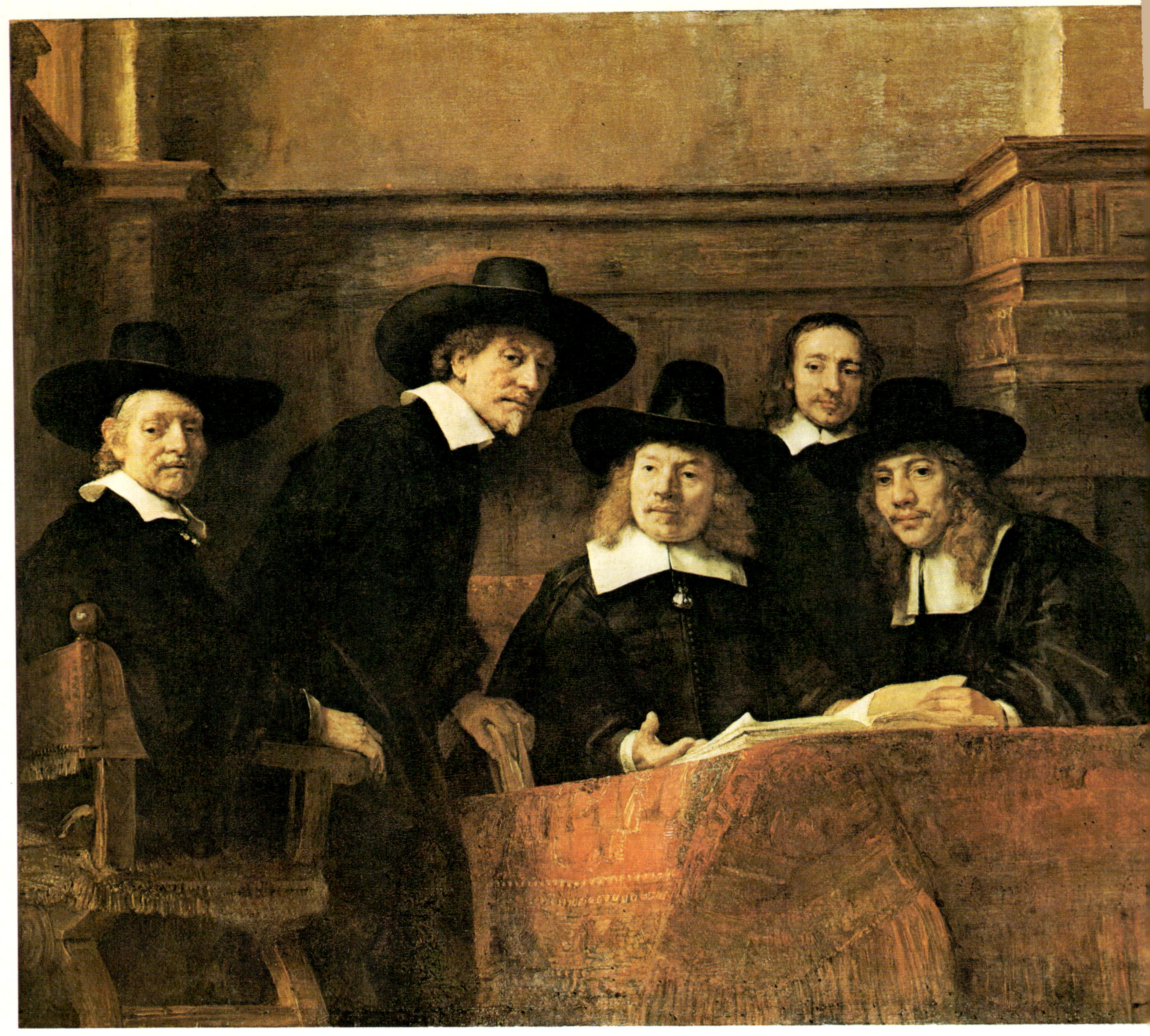

Plate 92
The Syndics of the Clothworkers' Guild
dated 1662
oil on canvas
$75\frac{1}{4} \times 109\frac{3}{4}$ in (191.5 × 279 cm)
Rijksmuseum, Amsterdam

From the time that the artist delivered the picture to his clients until 1808 it hung in the Cloth Hall at Amsterdam. Lent by the City of Amsterdam to the Rijksmuseum ever since.

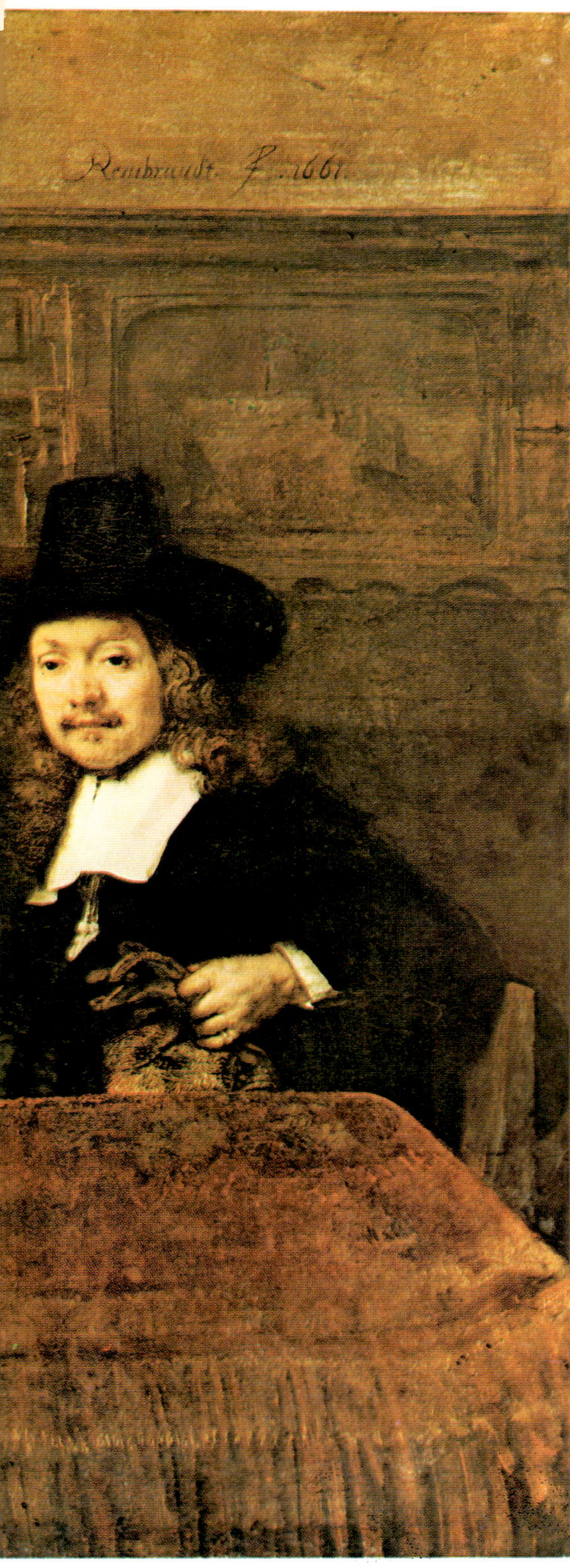

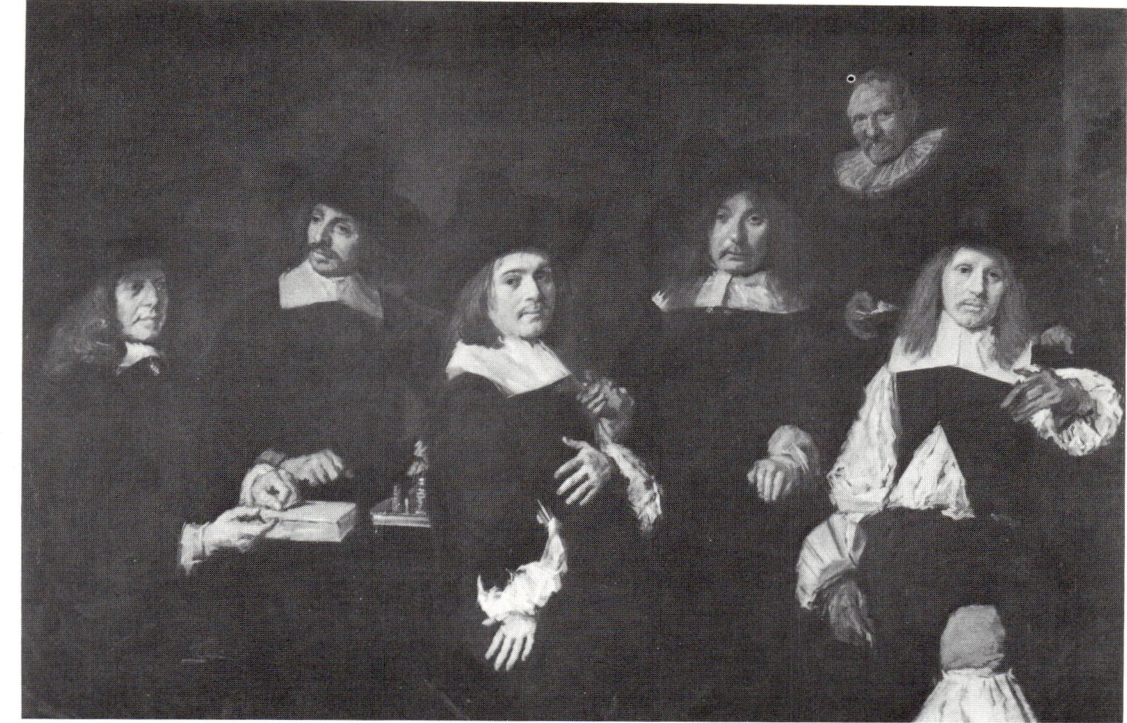

category of the group portrait in a general sense, but *The Syndics of the Clothworkers' Guild* (plate 92) of 1662, in the Rijksmuseum, Amsterdam, is the only straight group portrait that he seems to have painted. As in the Trip portraits the technique is sober–there are none of the eccentricities which mark so many of his later paintings. Only the red tablecloth has been used as an excuse for a display of texture and colour. A comparison with *The Governors of the Old Men's Almshouse, Haarlem* (plate 93) by Frans Hals, in the Frans Halsmuseum, Haarlem, which dates from about 1664, is inevitable. As a recipient of public charity Hals was emotionally involved with his subjects, and the resultant exposure of their weaknesses as people was devastating. The fact that committees concerned with the dispensation of public charity often lack humanity has been for ever recorded on this highly disconcerting canvas. The Rembrandt is observed with so much more objectivity. The old men have gentle, intelligent faces; both learned and serene, they sit round their table in a solid phalanx of black and white costumes, while the tablecloth sets off their sober dignity. This picture has none of the depressing quality associated with Rembrandt's late work.

The *Old Woman as the Magdalen (?)* (plate 94) of 1663, in the Musée Départemental des Vosges at Epinal, has a grave, decayed feeling, which leaves the spectator depressed, and this is even more strongly felt in the last self-portraits when Rembrandt seems to have been obsessed with his own approaching death and with recording his decaying features in an inimitably joyless way.

The last in the series of pictures which went to Don Ruffio is the

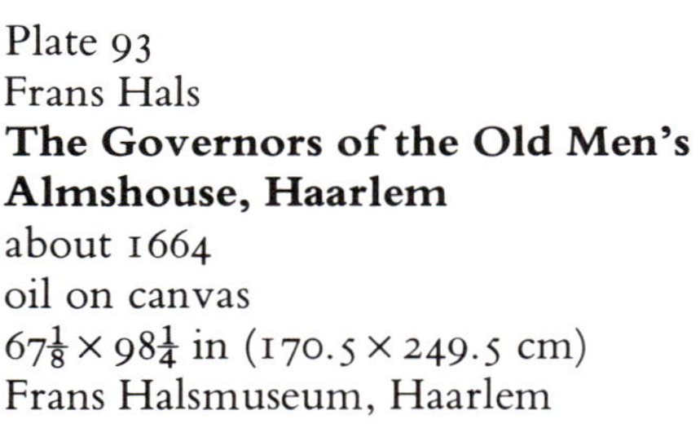

Plate 93
Frans Hals
The Governors of the Old Men's Almshouse, Haarlem
about 1664
oil on canvas
$67\frac{7}{8} \times 98\frac{1}{4}$ in (170.5 × 249.5 cm)
Frans Halsmuseum, Haarlem

In the Old Men's Almshouses, Haarlem, since it was painted until 1862 when it was transferred to the Frans Halsmuseum.

Homer Dictating to a Scribe (plate 95) of which a fragment survives in the Mauritshuis in The Hague. The extent of the whole composition is known from the drawing in the Nationalmuseum, Stockholm (plate 96). The drawing shows the poet in almost the same attitude as he appears in the painting, while the scribe plays a relatively minor part in the composition. Although the picture, dated 1663, predates *The Jewish Bride* (plate 97), the technique is rather similar. Shorn of the scribe the fragment has never been much appreciated since the single figure, as it now is, lacks the interest of the relationship between two or more human beings. In spite of this the *Homer* is a deeply felt picture where all the wisdom, learning and talent of the historian-poet is embodied in the sad expression on the face. There is none of the pernickety feeling, which many of those of great learning have in old age, but rather an increased breadth and understanding of the world. Perhaps in this *Homer* Rembrandt unwittingly had himself in mind. His own art has achieved a breadth and wisdom which it

Plate 94
An Old Woman as the Magdalen (?)
dated 1661
oil on canvas
$42\frac{1}{8} \times 31\frac{7}{8}$ in. (107 × 81 cm)
Musée Départemental des Vosges, Epinal

Belonged to the Princes of Salm-Salm in the 18th century. Most of the collection was destroyed by fire in the town hall at Epinal in 1808 following its seizure at the time of the French Revolution. This picture was one of the few to escape the fire and has been preserved in the museum at Epinal ever since.

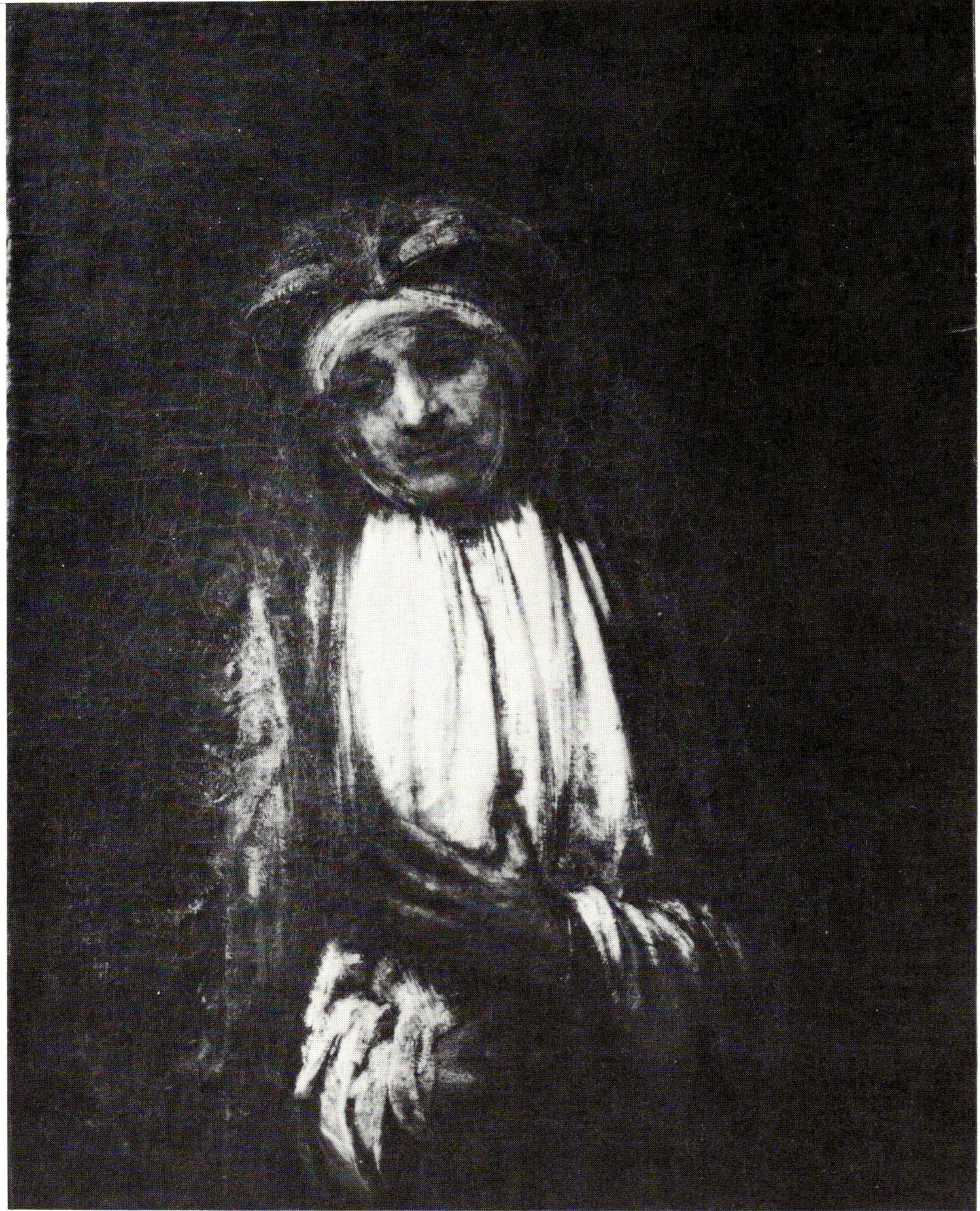

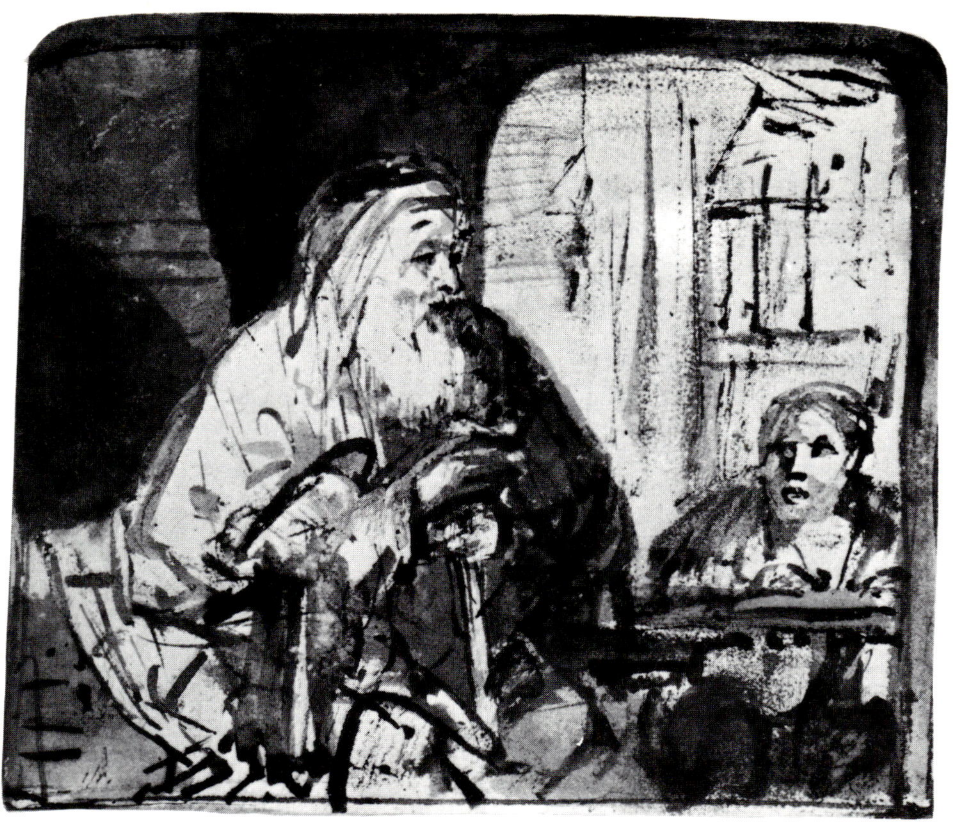

Plate 95
Homer Dictating to a Scribe
about 1662–63
pen and brush with brown and grey wash
$5\frac{3}{4} \times 6\frac{1}{2}$ in (14.5 × 16.7 cm)
Nationalmuseum, Stockholm

Acquired by the Nationalmuseum from the T. Sergel Collection. Sergel was a Swedish sculptor of considerable talent who worked in Rome in the 18th century.

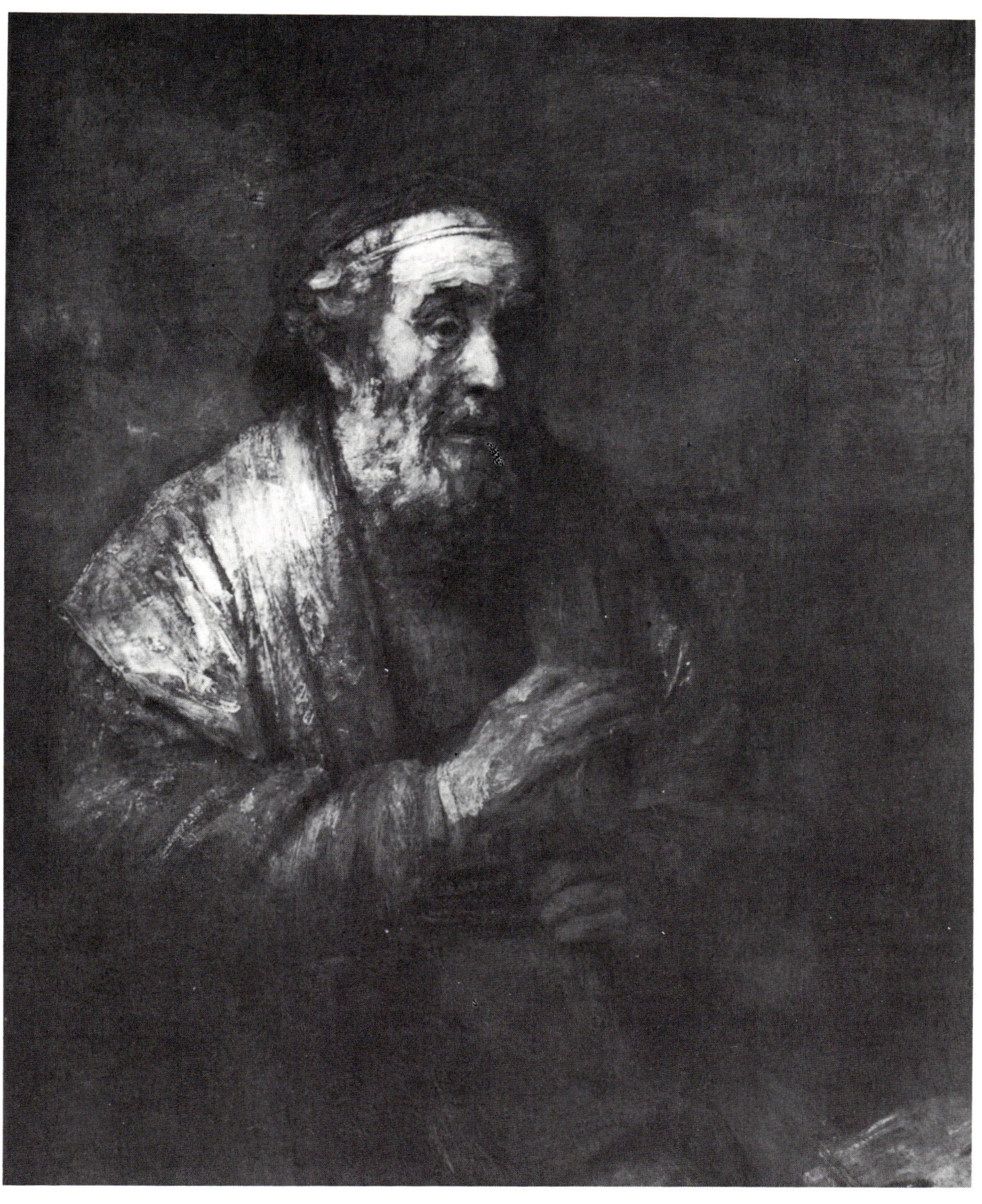

Plate 96
Homer (fragment)
dated 1663
oil on canvas
$42\frac{1}{2} \times 32\frac{1}{2}$ in (108 × 82.4 cm)
Mauritshuis, The Hague

Almost certainly painted for Don Ruffio in Sicily, but it is not known when it left his collection. Bought for the sum of 12 shillings by a certain Mr S. T. Smith in England in the 19th century. Acquired by the Mauritshuis from Mr Humphrey Ward of London in 1894.

Plate 97
An Unidentified Couple
The Jewish Bride
dated 1665
oil on canvas
48 × 65¾ in (121.5 × 166.5 cm)
Rijksmuseum, Amsterdam

Known only since the 19th century. Sold in Amsterdam in 1825 and then in the Van der Hoop Collection. Bequeathed by him to the City of Amsterdam in 1854 and lent to the Rijksmuseum since 1885.

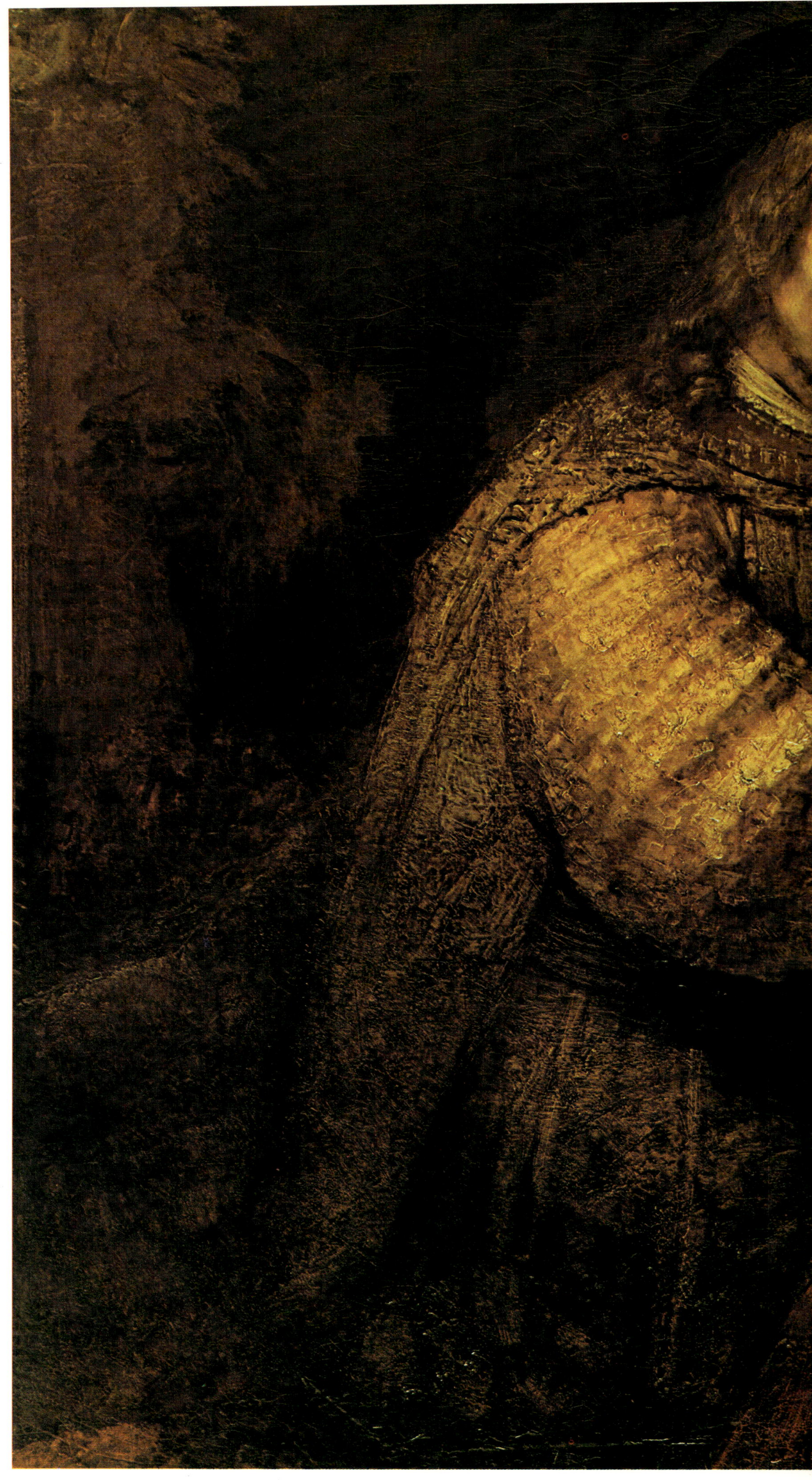

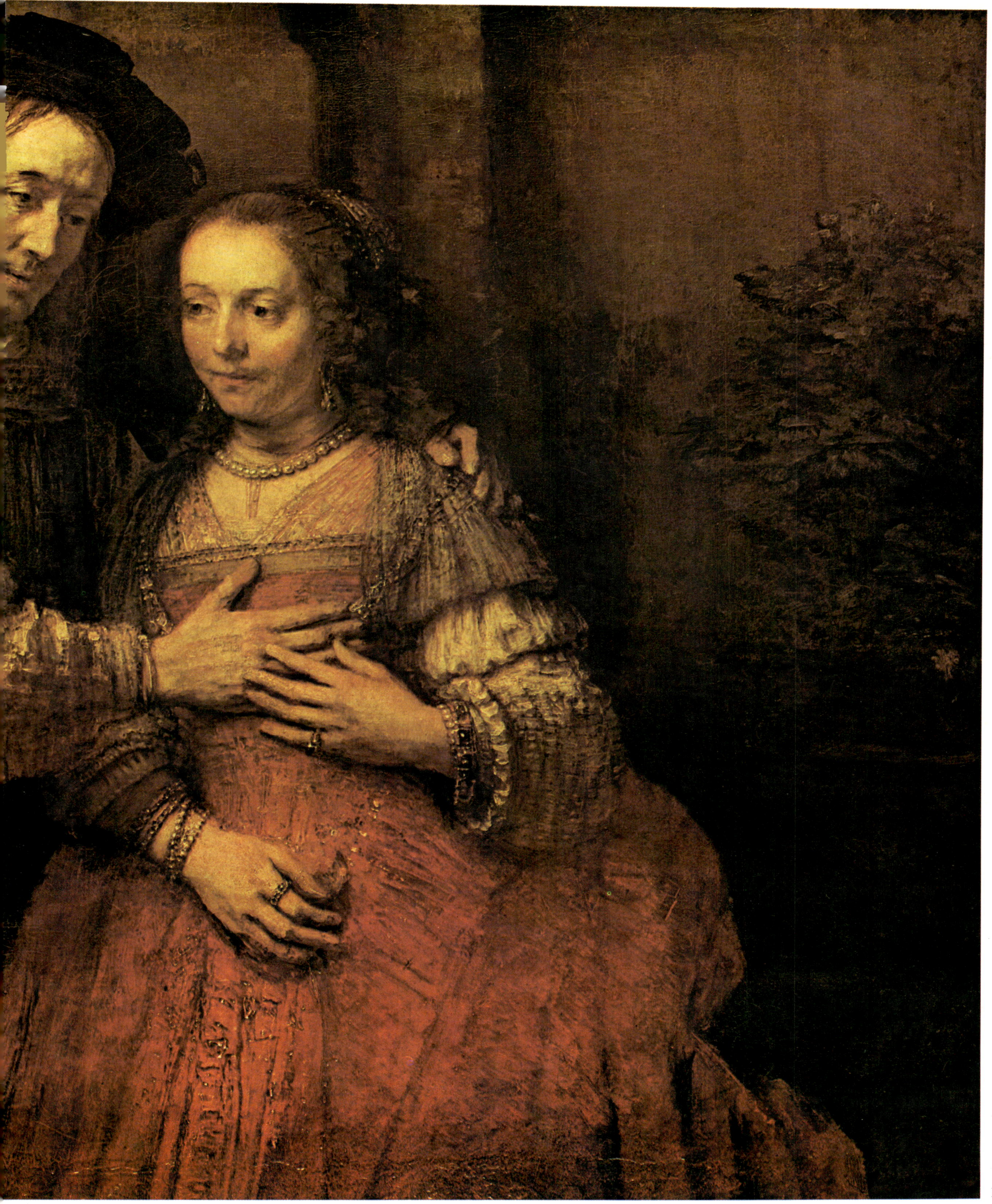

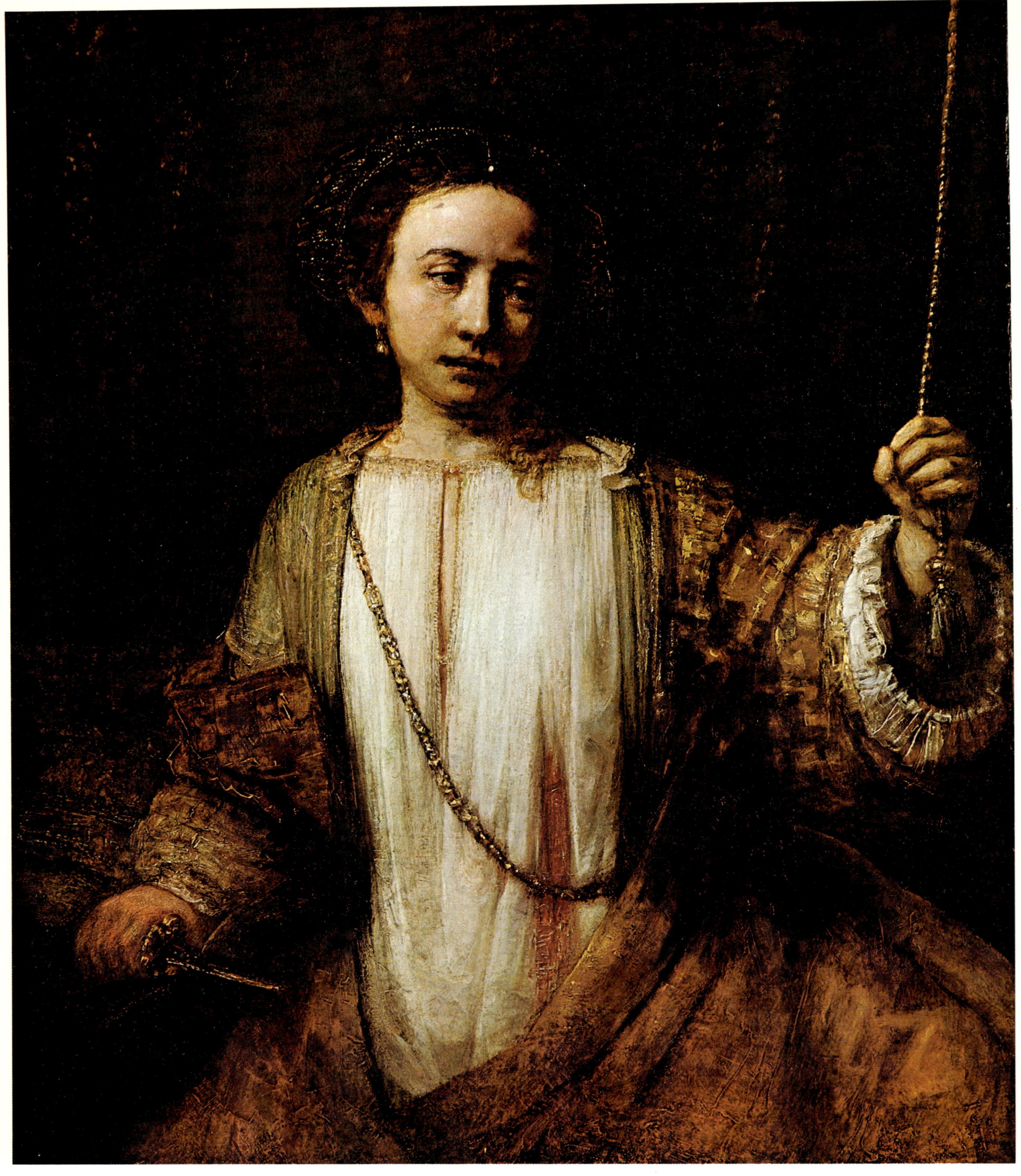

Plate 98
Lucretia Stabbing Herself
dated 1666
oil on canvas
$41\frac{1}{4} \times 36\frac{5}{8}$ in (105 × 92.5 cm)
Institute of Arts, Minneapolis

In 1854 in the Wombwell Collection. Subsequently it was in the H. V. Jones Collection, Minneapolis, and from that collection it passed to the museum.

had lacked in his younger days; but sadly there is still the feeling that he was beginning to lose his grip, a certain slackness in the painting of the hands, and the occasional imperfectly directed brushstroke in the lower part of the sleeve.

One of the artist's best-loved pictures is *The Jewish Bride* (plate 97) in the Rijksmuseum, Amsterdam, which is generally dated about 1665. The high reputation of this picture is understandable, as it is one of the purest statements in paint about two people who love each other. Both the sitters have an air of total satisfaction, both with the world and with each other. As in the Frick self-portrait (plate 79) all the edges of the picture are blurred, and only the faces and the hands are really in focus. All those who stop before this picture are rivetted by the famous golden sleeve of the man. Delight in a sleeve for its own sake was no new thing. Titian's *Portrait of a Man* in the National Gallery, London, which is an exercise in the painting of a sleeve, had passed through an Amsterdam saleroom in the 1630s where Rembrandt must have seen it. Here the Italian's image is, quite naturally, totally transformed into something which seems to have an extra presence, as well as being a bulky and soft object which exists in its own right.

The *Lucretia Stabbing Herself* (plate 98) of 1666, in the Minneapolis Institute of Arts, has never caught popular attention partly because of its relatively obscure subject-matter, and partly because it lacks the intense quality of so many of the pictures of ten years earlier. As is sometimes found at this end of his career, Rembrandt has concentrated on the poetic side of the subject. The beautiful woman has been wronged, and she is about to take her own life in shame. The painting has the usual encrusted texture, and in spite of the fact that this is not one of his very greatest works it remains touching in its quiet melancholy.

The pair of portraits, an *Unknown Man* (plate 99) and an *Unknown Woman, His Wife* (plate 100) in the National Gallery, Washington, normally dated as late as about 1668, form the swan song of the artist's conventional portrait style. The couple are solemn, dressed fashionably, but in good taste, neither too flashily nor deliberately dowdily. The artist has lavished a good deal of attention on the portrait of the wife who carries an ostrich feather. Her eyes are sad and have a watery feeling, as if she were about to cry, not at some disaster, but out of world-weariness. Her husband is less serene: his face has been lined by an interesting life and he is both lively and solid. His hands are in a gesture of movement, while those of his wife are in repose. In their quiet way, so much more so than usual, these two pictures reveal a too easily forgotten Rembrandt. All the myth of his failures, all the grandeur of his

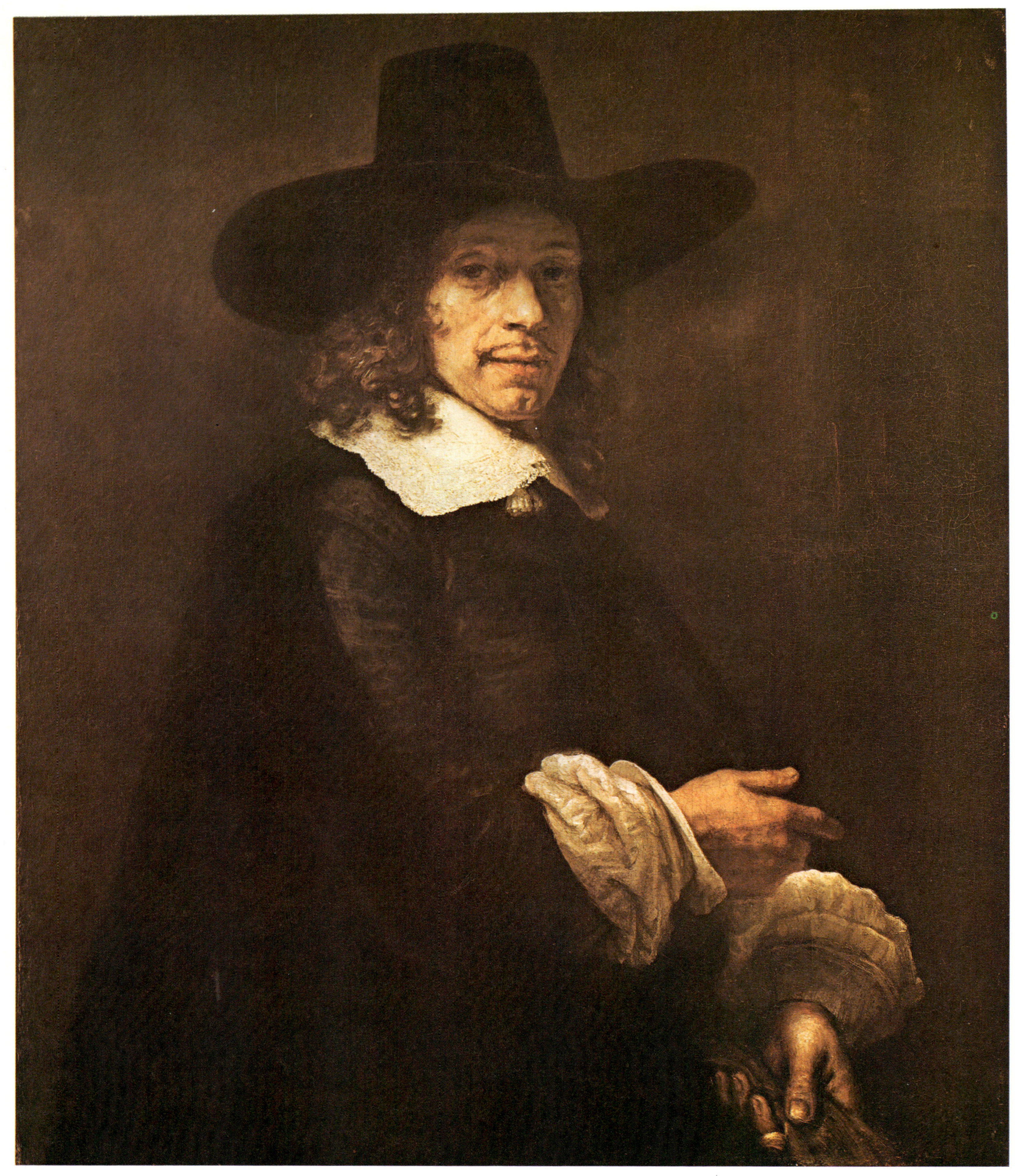

Plate 99 *see page 122*

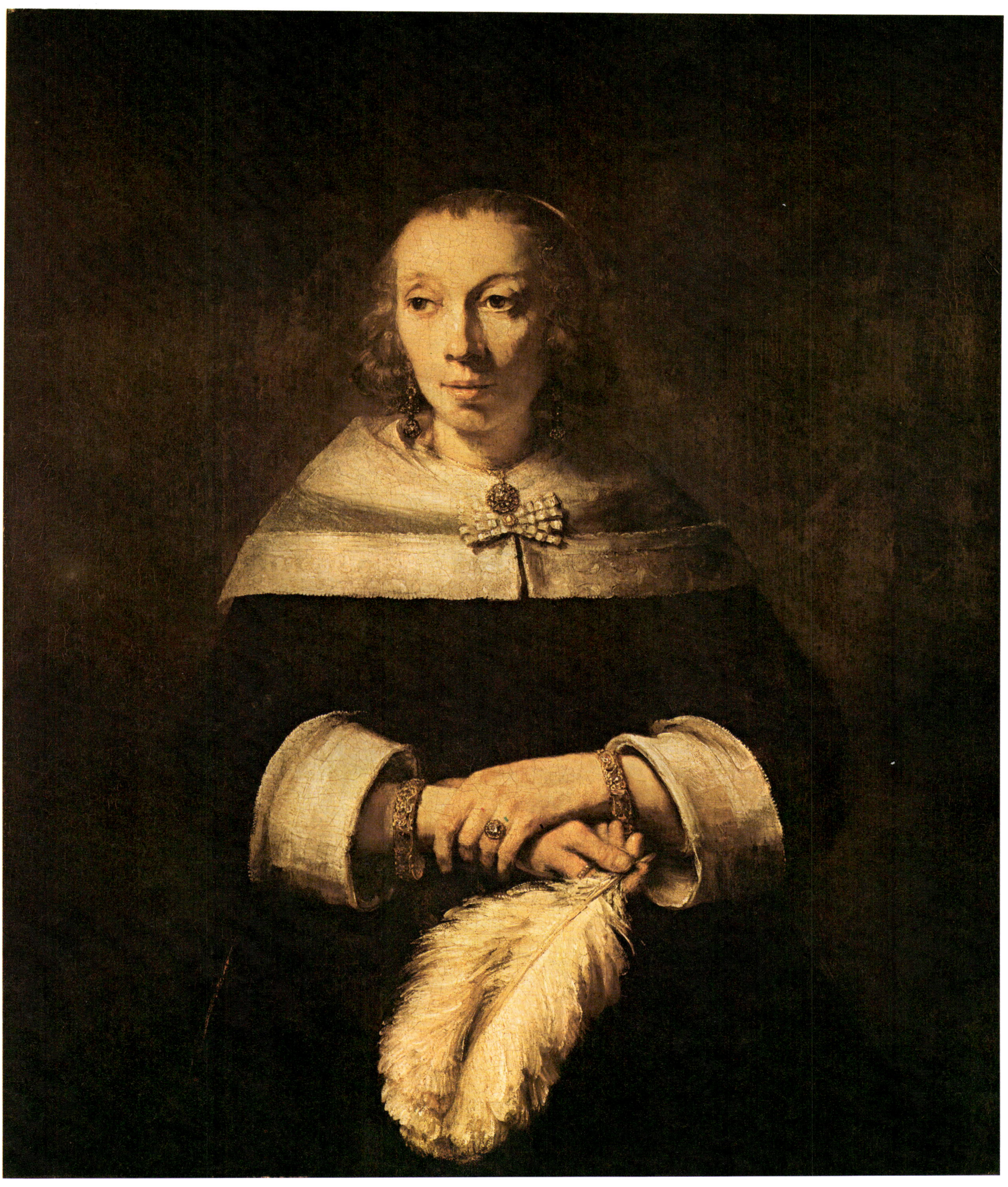

Plate 100 *see page 122*

Plate 99
An Unknown Man
about 1668
oil on canvas
$39\frac{1}{8} \times 32\frac{7}{8}$ in (99.5 × 83.5 cm)
National Gallery of Art, Washington
Widener Collection

Plate 100
An Unknown Woman, His Wife
about 1668
oil on canvas
$39\frac{3}{8} \times 32\frac{3}{4}$ in) 100 × 83 cm)
National Gallery of Art, Washington
Widener Collection

Completely unknown until both appeared in the collection of Prince Felix Youssoupoff in Russia at the end of the 19th century. Acquired by Joseph E. Widener of Philadelphia at the time of the Russian Revolution of 1917 and subsequently presented to the National Gallery with the rest of his collection.

religious and mythological pictures are irrelevant here. This is no final statement about humanity–he was capable of that as well–but a discreet record of two rather ordinary people, whose faces ring down the ages because they were painted by a man who sometimes forgot his own rather important preoccupations and who settled down to produce an unpretentious but enduring masterpiece.

The *Family Group* (plate 101) in the Herzog Anton Ulrich-Museum at Brunswick must be one of the last pictures that he painted. It is very much more detached from the world than might be expected. The strong emotions have disappeared and have been replaced by a gentle interpretation of the woman and her three children. Paterfamilias looks on benignly, while mother has her favourite child on her knee. The textures in this picture are quite astonishing, as the textiles are painted with such breadth that they no longer give the impression of being cloth, but remain as richly applied paint. The hands are hardly drawn at all: they are just approximations. Only the faces have any real detail. There are the same glazes of brilliant red and gold found in *The Jewish Bride* (plate 97) and the same slight inclination of the heads towards each other. Although not the archetypal bourgeois happy family–there is too much of the artist's innate melancholy for that–there is the impression that the family is at peace with itself. This is all the more of a miracle because we know that the artist was not in this state of mind at all if his self-portraits are taken as evidence.

Everybody has their own special definition of greatness in art, but there are few who would not admit, albeit sometimes grudgingly, that Rembrandt comes into this category. Yet this has not always been so well established as we would like to think. Rembrandt angered Ruskin, that most sensitive and yet most prejudiced of critics, because he mistrusted his shadows. The apostle of Turner was bound to be resentful when faced with the mystery of shadow rather than the clear and definable light of day.

On a superficial level Rembrandt is easy to appreciate. His message comes across immediately–the pictures speak. An example of this is that incredible room in the Glasgow Art Gallery which is full of excellent Dutch pictures of many different types but which is dominated by the *Man in Armour* (plate 67) in a way which makes all the other pictures look like carefully organised jigsaw puzzles. The Rembrandt envelopes all the elements in the picture in a kind of atmosphere in a manner which no other Dutch artist had even thought about, let alone attempted. On a deeper level, once the brilliance of technique is understood, once the difference from his contemporaries is grasped, there is much more to find. This is the area which leads to misunderstanding.

The taste of the present writer would lead him to mistrust the overtly emotional in painting, in the belief that in most cases deliberate rather than innate statements of emotion lead to the banal. In Rembrandt's case there was both. He was innately emotional in the sense that he was responsive to the human condition, whether it was the unmentionable, like the drawing of the *Woman Urinating* in the Albertina, Vienna, and in the etching of a couple copulating, or, more agreeably, his ability to tell the Bible story in human rather than abstract and ideal terms. His response to nature, unadulterated by man, was innate, as so many of his unpretentious landscape drawings show. More important than this was his continual observation of the effect of old age both in himself and in others. This is a thread which appears right through his career. As a young man many of his wealthy sitters were elderly, and in old age he had himself.

On the negative side it is seldom realised that Rembrandt lacked the one thing that Renaissance man had rediscovered from Antiquity–*joy* in the visual world. He was incapable of singing a paean of praise for its own sake. It is perhaps unfair to cite Botticelli's *Primavera* in the Uffizi, Florence, in this context, but the 15th-century Florentine took a delight in nature as well as being curious about it. Rembrandt had curiosity in abundance, but he lacked, most of the time, a sense of happiness and breadth which imbues so much of the art of the Italian Renaissance with its lasting quality. Inevitably, living in the bourgeois, commercial-minded, rainy (by Italian standards) Amsterdam, Rembrandt was unlikely to concentrate on the brighter side of man's soul. A very high proportion of his surviving paintings depict overweight, phlegmatic, self-satisfied and successful Dutchmen, whose faces have rung down the centuries because they happened to have chosen Rembrandt as the artist to paint their portraits. Rembrandt penetrated deep into this very solid God-fearing society, not exposing evils like a moral commentator, but recording the good and the bad in his sitters as their faces showed it. There is very little social consciousness, none of the preoccupation with the nobility of character which rank conveys on its recipient as with Van Dyck, in whose portraits lesser mortals usually have coarser faces. Rembrandt saw man not as an optimistic and basically joyful being with a better future than past, but as a sorrowing creature who had to learn to adjust to the evils and imperfections of the world and make the best of them. It is only when all his qualities, and indeed his failings, are taken together, that there is the realisation that his contribution to mankind makes him richly deserving of a place with the gods.

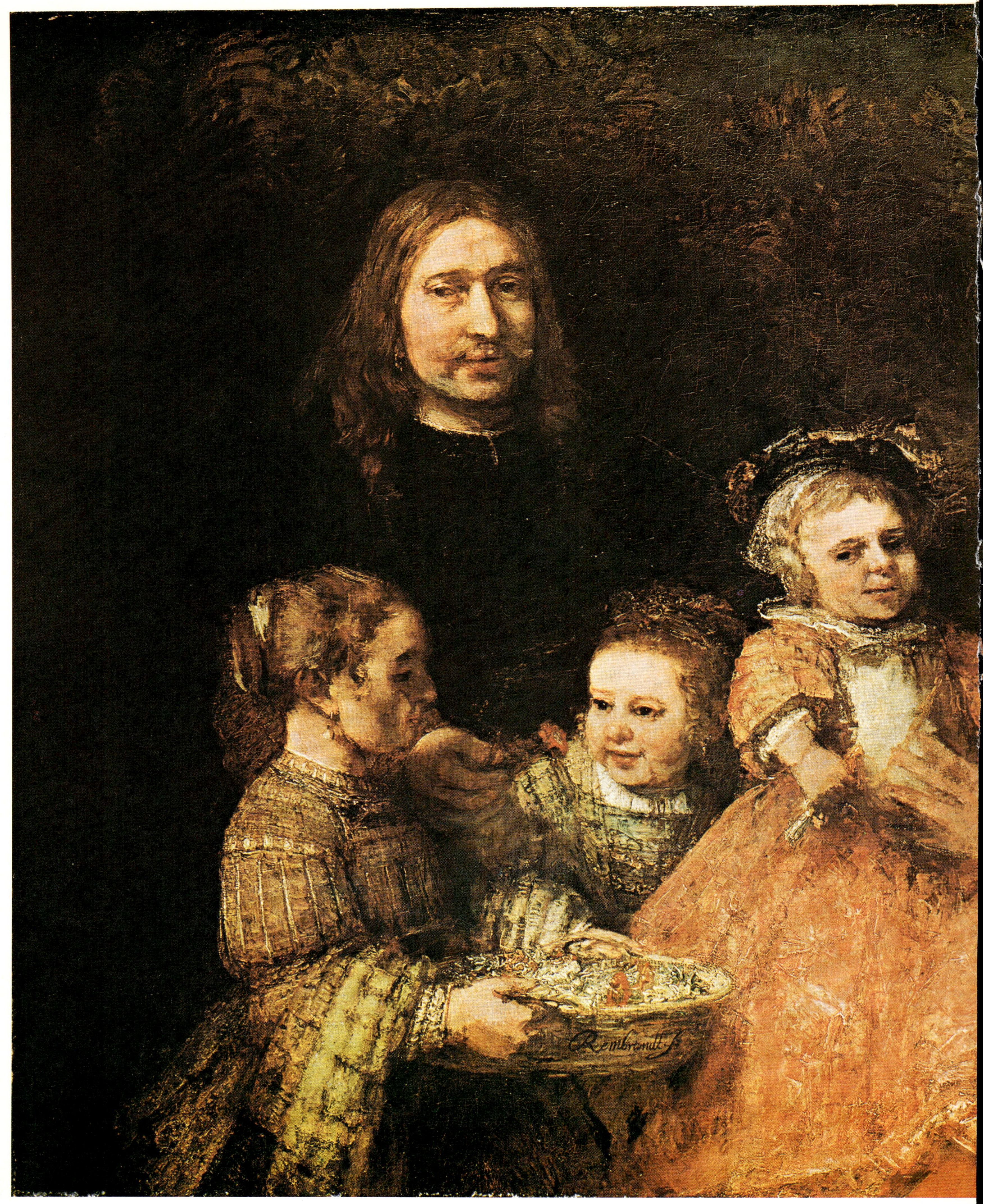
Rembrandt f.

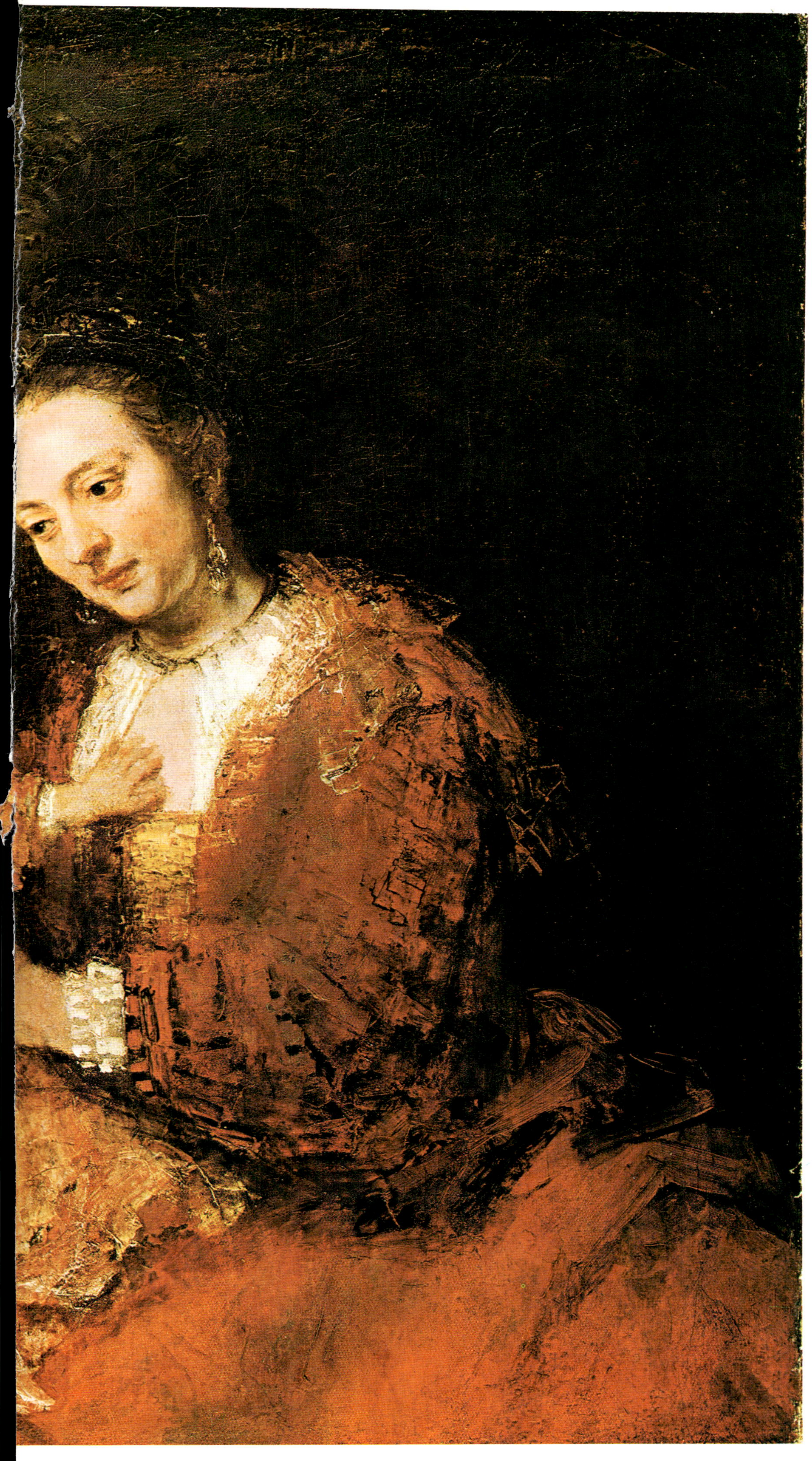

Plate 101
Family Group
about 1668–69
oil on canvas
$49\frac{5}{8} \times 65\frac{3}{4}$ in (126 × 167 cm)
Herzog Anton Ulrich-Museum, Brunswick

Recorded in the picture gallery of the Dukes of Brunswick in 1737 where it has remained ever since.

Index

Numbers in bold type refer to captions

Acknowledgments

Plate 39 is reproduced by gracious permission of Her Majesty the Queen. The following plates are reproduced by permission of the Trustees of The British Museum, London 8, 58, 59; by permission of the Governors of Dulwich College Picture Gallery 11, 91; by courtesy of the Trustees, The National Gallery of London 17, 25, 63, 88, 89, 90; by permission of the Trustees of the Chatsworth Settlement 27, 31; by courtesy of The Greater London Council as Trustees of the Iveagh Bequest, Kenwood 82.

Art Gallery and Museums, Brighton 5; Art Gallery, Glasgow 19, 67; Ashmolean Museum, Oxford 66, 75; Barber Institute of Fine Arts, University of Birmingham 28; Bayerische Staatsgemäldesammlungen, Munich 48; Blauel, Munich 18; Boymans-van Beuningen Museum, Rotterdam 65; City Art Gallery, Leeds 57; County Museum of Art, Los Angeles, 4; Courtauld Institute, London 31, 44, 74; Devonshire Collection, Chatsworth, 27; Dulwich College Picture Gallery, London 11, 91; Henry Ely, Aix-en-Provence 80; Frans Halsmuseum, Haarlem 93; John R. Freeman & Co. (Photographers) Ltd, London 8, 58, 77; Copyright the Frick Collection, New York 10, 69, 79; Gulbenkian Foundation, Lisbon 68; Hamlyn Group Picture Library 32, 59, 61; Herzog Anton Ulrich-Museum, Brunswick 101; Hunterian Museum, University of Glasgow 36; Institute of Arts, Minneapolis, Minnesota 98; Isabella Stewart Gardner Museum, Boston, Massachusetts 13, 33; Iveagh Bequest, Kenwood, London 82; Konstmuseum, Gothenburg 87; Lauros-Giraudon, Paris 30; Lichtbildwerkstätte 'Alpenland', Vienna 70; Mauritshuis, The Hague 1, 7, 12, 96; The Metropolitan Museum of Art, New York, 51, 60, 78; Musée Départmental des Vosges, Épinal 94; Musées Nationaux, Paris 2, 86; National Gallery, London 17, 25, 63, 88, 89, 90; National Gallery of Art, Washington D.C. 54, 81, 99, 100; National Gallery of Ireland, Dublin 49; National Gallery of Scotland, Edinburgh 16, 52; Nationalmuseum, Stockholm 43, 84, 95; Phaidon Press Limited, London 15, 26, 64; Photographie Giraudon, Paris 3; Gerhard Reinhold, Leipzig-Mölkau 12, 29, 37; Rembrandthuis, Amsterdam, 55; Rijksmuseum, Amsterdam 9, 41, 46, 62, 71, 72, 73, 83, 92, 97; Staatliche Graphische Sammlung, Munich 40, 85; Staatliche Kunstsammlungen, Dresden-Kupferstich-Kabinett 23; Staatliche Kunstsammlungen, Kassel 42, 76; Staatsgalerie, Stuttgart 6; Städelsches Kunstinstitut, Frankfurt 20, 45, 47; Walter Steinkopf, Berlin 21, 24, 38, 50, 53; Teyler Museum, Haarlem 34; Victoria and Albert Museum, London. Crown Copyright 35; The Walker Art Gallery, Liverpool 14, 56.

Bibliography

A complete bibliography of Rembrandt would fill a book very much longer than this one.

There is still no fully researched catalogue raisonnée of the paintings, but the best study remains:

A. Bredius, *The Paintings of Rembrandt*, Vienna, 1935 (English edition London, 1937). This book was revised and brought up to date with new locations and many disputed attributions by Horst Gerson, London, 1971.

For the history of the individual pictures and notes on their condition many current museum catalogues are the best source of information. Particularly recommended are the London National Gallery *Catalogue of the Dutch School*, 1960, by Neil Maclaren, and the catalogue of the Paris Petit Palais exhibition, *Le Siècle de Rembrandt: Tableaux Hollandais dans les Collections Publiques Françaises*, 1970–71.

For the drawings the excellent and thorough work of the late Otto Benesch has not been superseded:

O. Benesch, *The Drawings of Rembrandt, A critical and chronological catalogue*, 6 vols, London, 1954–57.

For the etchings the standard work is now:

Christopher White and Karel G. Boon in F. W. H. Hollstein, *Dutch and Flemish Etchings, Engravings and Woodcuts, Vol. XVIII*.

There are many good short introductions to the artist. For the patrons and biography, Christopher White, *Rembrandt and His World*, London, 1964, is recommended, while a highly individual approach is found in Kenneth Clark, *Rembrandt and the Italian Renaissance*, London, 1966.